SOLAR RETROFIT
Adding Solar to Your Home

Daniel K. Reif

BRICK HOUSE PUBLISHING COMPANY
Andover, Massachusetts

Special thanks to the Center for Ecological Technology (CET) for the use of slides from their file.

Published by Brick House Publishing Co., Inc.
34 Essex Street
Andover, Massachusetts 01810

Production credits
Editor: Jack Howell
Cover design: Cela Wright
Illustrations: Barbara Putnam
Copy editing: Carol Higgins
Manuscript revision: Diana Amsterdam, Wordworks
Typesetting: Neil W. Kelley
Production supervision: Dixie Clark Production

Printed in the United States of America
Copyright © 1981 by Daniel K. Reif

All rights reserved

We recommend care and adherence to standard construction safety procedures. Use welding glasses or the equivalent to protect your eyes when working with power tools. Neither the publisher nor the author takes responsibility for accidents that may occur during the building or use of any of the projects described in this book.

No part of this book may be reproduced in any form without the written permission of the publisher. (Use of illustrations by Barbara Putnam also requires permission of the artist.)

Library of Congress Cataloging in Publication Data
Reif, Daniel K.
  Solar retrofit.
    Bibliography: p.
    Includes index.
    1. Solar heating. 2. Dwellings—Heating and ventilation. I. Title.
TH7413.R43   697'.78   80-39801
ISBN 0—931790—50—6
ISBN 0—931790—15—8 (Pbk.)

To Linda, Ann, Jack, Fannie, and Harry

CONTENTS

1 SOLAR! 1

Getting the Most from Your Solar Heating System   6   Choosing the System   9
Constructing and Using a Solar Shading Mask   16
Systems Selection Worksheet   24   Safety   28
Solar Terminology   28

2 DIRECT GAIN   30

How It Works   30   System Strategies   31
Materials   37   Construction   40
Insulating Shades   47   Maintenance   53

3 THE THERMOSIPHONING AIR PANEL (TAP)   57

How It Works   57   System Strategies   59
Materials   61   Construction   65
Maintenance   80   Performance   82

4 THE ATTACHED SOLAR GREENHOUSE   84

How It Works   84   System Strategies   87
Design   92   Materials   98
Construction   105   Maintenance   120

5 THE HORIZONTAL AIR FLOW ACTIVE COLLECTOR 122

How It Works 122   System Strategies 125
Materials 126   Construction 130
Maintenance 146   Performance 146

6 IDEAS FOR IMPROVING PERFORMANCE 148

Reflectors 148   Wind Barriers 149   Summer
Shading 151   Solar Window Greenhouse 154
Improving TAP Performance 156

7 FUNDAMENTALS OF SOLAR 160

Heat Loss 160   Solar Heat Gain 165
Heat Storage 169

APPENDICES

1 Caulking 175

2 U-Values of Windows 177

3 Insulating Values of Materials 178

4 Clear Day Insolation Data 184

BIBLIOGRAPHY 199

ACKNOWLEDGMENTS

The solar space heating designs presented here were initially developed by Dick Howe, Shelly Klapper, Barbara Putnam, and me for the 1979 New England Project S.U.E.D.E. (Solar Utilization, Economic Development and Employment). Total Environmental Action, Inc. of Harrisville, New Hampshire served as solar consultants on the project especially Joe Kohler, Dan Lewis, Winslow Fuller, Charles Michal, Peter Temple, Lisa Heschong and Dan Scully. Jeremy Coleman, Vic Reno, Nancy Hazard and Terry Fenton provided additional technical assistance. Administrators for New England S.U.E.D.E. were William Frye of the Total Environmental Action Foundation; Ned Nisson and Laura Dubester of the Center for Ecological Technology, Pittsfield, Massachusetts; and Dennis Jaehne and Merillee Harrigan of the University of Massachusetts at Amherst. Jennifer Harris and Ken Allen provided administrative support to the project.

The solar heating systems described in this book were constructed throughout New Hampshire and Massachusetts as part of the New England S.U.E.D.E. project. In Berkshire County, Massachusetts, I designed 30 of these systems. Anastas Pollock, Michael Richardson, Alan Rivenson, Edward Williams, Leona Lavallee, Michael Sinopoli, Denis Banister, and Habib Chalfin constructed them. During the six-month construction phase, Anastas and I worked closely to refine the initial designs as they are presented here.

Kenneth Kerber and Paul Gerard have been a source of continuous encouragement.

Special thanks go to my wife, Linda, for her important insights and her warm support.

1
SOLAR!

Many homeowners fight a constant winter battle between the need to stay warm and the reluctance to spend a lot of money on fuel.

How can we maintain comfortable home temperatures without spending exorbitant amounts of money? Obviously it is essential to insulate and weatherize homes and conserve energy whenever possible. In the years to come, these techniques must go hand in hand with another: the use of solar.

Solar heating, combined with insulation, weatherization, and conservation, can save half the energy we now use to heat our homes.

This book provides step-by-step instructions for building effective and economical solar space heating systems on new and existing homes. Four systems are described: Direct Gain, Thermosiphoning Air Panel (TAP), Horizontal Air Flow Active Collector, and Attached Solar Greenhouse. Each type of system has been built many times for material costs of $300 to $2000 (1980 prices). *One or more of these systems is appropriate for over half the homes in the United States.* With carpentry skills equal to those of most do-it-yourself carpenters, you can construct any of these systems in several weekends. The instructions in this book make efficient solar heating available to everyone.

Does solar work? Indeed, the amount of solar energy that comes through a south-facing insulated glass window during

Fig. 1-1 This south-facing sunporch makes an efficient and beautiful Direct Gain solar heating system. (Photo by Michael Sinopoli)

the day *is greater than the amount of heat lost* through that same window during an entire day and night. This is true even in severely cold and cloudy climates. In fact, the simplest, most cost-effective solar space heater is an insulated glass south-facing window, especially one with insulating shades for nighttime use.

Each of the systems presented here has been designed to use materials that are readily available at local lumber yards, hardware stores, and glass shops. For materials which are somewhat more difficult to locate, I have listed either sources of the material or information about the nearest distributor. Prices vary considerably depending on quantity of purchase,

Solar! 3

Fig. 1-2 Thermosiphoning Air Panels (TAPs) such as these can be constructed in two or three weekends. (Michael Richardson, designer; Anastas Pollock, builder; photo by Anastas Pollock)

geographic region, and inflation. For general cost estimates, I have provided cost per unit and cost per square foot for each of the systems.

The percentage of total useable heat that can be derived from these solar systems varies according to such factors as amount of heat needed, size and efficiency of the solar collector, use of thermal storage, and climate. Cold climates, even those with considerable cloud cover, are often the best for solar space heating because when fuel use is high, a savings of just 30 percent can be a real boost. Conversely, in warm, sunny climates—although they are ideal for solar collection—it might be necessary to get 90 percent of your heat from

Fig. 1–3 TAPs provide supplementary solar heat to the kitchen.

Fig. 1–4 An Attached Solar Greenhouse makes a beautiful addition to any home (Hobie Iselin, designer and builder.)

Fig. 1–5 Horizontal Air Flow Collectors are an ideal type of solar heating when the collectors are separated from the area to be heated. (Photo by Nancy Hazard)

solar to show a similar monetary savings. For example, saving 30 percent on a $1000 fuel is the same in dollars as saving 90 percent on a $333 fuel bill.

One of the factors influencing solar efficiency is thermal storage—that is, the capacity of a solar installation to store heat for later use. In solar retrofits (adding a solar system to a home), thermal storage possibilities are generally limited. Without thermal storage, indoor temperatures can rise above 80° F in spring and fall. Venting this occasional overheating reduces year round collector efficiency. These facts should be considered in building your solar installation, especially if you live in a warm climate where overheating may be a problem.

For each dollar you invest in solar energy, you get a cost benefit savings. In some cases you can receive an equal payback through energy savings within the first year. More often, economic benefit will be realized over several years of energy savings; in time you will gain interest on the money and labor you invested.

The percentage of interest you receive depends on several factors. How much money per year did you previously spend on fuel? What has the cost of fuel been? What will it be? How many additional energy saving steps—such as adding insulation and weatherstripping—have you taken? What is the cost of these steps? This book helps you increase the value of your investment because it enables you to do your own building. You will realize the benefits of your labor year after year when you do a "hands on" solar project.

The solar revolution is just one part of our battle to save fuel. Weatherization—insulation and weatherstripping, for example—is necessary to make solar use successful. When you invest in solar, you need a heat-tight house to make it work effectively. Proper insulation and weatherstripping help hold the solar heat captured during the day long into the night.

This book is designed to take the mystery out of solar heating and make the sun's energy accessible to everyone.

Getting the Most from Your Solar Heating System

Your lifestyle has a significant effect on the amount of money you save from any solar retrofit system. Similar houses with identical solar retrofits have shown substantially different savings. Solar retrofitting is not an excuse to turn up the thermostat. It is, rather, a viable method by which we can conserve energy, save money, control heating supplies—and be less dependent on uncertain sources of fuel in the future.

Maximum benefit can be achieved from solar retrofits by decentralized heating—solar heating only a portion of your home. Using available solar energy to heat daytime living spaces—whether by Direct Gain, TAP, Horizontal Air Flow Active Collector, or Attached Solar Greenhouse—you will have cozy, warm rooms on sunny, cold winter days. Being thermally comfortable in some rooms, you can keep the rest of your house at a lower temperature.

The concept of decentralized heating is already common among energy conserving people. Owners of wood stoves, for instance, save money not only by using wood, an often lower-cost fuel, but also by not heating all of the rooms in their house equally, thus reducing overall fuel consumption. The reduction is most dramatic in large, moderately and poorly insulated houses where uniformly maintained temperatures demand significant heat input to offset heat losses.

For example, it is not necessary to heat bedrooms to 65°F during the day. Nor is it necessary to heat recreation and activity rooms to the same temperature as other daytime rooms. The concept of equal heat throughout the house is compatible only with low heating fuel prices. Centralized heating systems are popular with builders and banks because, with only one thermostat and a few heating system controls, they are *initially* less expensive. Despite lower installation costs, in the long run, centralized heating systems are not cost-effective.

Each of the four solar heating systems described in this book can be used to decentralize existing residential heating systems, providing thermal comfort *where it is most needed*. For example, with an Attached Solar Greenhouse, the adjoining room receives much of its heat from the greenhouse on a sunny day with the use of a fan near the greenhouse ceiling and a return air vent along the floor. Occupants naturally congregate to the warm and sunny space near the greenhouse. A house thermostat placed *within* this solar-tempered room will not trigger the house furnace to turn on as long as the temperature setting is maintained by the solar-heated greenhouse. Thus, we can "fool" the thermostat.

When the temperature in the solar-tempered room drops to below the thermostat setting, the conventional heating system comes on, delivering a moderate amount of heat to the entire house until the thermostat setting is reached. Solar-tempered rooms always remain warmer than the rest of the house as long as there is some net heat gain from the solar heating system. The temperature of rooms adjacent to the solar-tempered room can be roughly regulated by opening and closing doors, while the spaces furthest away will be denied solar heat. Usually the bedrooms are furthest away and correspondingly need the least daytime heat.

In conjunction with an energy-conscious lifestyle, a decentralized heating system can maintain several different levels of thermal comfort simultaneously. Even with a moderate size collector and without the benefit of heat storage for night use, this simple decentralized approach can decrease a large portion of the daytime heating needs for the entire house. Thus, the homeowner can be comfortable while saving more money than would be saved by distributing the solar heat throughout the house.

Sizing your collector

The efficiency of your solar heating system depends largely on the size of the collector. While it must be large enough to supply the heat needed, a too-large collector will have diminishing returns.

Doubling the collector size may not double the total useful solar heat. Using the graph below, compare the useful solar heat obtained from a 150 square foot collector to that obtained from a 300 square foot collector.

In the average house, with a Direct Gain or Attached Solar Greenhouse system you can add up to 150 square feet of south-facing double glazing with insulating shades for nighttime use. With a greenhouse system, this assumes that all the heat collected from the greenhouse is delivered to the house. If some of the solar heat is stored in the greenhouse, you can substantially increase collector size without decreasing effectiveness. If you install a Thermosiphoning Air Panel or Horizontal Air Flow Active Collector you can add up to 200 square feet of solar collector.

In most solar retrofits, architectural considerations limit the size of the collector to within these dimensions.

These figures are based on the assumption that the solar heat will be distributed throughout the house. When solar heating only a portion of your home (decentralized heating) you must either reduce these dimensions by as much as 50

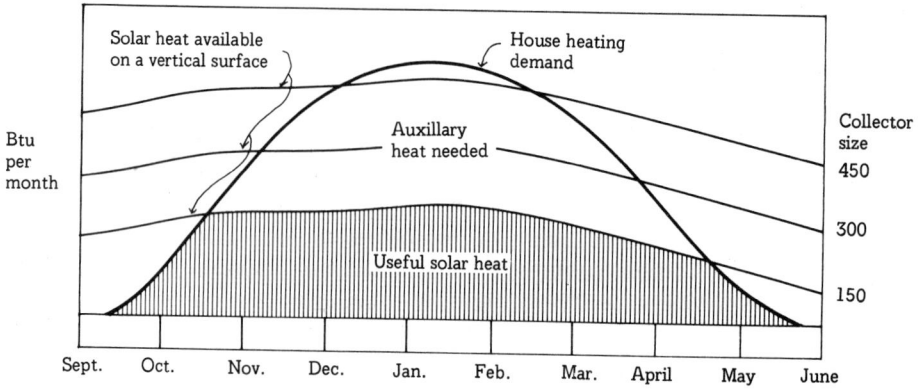

Fig. 1-6 Useful solar heat for a 150-square foot vertical solar collector. (Courtesy of *The Solar Home book*, Brick House Publishing Co.)

percent or add thermal storage; otherwise overheating or need for venting may result.

The amount of heat gained from each square foot of collector is reduced if the collector is so large that it supplies more heat than is needed during the day and there is no thermal storage to store the excess. The point at which you receive diminishing returns from your solar heating system depends on the climate and your house heating demand. When the collector is moderately sized, the heat produced can almost always be used, even in the spring or fall. If the collector is larger, the additional area is beneficial only in colder weather or with thermal storage. Larger-than-average collectors are appropriate only in severely cold climates, or when thermal storage is carefully integrated into the solar heating system.

Choosing the System

Selecting the solar heating system or combination of systems that is best for your situation is a major decision. Before you begin construction, carefully consider each system and be sure that you understand how it suits your home and your energy needs.

This book is both a general primer and a construction manual. It contains all the information you need to make an intelligent choice of systems, plus some special features to make selection easier. Don't jump ahead. Before you decide which system to construct, read the entire book so you are thoroughly acquainted with the basic principles of solar energy and the potential advantages and disadvantages of each of the four systems. Visiting houses with completed systems similar to those you are considering will provide additional insight. You can often locate such houses through local solar energy dealers or newspaper articles.

To help you conduct a thorough solar analysis of your home, I've designed and included some special tools: a *Systems Selection Worksheet* and instructions for building a solar shading mask. These tools are discussed in this chapter. But again, while you should read about them for a basic understanding, don't try to use them until you have read through the entire book and are ready to make your choice.

10   Solar!

In some cases your decision will be clear; if more than one system is appropriate the choice may be difficult. Sometimes a combination of systems is ideal. When you have made a decision, turn to the section dealing with the system(s) of your choice—and build it!

Site analysis

Your site is one of the most important factors determining both the best solar heating system(s) for your house and the amount of heat your system will produce. To find the best location for your solar heating system you will need to perform a thorough site analysis of your south wall. The solar heating systems presented in this book are designed to be added to a south wall, except for the Attached Solar Greenhouse, which can be extended from an east, west, or south

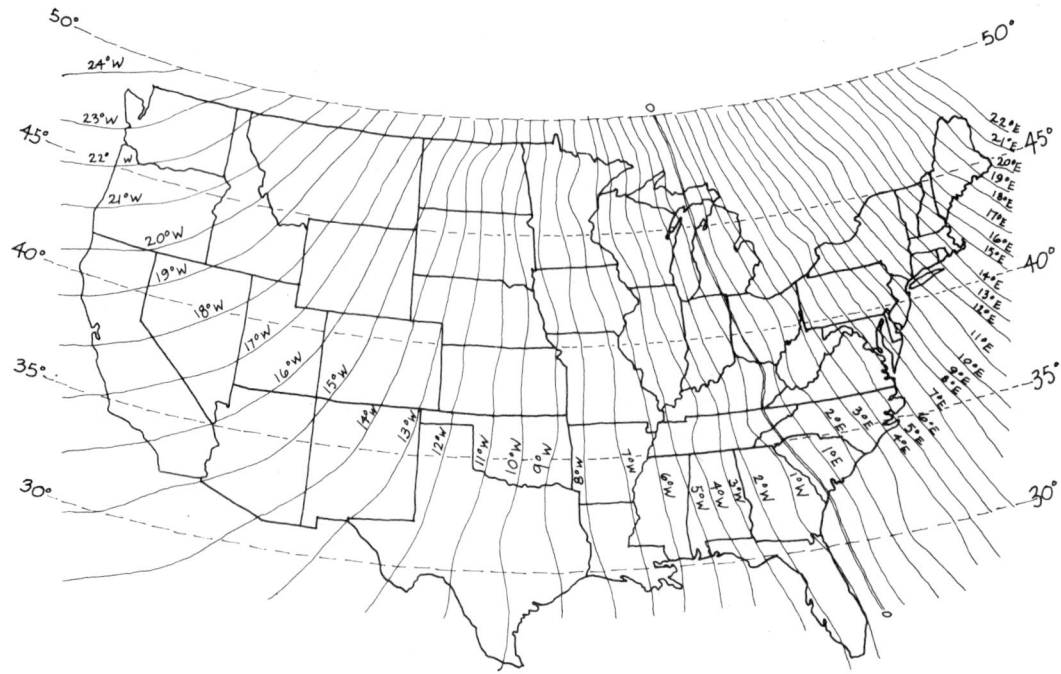

Fig. 1–7 Map of the United States indicating magnetic variation away from *solar south*. *Source*: Isogonic Chart of the United States, U.S. Department of Commerce, Coast and Geodetic Survey, 1965.

wall. Some other solar systems, not covered here, are mounted on south-facing roofs or freestanding away from the house.

There are two criteria for determining the solar potential of a wall area: the orientation of the wall away from *solar south*—the east-to-west position of the sun at midday—and the amount of shading on the wall during the heating season. The information you collect from studying your south wall should be added to the *Analysis* section of the *Systems Selection Worksheet*.

Orientation of your south wall

At midday, go outside and stand at the south side of your house. To find *solar south* you must first find out what time the sun rises and sets on that day. Exactly halfway between sunrise and sunset, the sun's east to west position is directly *solar south*. The shadow of a vertical stick at midday points directly away from solar south.

Note: If you live near a time change zone line, actual sunrise and sunset in your area may vary by as much as one half hour from that stated for your time zone. For an exact location of solar south, you must use the exact sunrise and sunset times at your site. To check the direction of solar south, the shadow of a vertical stick is shortest when the sun is directly solar south.

You can also find solar south using a compass, but you must first compensate for the fact that the location of solar south can vary from magnetic south. Use the magnetic variation map to find your magnetic variation.

If you live near the line of zero variation, running from Lake Michigan to Georgia, magnetic south and solar south are in the same direction. If you live *east* of this line, magnetic south is to the *left* (east) of solar south; and if you live to the *west* of this line, magnetic south is to the *right* (west) of solar south.

Once you have located solar south, stand with your back *flat* against the south wall. Point one arm straight ahead and the other arm toward *solar south*. (Both arms should be at the same height.) The size of the angle between your arms is the number of degrees your south wall is oriented away from solar south.

12 Solar!

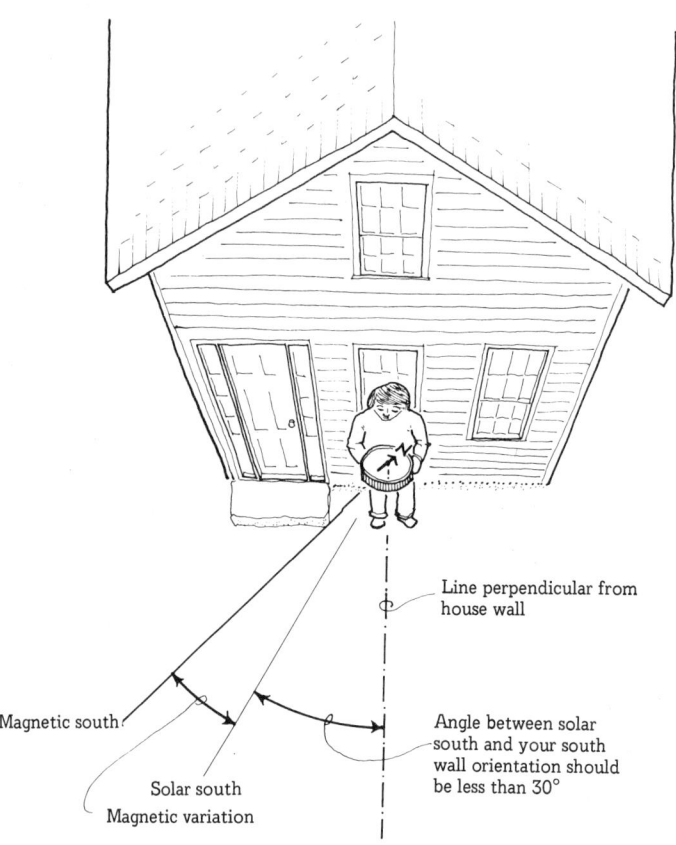

Fig. 1–8 Finding the orientation of your south wall

Maximum solar efficiency demands that the collector surface be oriented within 30° east or west of solar south. Collectors oriented beyond these limits have reduced winter heating efficiency and are more apt to provide excessive heat in the spring and fall. The east and west sides of your house receive more than twice as much solar energy in summer than they do in winter, while south walls (in latitudes north of 40° North) receive nearly twice as much solar energy in winter as they do in summer.

Slight easterly or westerly collector orientations can have unique advantages or disadvantages, depending on your exact site. An easterly orientation has the advantage of supplying heat earlier in the morning, while a westerly exposure

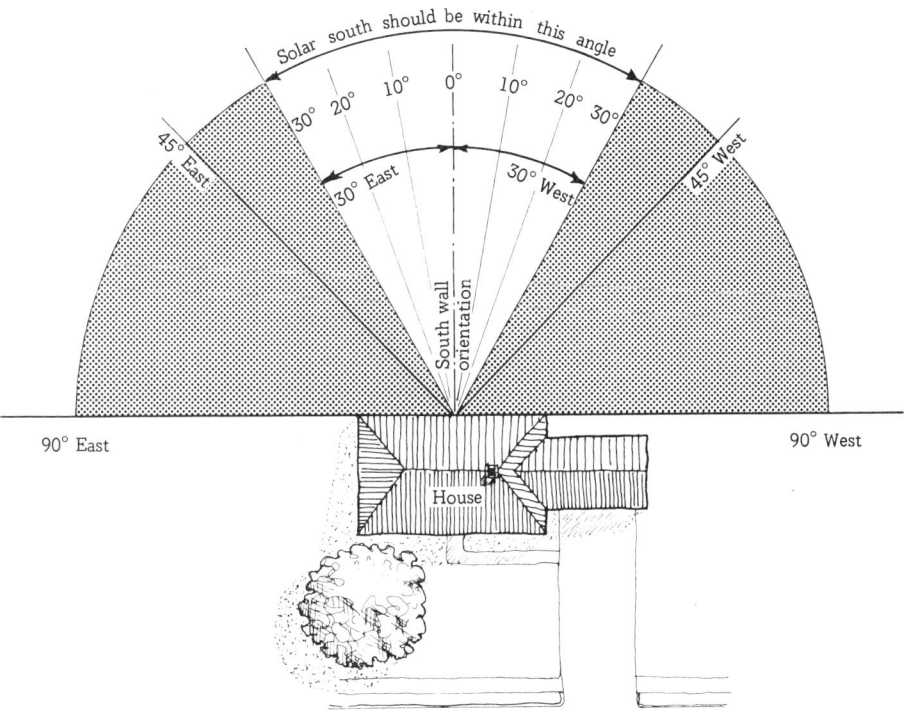

Fig. 1–9 Orientation of your south wall

gives you a little extra heat just before the cold night arrives. Of course, local weather conditions such as frequent morning fogs or afternoon clouds can also be an influence.

Shading of either the morning or afternoon sun is another consideration in determining a collector's optimum orientation. When the morning winter sun is shaded, a slightly western orientation is preferable, while shading of the afternoon winter sun makes a slightly eastern exposure ideal.

Shading

Look at your south wall. This is where a Direct Gain, TAP, or Active Collector would be placed. For an Attached Solar Greenhouse, the glazing would be located several feet from the south wall; therefore, you will also want to evaluate this area. You need to determine which areas of your south wall are *not shaded from the low winter sun.*

Note: Shading from nearby obstructions such as bushes, a chimney, roof overhang, or a part of your house that juts out, changes considerably if you move several feet sideways or vertically along the south wall.

While standing where the collector surface would be, imagine the path of the winter sun as it rises in the southeast, reaches its highest point at midday, and sets in the southwest. Shading of the morning or late afternoon sun is not nearly as crucial as shading of the strong midday sun. Winter shading from deciduous trees is less than winter shading from evergreens or from solid obstructions, such as the house next door. If you are evaluating your site in summer, spring, or fall, remember that shadows cast by the low winter sun will be much longer than those cast during the other seasons. If your potential site has shading of no more than 20 percent of the morning or afternoon sun, or 10 percent of the sun between 10:00 A.M. and 2:00 P.M., and your south wall is oriented within 30° east or west of solar south, you have a good solar site!

If you are uncertain about the amount of winter shading on your wall or want a more exact sighting of the sun's path, you can construct a *solar shading mask*. This device lets you *see* the sun's path throughout the heating season. Instructions for constructing a solar shading mask are included in this chapter.

Please note, sites with no shading at all are rare and certainly 10 percent shading is acceptable. Don't cut down a 100-year-old tree to decrease shading by a few percentage points.

Direct Gain, TAP and Horizontal Air Flow Active Collectors are designed with vertical glazing. This is because *vertical glazing receives a maximum amount of sunshine during the winter, and very little in summer.* In winter, the reflection of sunlight from the ground, especially when it is covered with snow, increases the amount of sunshine striking the collector by as much as 30 percent. This reflection compensates for the fact that the collector surface is not perpendicular to the sun's rays. In fact, with good ground reflection vertical glazing outperforms sloped glazing. Because the sun's path is much higher in the sky in summer than it is in winter, little of the summer sun strikes vertical, south-facing

Solar! 15

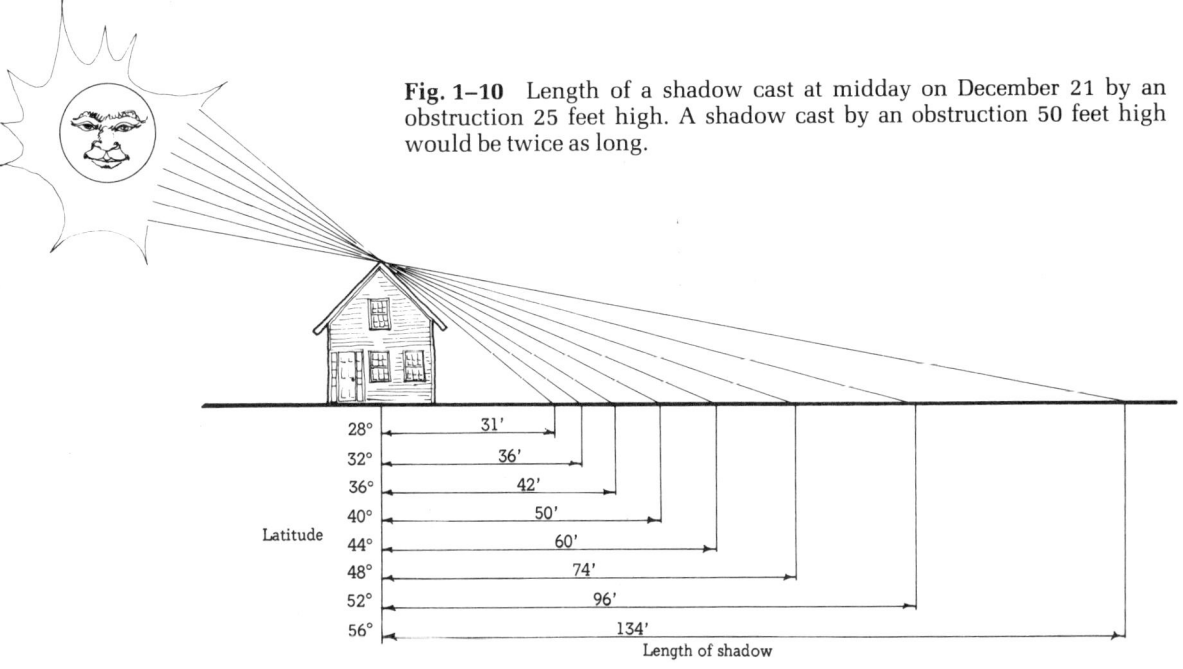

Fig. 1–10 Length of a shadow cast at midday on December 21 by an obstruction 25 feet high. A shadow cast by an obstruction 50 feet high would be twice as long.

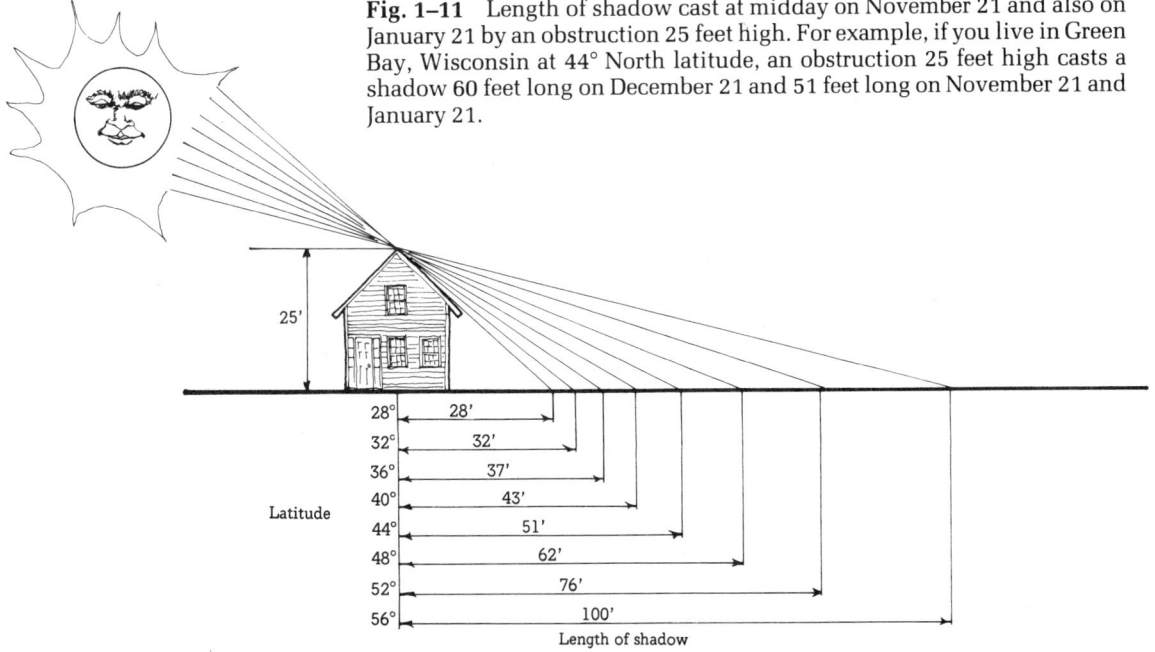

Fig. 1–11 Length of shadow cast at midday on November 21 and also on January 21 by an obstruction 25 feet high. For example, if you live in Green Bay, Wisconsin at 44° North latitude, an obstruction 25 feet high casts a shadow 60 feet long on December 21 and 51 feet long on November 21 and January 21.

surfaces. Therefore, heating of the house and collector is minimized.

Note: Since vertical collectors are designed for optimum winter heating and minimum summer heating, they are not suitable for year-round heating needs such as household water heating.

Constructing and Using a Solar Shading Mask

The solar shading mask can be constructed in several hours for material costs of about $5.00. It is an excellent tool for performing a thorough shading analysis and is especially helpful for evaluating questionable solar sites. When you are finished with your site analysis, the mask is a great present for a friend.

Shading Mask Materials

1. 14½" long, 1" × 8" pine board
2. 12" long, 1/2" diameter wood dowel
3. 24" × 20", .005" (or thicker) clear acetate sheet
4. 12 - 1/2" pan head wood screws with 1/2" washers
5. 24" × 2" piece of cardboard

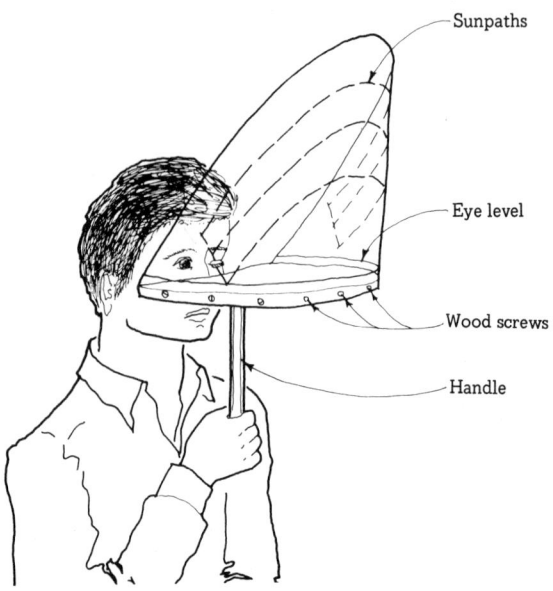

Fig. 1–12 Looking through a shading mask

Shading Mask Tools

1. drill
2. sabre saw or keyhole saw
3. black marking pen
4. screwdriver
5. ruler
6. string (for drawing 14½" diameter circle)
7. glue
8. 1/8" graph paper (4 sheets)
9. Sun Path Chart and Magnetic Variation Map (provided in this book)

Construction

Base and handle

1. Using a pencil tied to a string, draw a 14½ in. diameter semicircle on the 1 in. × 8 in. × 14½ in. board.
2. Mark the point 3½ in. from the edge and equidistant from the sides.
3. Cut the board to form a semicircle.
4. Drill a 1/2 in. hole at the center point, and glue the end of the 1/2 in. dowel into this hole, to make the handle.
5. Drill 1/16 in. screw holes every 2 in. along the curved edge of the semicircle, as shown.

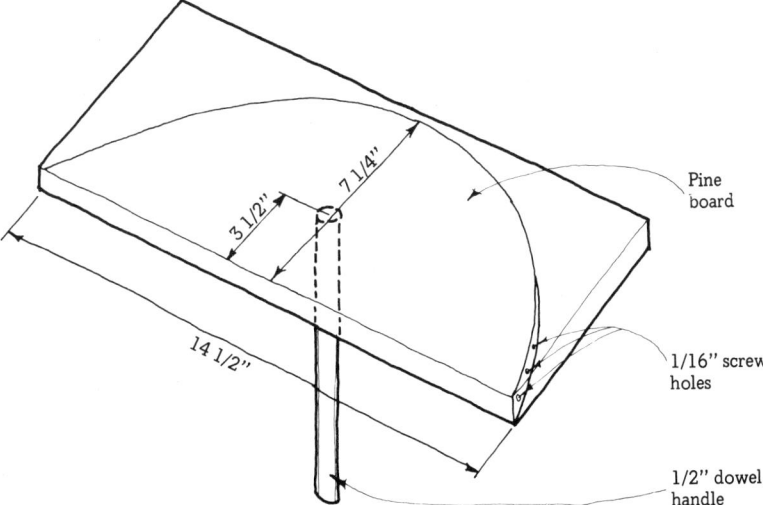

Fig. 1–13 Shading mask base and handle

Drawing sun paths

1. Join three 8½ in. × 11 in. sheets of 1/8 in. graph paper to make one 11 in. × 24 in. sheet.
2. Find the Sun Path Chart (Figure 1–16) for the latitude nearest yours. (You can determine your latitude from Fig. 1–7.
3. Using a ruler, draw the Solar Altitude–Solar Azimuth Graph according to the dimensions in Figure 1–14. Solar Altitude is the height of the sun above the horizon. Solar Azimuth is the east-to-west position of the sun.

   Note: Solar Altitude spacing varies for each 10° interval.
4. Draw the Sun Path Chart for your latitude onto the 11" × 24" graph paper. The easiest way to do this is to mark a dot on the graph paper on each Solar Azimuth line where the curve of the sun paths cross that Azimuth. Then, simply connect the dots to form the correct curves.
5. Find your location on the Magnetic Variation Map. Read the number of degrees variation and the direction—east or west. Remember that if you are east of the zero variation line your magnetic south line is *left* of the solar south line, or if you are west of the zero variation line your magnetic south line is *right* of the solar south line. Draw a dotted vertical line crossing the horizon line representing magnetic south for your location.
6. Trace the sun paths, solar and magnetic south lines, and horizon line on to the acetate from the prepared graph paper. Label each of the sun paths by month, solar and magnetic south, horizon line, and east and west.
7. Use the screws, washers, and cardboard to attach the finished acetate sheet to the base.

   Note: The horizon line should be at eye level when your nose is resting on the wood base. The distance from the horizon line to the base should be approximately 1½ in.)
8. Cut away excess acetate about 1/2 in. above the highest sun path to add rigidity to the acetate sheet.

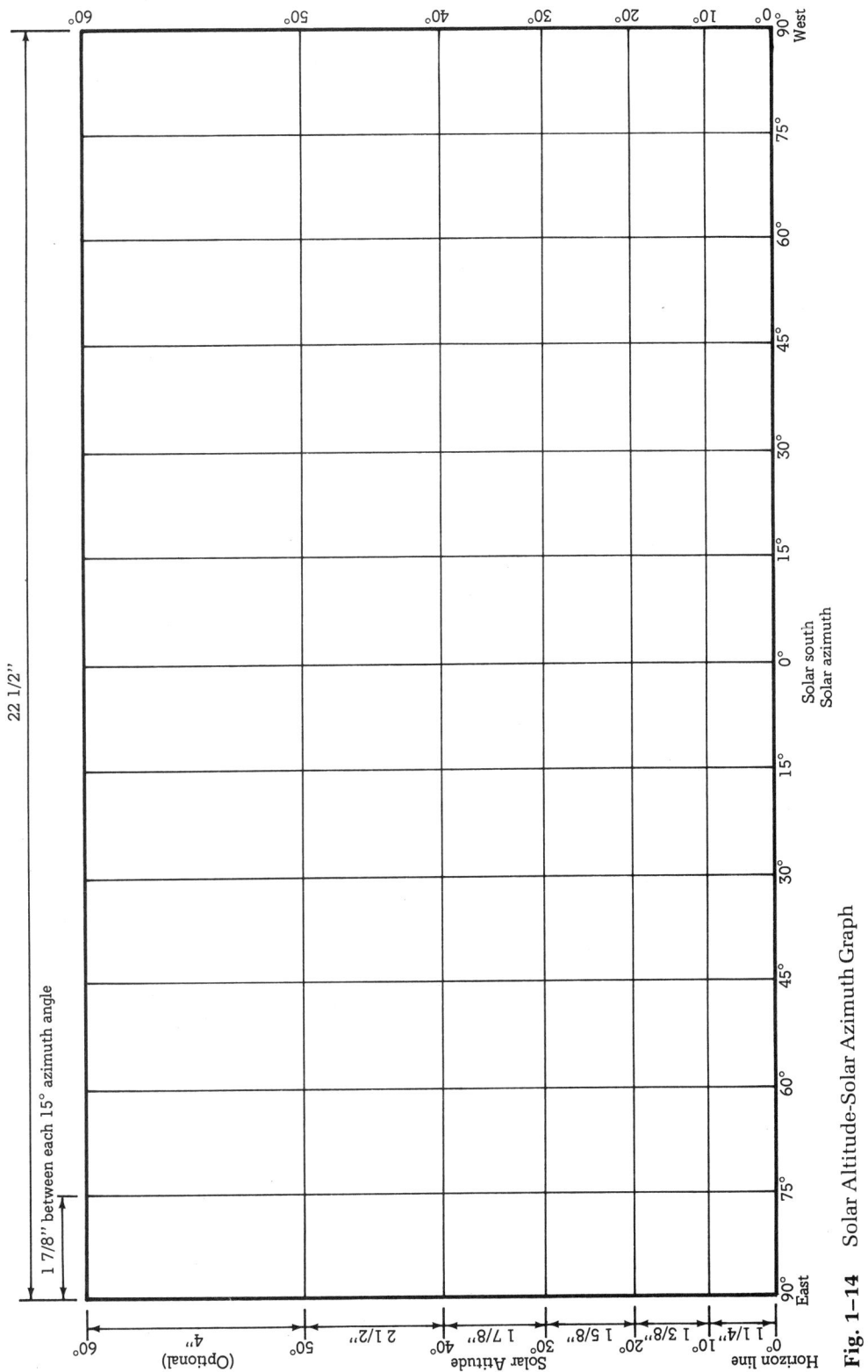

Fig. 1-14 Solar Altitude-Solar Azimuth Graph

20 Solar!

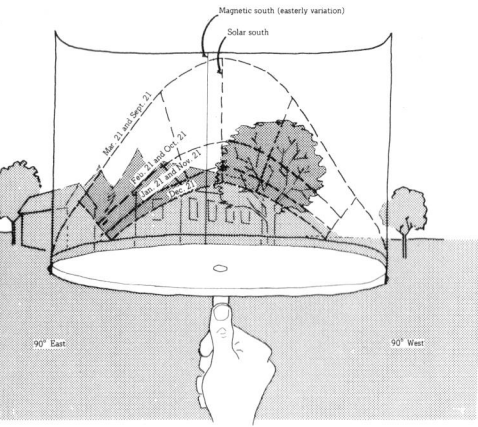

Fig. 1–15 Sun paths as viewed through a shading mask.

Using the solar shading mask

To determine the amount of shading on a south wall area, stand with your back in line with the potential solar collector installation. Place the wood base of the shading mask under your nose, so that your eye level is at the same height as the *horizon line* on the mask. Using a compass, locate magnetic south and aim the *magnetic south line* on the mask toward magnetic south. Note the difference between solar south and magnetic south. Make certain you are holding the base of the mask level.

View the sun's path in each of the heating season months and see when the sun will be shaded. Move to several different areas of the south wall and compare the amounts of shading. Remember that shading of up to 20 percent of the morning or afternoon, or 10 percent of the sun between 10:00 A.M. and 2:00 P.M. is common and acceptable.

Fig. 1–16 Sun paths for Northern latitudes.

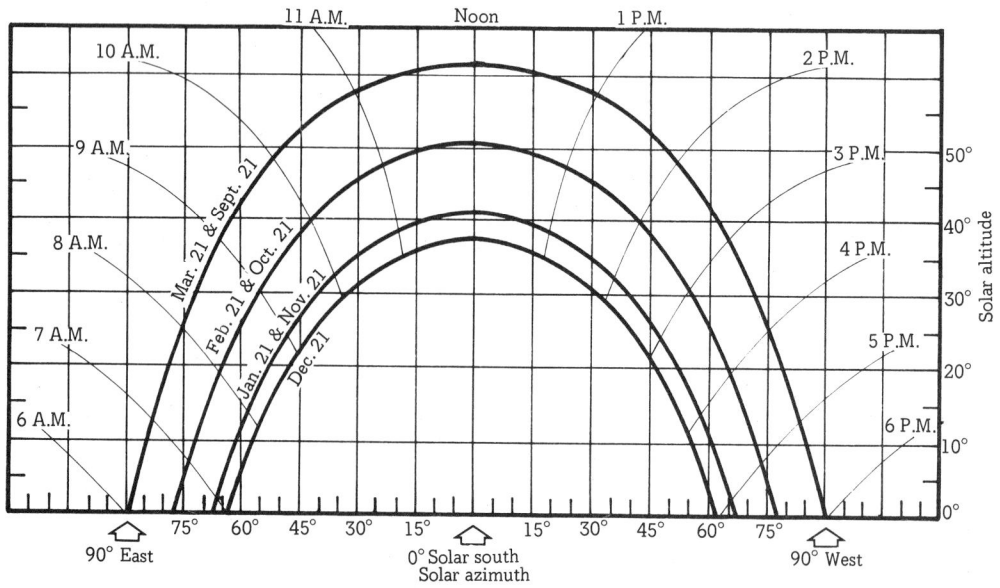

a) 28° North latitude.

Solar! 21

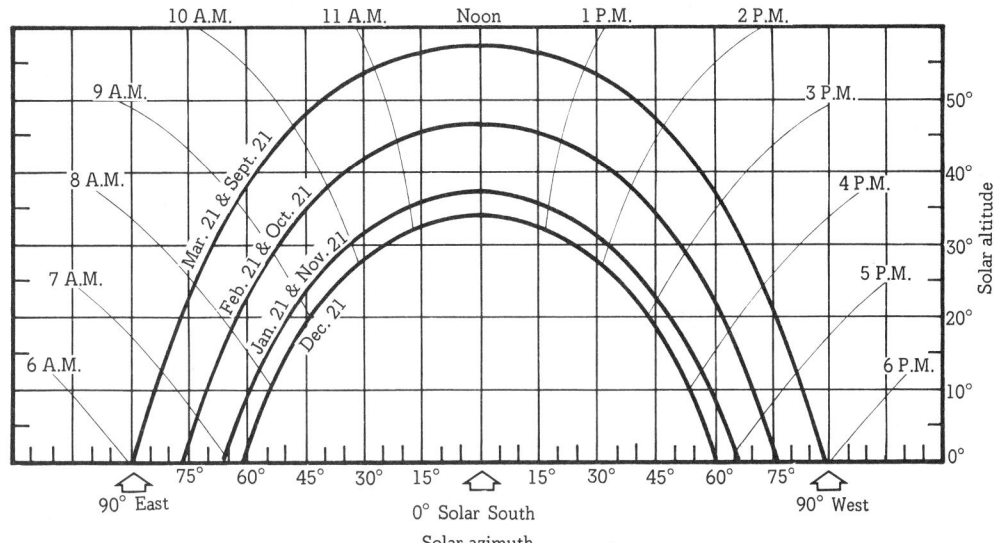

b) 32° North latitude.

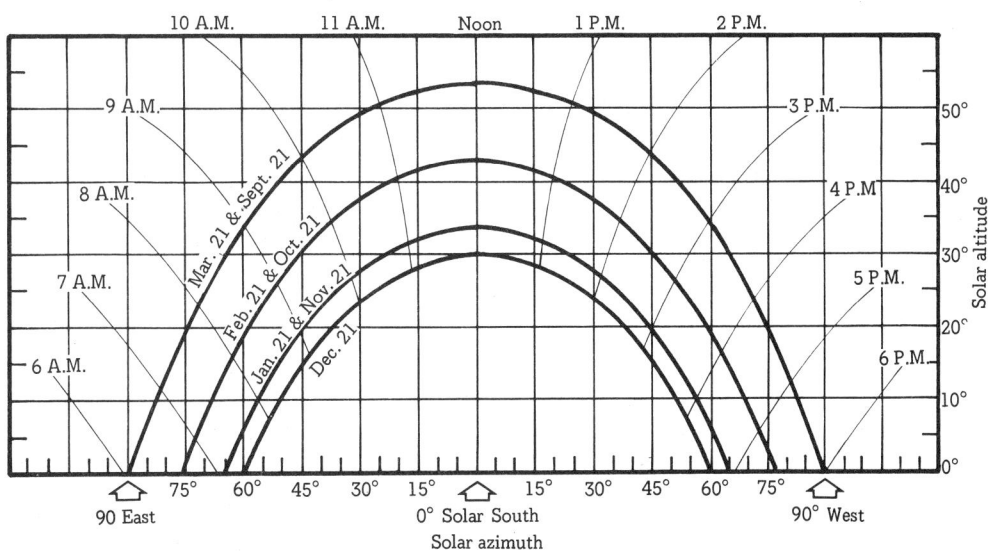

c) 36° North latitude.

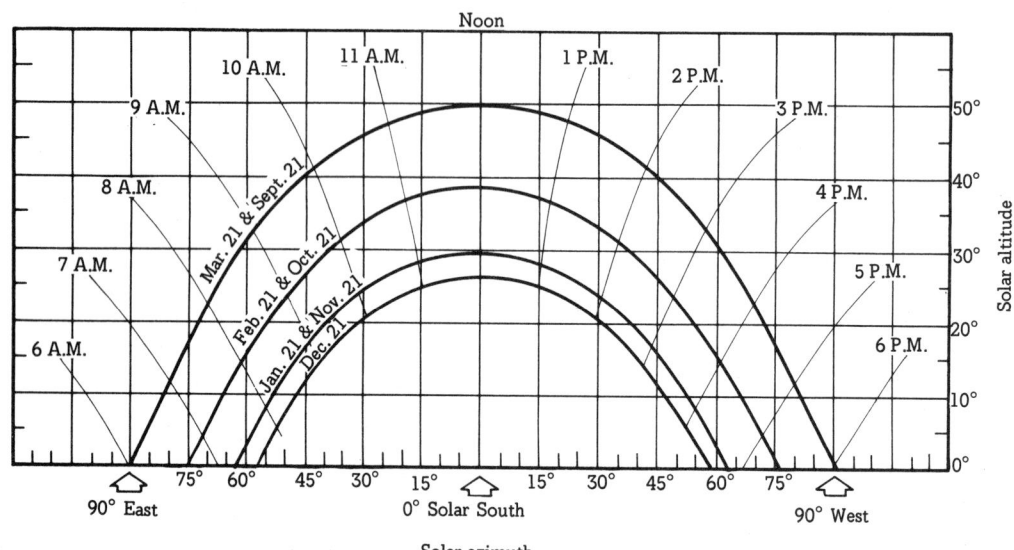

d) 40° North latitude.

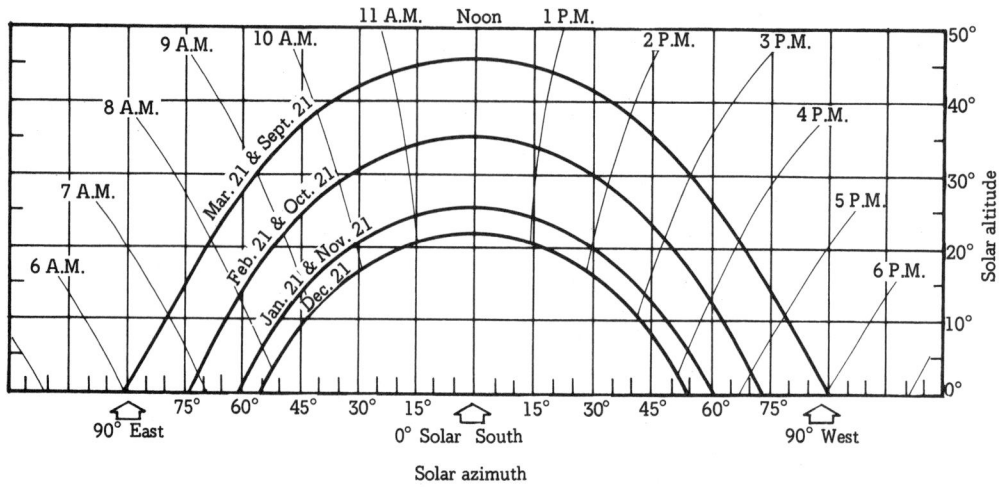

e) 44° North latitude.

Solar! 23

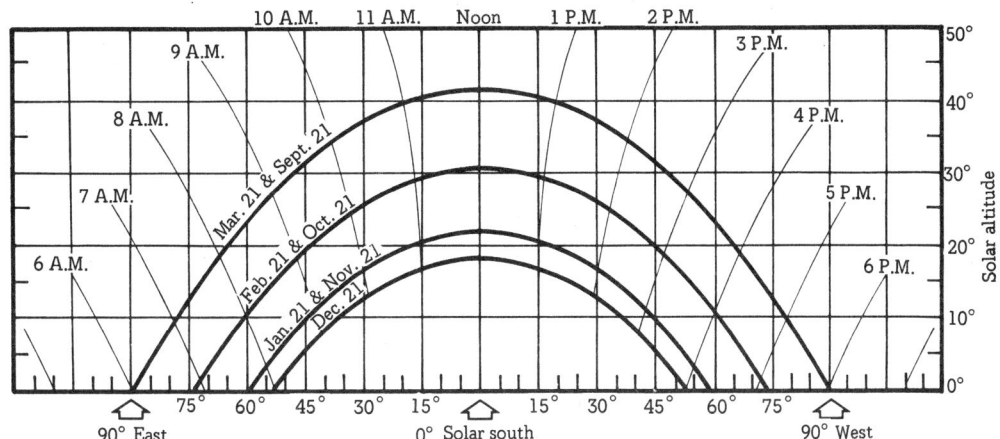

f) 48° North latitude.

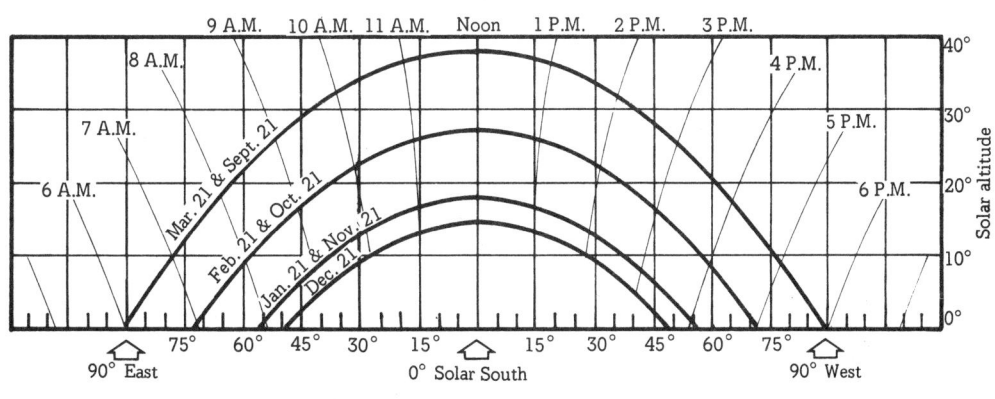

g) 52° North latitude.

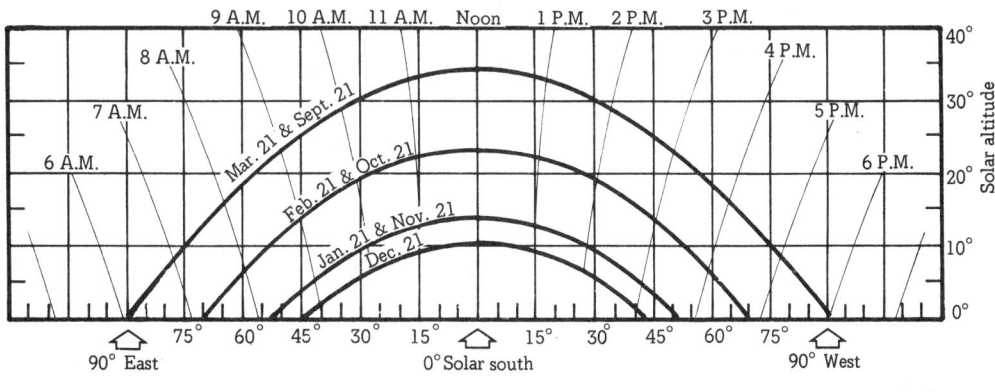

h) 56° North latitude.

SYSTEMS SELECTION WORKSHEET

This worksheet is designed to help you choose which solar heating system(s) to build. First, circle the appropriate letters on the *Analysis* section of the worksheet. After you have answered all the questions, match your answers with the letters on the *Selection* section of the worksheet to determine the best solar heating system(s) for your needs. In many cases, more than one system will be appropriate. Sometimes a combination of systems is best. You should base your final decision on a complete reading of this book and on the tastes and preferences of members of your household.

Analysis *Site analysis of the south wall*

1. The orientation of your south wall is:
   a. Within 30° of solar south
   b. 30° to 45° east or west of solar south
   c. More than 45° east or west of solar south

2. The amount of shading on the south wall during the heating season is:
   a. 0 to 10 percent
   b. 10 percent to 20 percent
   c. More than 20 percent

3. Your view to the south is:
   a. Excellent to good
   b. Fair to poor

Architectural analysis

1. Rooms on the south side of your house are:
   a. Used during the day, such as the kitchen or living room
   b. Used mostly at night, such as bedrooms or dining room

2. Construction of the south wall of your house is:
   a. Wood frame
   b. Masonry
   c. Metal (mobile home)
   d. Other

3. The unobstructed continuous flat wall area on the south wall is:
   a. Larger than 7 ft. 2 in. high by 14 ft. 11 in. wide
   b. Larger than 7 ft 2 in. high by 3 ft 2 in. wide
   c. Smaller than either of the above

4. Is the solar collector being built as part of a house addition?
   a. Yes
   b. No

Climate

1. The amount of sunshine in winter is:
   a. Sunny
   b. Partly cloudy
   c. Cloudy
   and the average winter temperature is:
   d. Cold
   e. Cool
   f. Mild

Economics

1. How much money do you want to invest in solar (including tax rebates and finance charges)?
   a. $150 to $300
   b. $300 to $1000
   c. $1000 to $1500
   d. $1500 or more

2. What is your goal for your solar system?
   a. Grow food as well as save fuel
   b. Save up to 30 percent of fuel costs
   c. Save more than 30 percent of fuel costs

Match the letters you circled for each question in the *Analysis* section to the letters in corresponding subsections of this worksheet section.   **Selection**

Site analysis of the south wall

1. If the orientation of your south wall is:
   a. You have an excellent solar site for all systems.
   b. You have a compromised site with a potential 15 to 25 percent loss of collector efficiency.
   c. Another side of your house is oriented closer to solar south.

2. If the amount of shading is:
   a. You have an excellent solar site!
   b. You have a good solar site for all systems.
   c. You have a fair to poor solar site. Consider moving the collector or removing the obstruction.
3. If your view to the south is:
   a. You have a good site for Direct Gain and Attached Solar Greenhouse systems (with transparent glazing).
   b. You have a good site for a TAP and a Horizontal Air Flow Active Collector. Or, Direct Gain and Attached Solar Greenhouse systems can be built with translucent glazing to obscure the view to the outside.

Architectural analysis

1. If the rooms on the south side of your house are:
   a. Your site is ideal for all systems with or without thermal storage.
   b. A Horizontal Air Flow Active Collector or Attached Solar Greenhouse with thermal storage are recommended; Direct Gain can be used with thermal storage. (Consider changing the function of one of these rooms so that it is used during the daytime.)
2. If construction of the south wall is:
   a. All of the systems can be built.
   b. Your site is good for Attached Solar Greenhouse and Direct Gain systems. (A "Trombe wall" system, not covered in this book, is also possible.)
   c. Your site is good for TAP, Direct Gain, and Attached Solar Greenhouse systems.
   d. Appropriate systems must be determined from a thorough analysis of each system.
3. If the size of unobstructed continuous flat wall area is:
   a. It is appropriate for all systems.
   b. TAP, Direct Gain and Attached Solar Greenhouse systems are possible.
   c. Direct Gain and Attached Solar Greenhouse systems are possible.

4. If the collector is being built as part of a house addition:
    a. Thermal storage can be integrated into the house addition; there is flexibility in choice of the system.
    b. Thermal storage and choice of appropriate systems may be limited.

Climate

1. If the amount of sunshine and average temperature in winter is:
    a./d. You can expect excellent performance from all systems.
    a./f. For a collector area over 100 square feet, thermal storage should be provided to improve system performance.
    c./d. Insulating shades must be provided on Direct Gain systems.
- For all other climates, follow general system guidelines.

Economics

1. If you want to invest:
    a. You can purchase materials for one TAP or small Direct Gain system.
    b. You can purchase materials for several TAP or Direct Gain systems, or a combination of these systems.
    c. You can purchase materials for more of the above or for a Horizontal Air Flow Active Collector.
    d. You can purchase materials for an Attached Solar Greenhouse system and/or combinations of the above systems.
2. If your goal for your system is:
    a. You should install an Attached Solar Greenhouse.
    b. You should install a Direct Gain, TAP or Horizontal Air Flow Active Collector system.
    c. You should install thermal storage integrated with a Direct Gain, Horizontal Air Flow Active Collector, or large Attached Solar Greenhouse system.

Safety Building the solar heating systems in this book requires good carpentry skills. You should know the proper procedures for performing the work described and be familiar with the potential hazards. Safety is based on knowledge, skill, and an attitude of care and concern.

Keeping your construction site neat and orderly makes the construction process both easier and safer.

Use the correct tool for the job and keep your tools in good working order. Poorly functioning or improper tools subject you to unnecessary dangers.

Wear safety glasses when using power tools or whenever the work involves hazard to your eyes. Also, wear shoes with thick soles to protect your feet from protruding nails.

Do not place tools overhead on ladders or anywhere else where they slip off and cause injury.

Lift heavy objects with the strength of your legs—not with your arms and back. Always stand close to the load and keep your back as vertical as possible. When the load is extra heavy or bulky, get help from friends.

Solar Terminology *Active solar heating* —Use of mechanical power (fans and/or pumps) to move collected heat.

Btu—The amount of heat needed to raise the temperature of 1 lb. of water 1° F. (Approximately equal to the heat from one wooden kitchen match.)

Collector—A system or device used to collect solar energy and convert it to heat.

Direct gain—Direct collection of solar energy, for example, with windows.

Double glazing—Two layers of glazing with an insulating air space between them.

Glazing—Translucent or transparent glass or plastic material that allows light to pass through.

Insolation—The total amount of sunlight—direct, diffuse, and reflected—that strikes a surface.

Insulation—A material that significantly reduces the transfer of heat.

Passive solar heating—Movement of collected heat using natural principles, without fans or pumps.

Retrofit—Adding solar heating (or cooling) to an existing building.

Thermal storage—Potential heat storage capacity. As the temperature of a material rises, it absorbs (stores) heat, which is given off as the material cools.

Thermosiphoning—The natural movement that occurs as warm air (or fluid) rises and cool air falls.

2

DIRECT GAIN

Direct Gain (Additional South Glazing) is the simplest approach to solar heating. A Direct Gain system consists of large amounts of insulated glazing added to the south side of your house and insulated shades or shutters for nighttime use.

How It Works Direct Gain works on the principle that more heat is gained during a sunny winter day through south-facing, vertical, insulated glazing than is lost through the glazing during both day and night.

The idea is to install a large amount of insulated glazing oriented toward the south; allow the winter sun's rays to be absorbed within the house; and insulate and weatherstrip tightly to trap the heat inside.

With Direct Gain, your house acts as a solar collector. During the day, the winter sun's rays pass through your south-facing windows. The sunlight that enters is absorbed by furnishings, walls, floor, and ceiling. When sunlight is absorbed it is converted to heat—solar heat. This process in turn heats the air in your house. When thermal storage is used, the sunlight directly strikes the storage material and warms it. Then the heat is slowly given off to the room as the storage cools.

Fig. 2–1 A Direct Gain sunporch (Hobie Iselin, designer and builder).

Direct Gain is ideal for rooms used during the day or, with thermal storage, for rooms used both day and night. Sites with reduced amounts of sunlight can benefit from Direct Gain as opposed to thermosiphoning and active collectors which use exterior absorber plates to collect solar heat. With thermal shades or shutters for night use, Direct Gain can be extremely effective, reducing auxiliary fuel use by 20 to 50 percent [1]. Unfortunately, the benefits of this system are often overlooked in favor of more complex solar heaters.

System Strategies

Fig. 2–2 Carefully evaluate the south side of your house to determine the most appropriate solar heating system.

The first step in installing a Direct Gain system is to *substantially increase the amount of south-facing insulated glazing*. For the average home, up to 150 square feet of south glazing with nighttime insulating shades will be effective. In sunny, cold climates, the amount of effective glazing can be increased. Beyond a reasonable limit, increased amounts of glazing can create undesirable effects—spring and fall overheating, and reduced savings from each square foot of additional glazing—unless the system is carefully engineered to suit your exact thermal needs.

Fig. 2–3 Before constructing the frame for insulated glass units, check the porch foundation to be certain that it extends below the frost line.

When adding substantial glazed areas, new framing members must be designed not only to secure the glazing, but to carry roof loads as well. For entirely glazed areas, racking stress must also be analyzed. If you have any doubts regarding the structure of the house, consult someone knowledgeable before proceeding.

So that most of the sunlight will be converted into heat rather than reflected back outside, the room to which you add glazing should be at least 12 feet in depth (distance from glazing to far wall). In narrow rooms, such as sunporches, the floor and walls that the sunlight strikes should be painted with medium to dark colors. Masonry floors are ideal if they are a medium to dark color and are not carpeted where the sun strikes. Medium to dark colored vinyl floor coverings work well. *All* furnishings, walls, and floors need not be dark, however, because sunlight that reflects from one object is likely to be absorbed by another object.

The room furnishings, walls, floor, and ceiling will give off heat as they cool slightly at night. This is *basic* thermal storage. Additional thermal storage can be used in Direct

Fig. 2–4 Interior of a sunporch

Gain systems if your house structure can support substantial additional weight and if the thermal storage will be in direct sunlight most of the day. Dark colored containers filled with water can be built into a window seat for effective storage.

At night, all thermal storage should be insulated away from the cold glazing and insulating shades should be placed securely over windows throughout the house. In this way, you save much of the heat captured during the day. Without nighttime insulating shades, the large glazed areas will lose a substantial amount of heat, resulting in cold drafts along the floor and radiant cooling which can make the room uncomfortably cold. Radiant cooling occurs as the cold glass surface draws heat from warmer objects around it, making anyone near the cold glass feel chilled.

Fig. 2–5 The completed Direct Gain system—an attractive sunporch (Photo by Edward Williams)

Instructions for constructing nighttime insulating shades are included in this chapter.

Advantages and Disadvantages

Because of its simplicity, additional glazing is ideal for use in conjunction with other solar heating systems. The primary material in Direct Gain systems—fixed and/or operable insulated glazing—is readily available in all sizes. For large areas fixed glazing is most economical, with several small operable windows (windows that open and close) added nearby for ventilation.

Direct Gain

Fig. 2–6 With *direct gain* each room can have its own solar collector.

You can buy fixed glazing at a moderate price in the form of sliding glass door replacement panels at lumber yards or glaziers. A 34 inch by 76 inch insulated glass unit or similar standard size costs about $60.

Each room with southern exposure can have its own Direct Gain collector. A slightly eastern exposure is ideal for morning direct gain to a kitchen, while a slightly western exposure may be ideal for watching winter sunsets. Additional glazing is a great way to take advantage of a good southern view.

Before building your Direct Gain system, you should consider several environmental factors. With large areas of transparent glazing, lack of privacy can sometimes be a problem. Also, strong winter sunlight can sometimes cause harsh glare, and may fade your furnishings. On the other hand, filling your house with sunlight in the middle of January has a very warming effect.

The total material cost for construction of a Direct Gain system is approximately $6 per square foot of insulated glazing. A weekend builder with one helper can install a Direct Gain system in about two weekends. Building or enclosing an existing south-facing sunporch is an excellent way to use Direct Gain solar heating.

Caution: Do not leave small children or pets unattended in small enclosed Direct Gain rooms (or solar greenhouses). Temperatures can reach 100°F even on partly sunny days, despite frigid outdoor temperatures.

Materials

Materials for Direct Gain systems are available at local lumber yards and glaziers. Because Direct Gain systems do not subject materials to extreme daily temperature changes, conventional construction materials and detailing can be used. Attention to detail and use of high quality materials, however, ensure the best performance.

Insulated glass is recommended for glazing because of its proven longevity and aesthetic value. Where ventilation is desired, use operable windows. Operable windows should be located high and low on several exterior walls to take advantage of prevailing summer breezes.

Plastic glazing can also be used effectively. Each type of plastic has unique characteristics that makes it appropriate for certain situations. Translucent plastic (or translucent glass) is suitable where privacy and reduced glare are desired. High impact strength plastic resists children's abuse. Plastic glazing can be cut to most shapes and sizes. However, special attention is often needed to install and maintain it, so check the manufacturer's directions before you use it.

Note: If you use translucent glazing, install transparent glazing in some areas so you can see through to the outside.

Large sheets of insulated glass are available in standard sizes of 28 inches by 76 inches, 34 inches by 76 inches, and 46 inches by 76 inches. A 34 inch by 76 inch sliding glass door replacement unit costs about $60 (glass only). Custom sizes are much more expensive. Low iron glass is best, because it

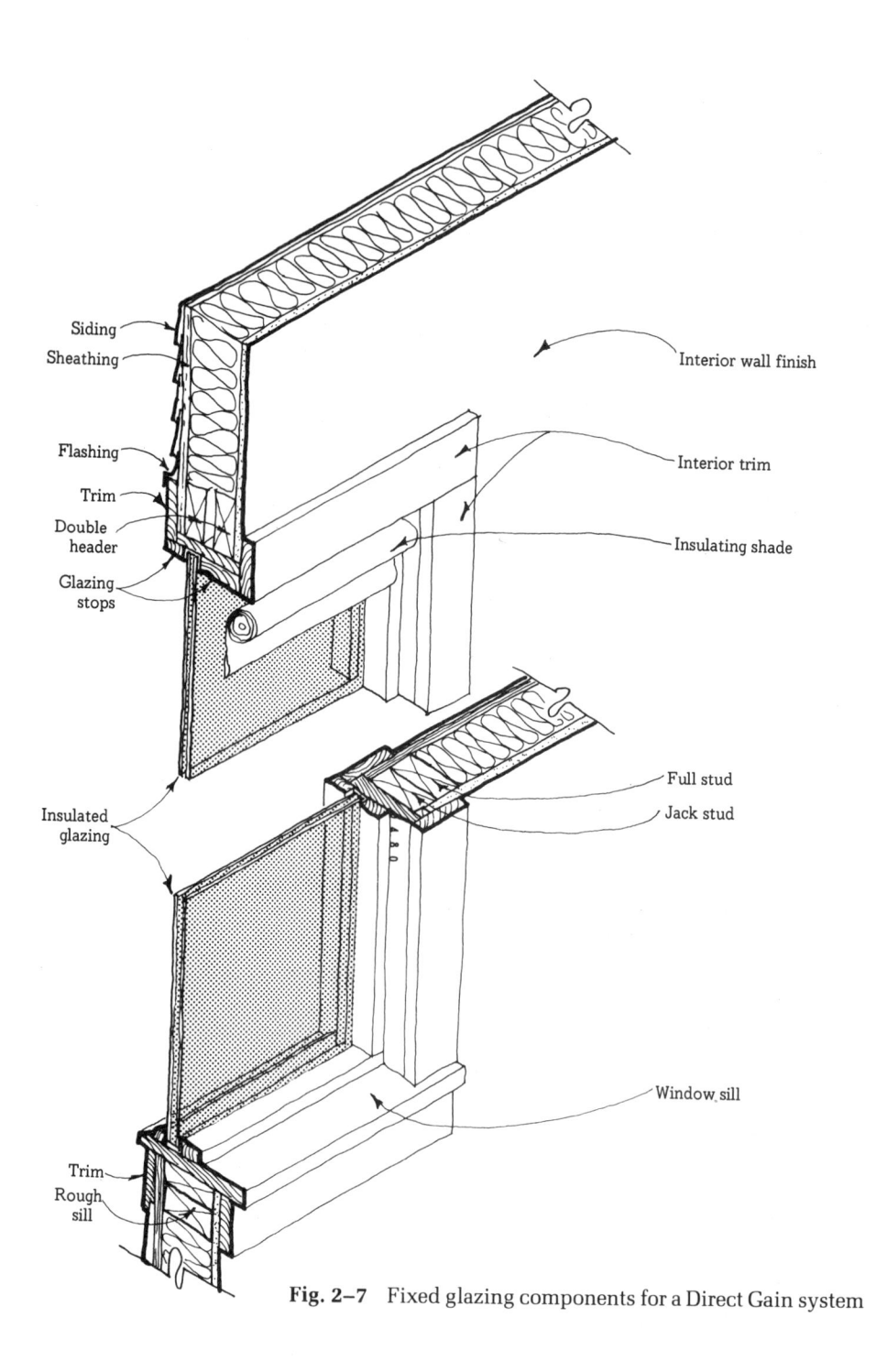

Direct Gain

Fig. 2–7 Fixed glazing components for a Direct Gain system

transmits more light than standard glass, but it is not readily available, and is expensive.

Acrylite is a double-walled, 5/8 in. thick acrylic plastic. It is translucent and has high impact strength. You can get Acrylite from Cyro Industries, 897 Route 46, Clifton, New Jersey 07015. It is available in sheets of 4 feet by 8 feet, 4 feet by 10 feet, and 4 feet by 12 feet and costs about $2.50 per square foot. Specifications, availability, and cost of other glazing materials are listed in Chapter 4 in the Attached Solar Greenhouse materials list.

Note: Fixed glazing systems can be constructed with various sizes and quantities of glazing. You must therefore

Direct Gain Materials List

Part	Dimensions	Quantity	Notes
full studs	2" × 4" × 8'		
jack studs	2" × 4"		
cripple studs	2" × 4"		
rough sill	2" × 4"		
header	2" × 4"		All wood must
mullion	2" × 4"		be straight
sill	1" × 8"		and true
head	1" × 5"		
jambs	1" × 6"		
stops	1" × 2"		
	1" × 4"		
trim	1" × 4"		
mullions	1" × 4"		
glazing cap	1" × 5"		
drip cap flashing			
glazing			
neoprene setting blocks	1/4" thick × 1" × 2"	2 per glazing sheet	available from glazier
neoprene spacers	1/8" thick × 1/2" × 2"	20 per glazing sheet	
caulk			latex or silicone
paint and primer			
nails	10d galvanized		
	16d galvanized		
	16d galvanized casing		
	6d galvanized casing		
insulation			

determine the specific sizes and amounts of materials needed for your design. Since the thickness of wall constructions varies, you'll need to determine the correct size of the sill, head, jamb, and stops for your wall thickness. In many cases, you will have to cut the depth of the wood to suit your exact needs.

Construction

Layout

Determine the best location on your south wall for your Direct Gain system. Consider appearance as well as thermal needs. Design your system to use fixed sliding glass door replacement panels in standard sizes, and/or fixed and operable windows. Where doors are needed, using insulated sliding glass doors with wood frames is a good way to add to your glazed area. Remember, each square foot of glazing up to approximately 150 square feet adds to the net heat gain.

Visualize all new glazed areas from both the interior and the exterior. Mark rough openings for all glazing on interior and exterior walls. If thermal storage is part of your design, thoroughly examine how it will aesthetically fit into your room. Be certain that thermal storage will be in direct sunlight most of the day, and check the floor structure to be sure it will support the weight of the storage material. Water, a popular thermal storage material, weighs 8.4 pounds per gallon.

Note: Before cutting exterior and interior walls, check to see if plumbing or wiring is enclosed in the wall area to be removed. Cut a small opening in the interior wall and look into the wall cavity. If plumbing or wiring is there, you will have to work around the pipes or wires or relocate them, according to local building codes.

Procedure

Note: Temporary supports must be provided before wall studs or any other structural members are cut.

1. Cut and remove the interior wall finishing within the rough opening.
2. Remove the wall insulation.

Direct Gain 41

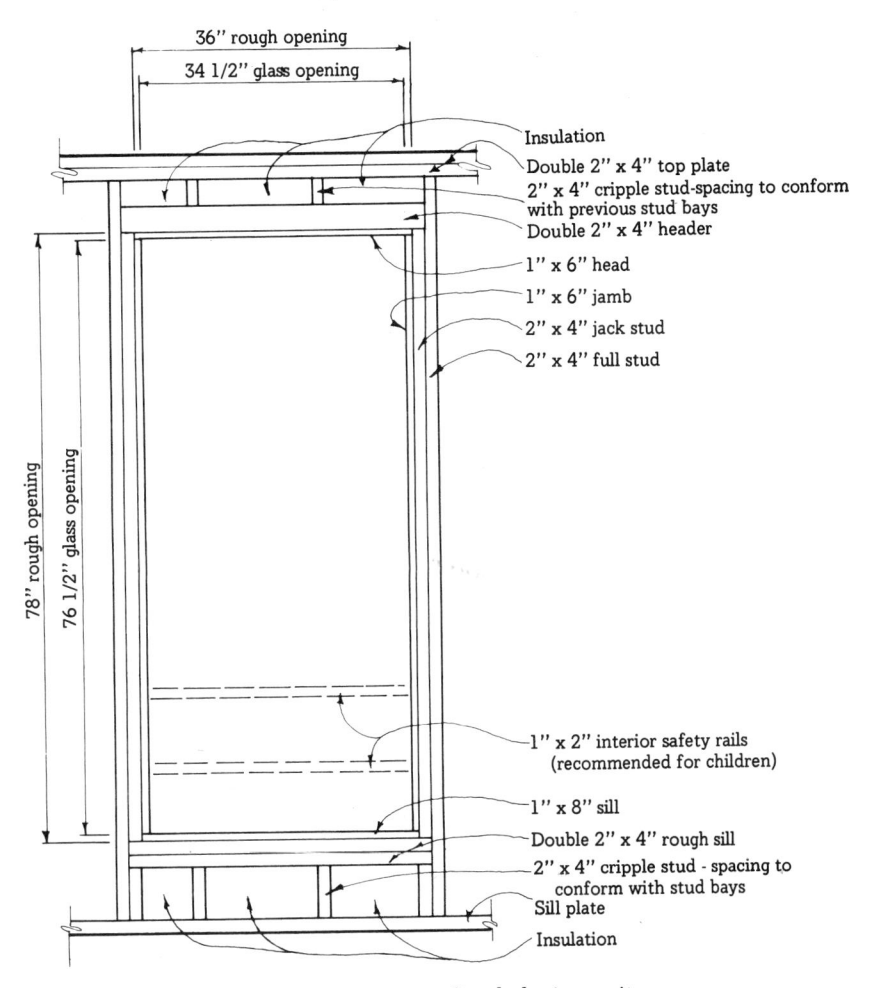

Fig. 2-8 Front view of a 34 in. × 76 in. fixed glazing unit

3. Hammer a nail through the sheathing and siding at each corner of the interior wall opening. Use these nails as a reference point to check the rough opening layout on the exterior wall.
4. Cut and remove the sheathing and siding. Make the sheathing opening the same size as the interior finishing opening. Cut the siding (leaving the sheathing) to allow for the 1 in. × 4 in. trim.

Direct Gain

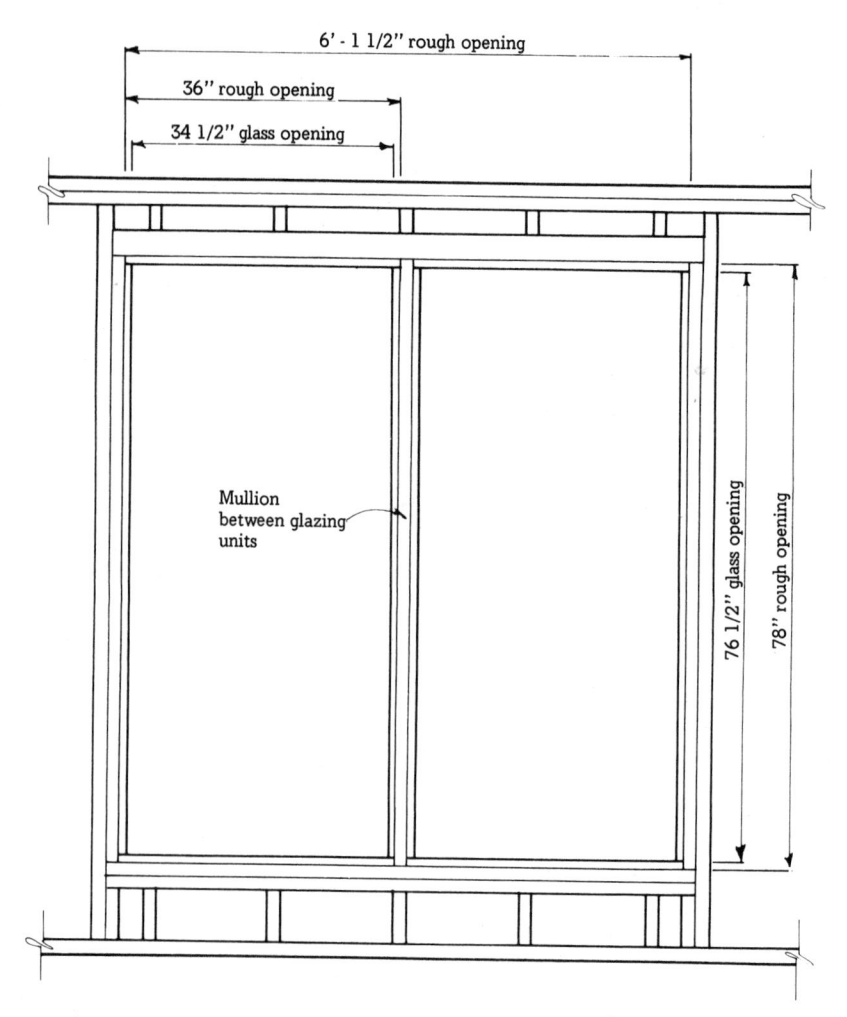

Fig. 2–9 Front view of two 34 in. × 76 in. glazing units

5. Clear the inside of the wall so the studs (full, jack and cripple), rough sill, and header can be placed in the wall cavity without obstructions.
6. Plumb, then nail full studs in place. Nail through the sheathing and interior finish where nails will be covered by 1 in. × 4 in. trim.
7. Nail the cripple studs, rough sill, jack studs, and double 2 in. × 4 in. header in place. The frame must be level and

Direct Gain 43

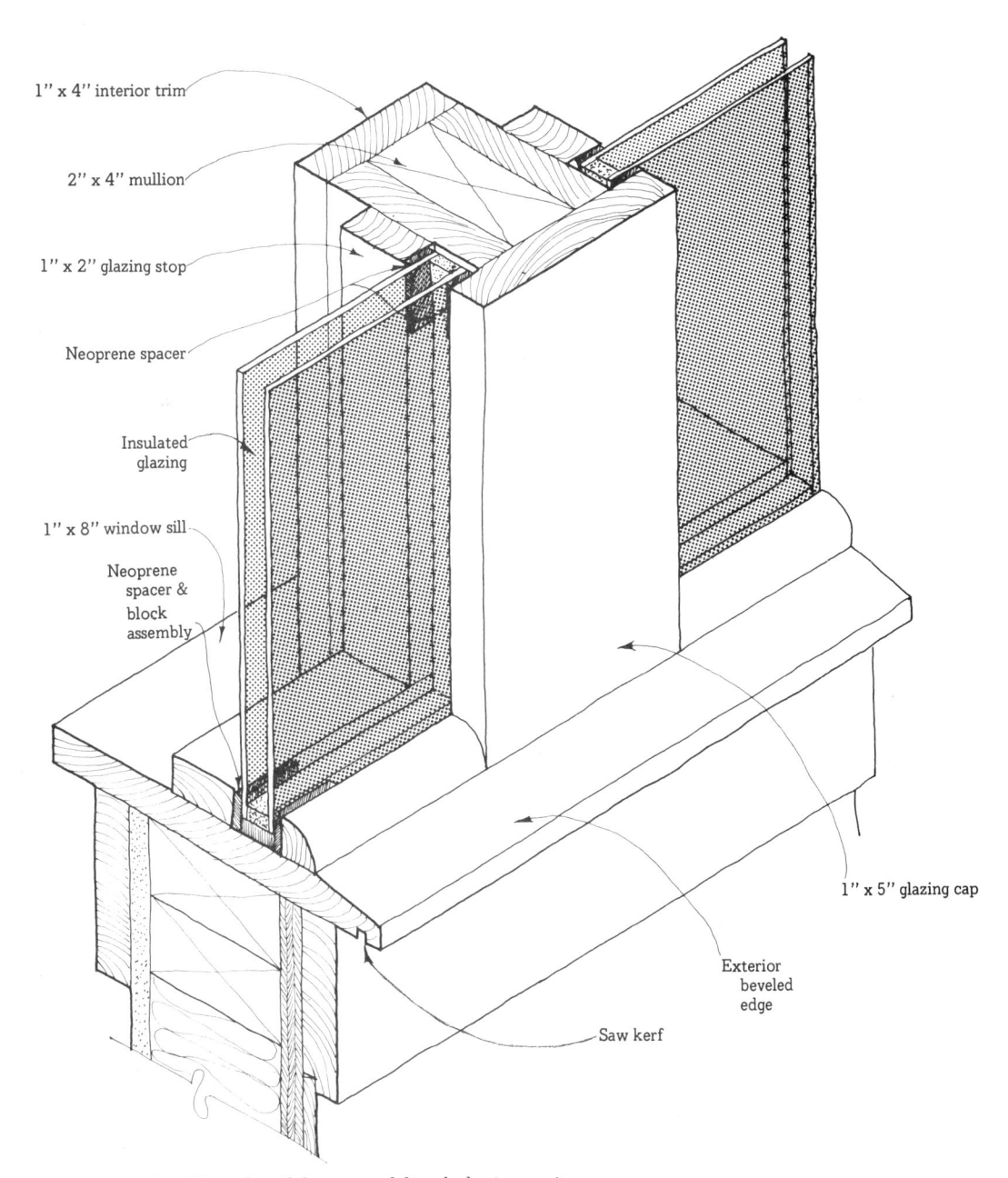

Fig. 2–10 Mullion detail for several fixed glazing units

Direct Gain

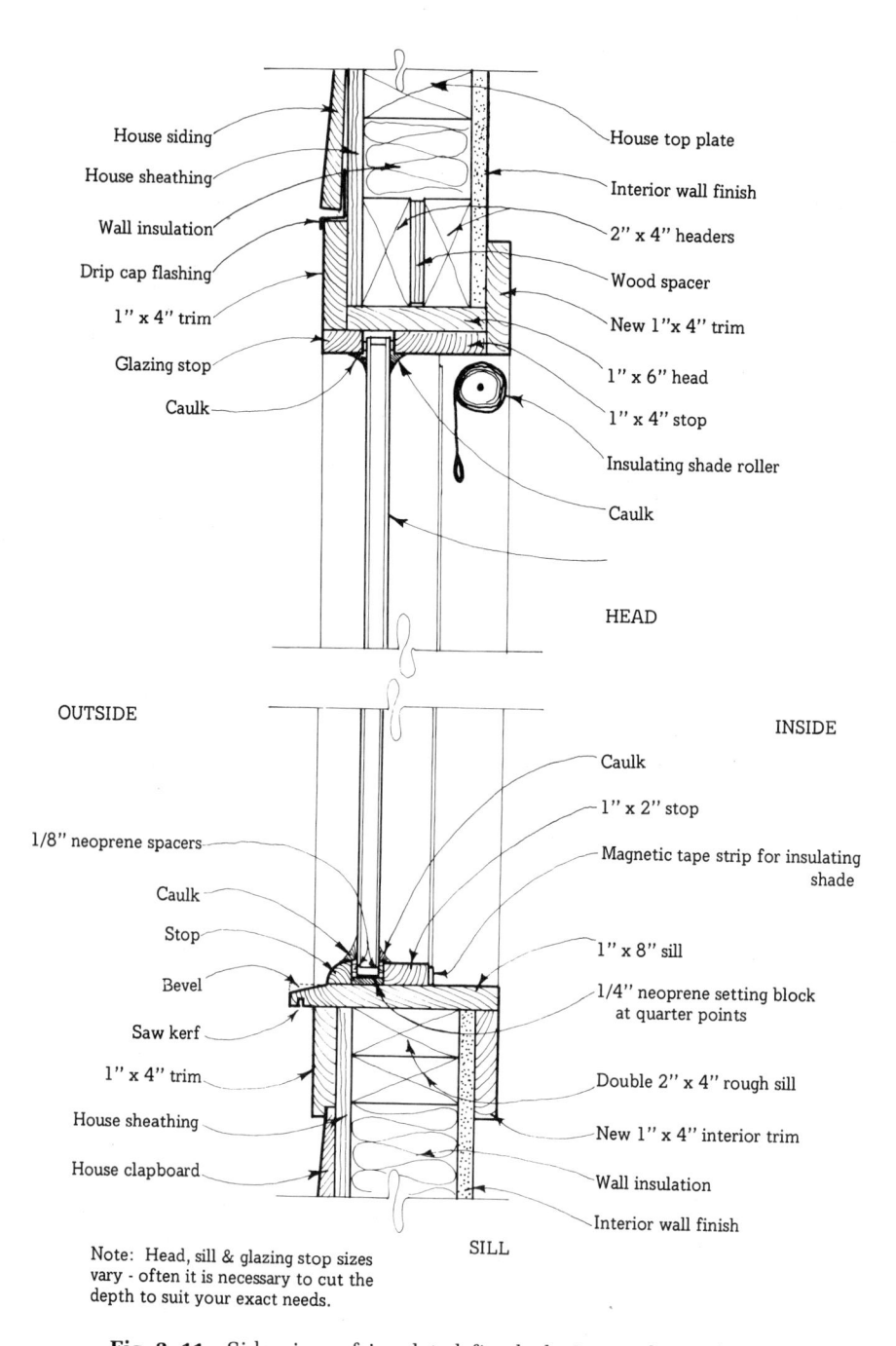

Fig. 2–11 Side view of insulated fixed glazing with insulating shade

Direct Gain 45

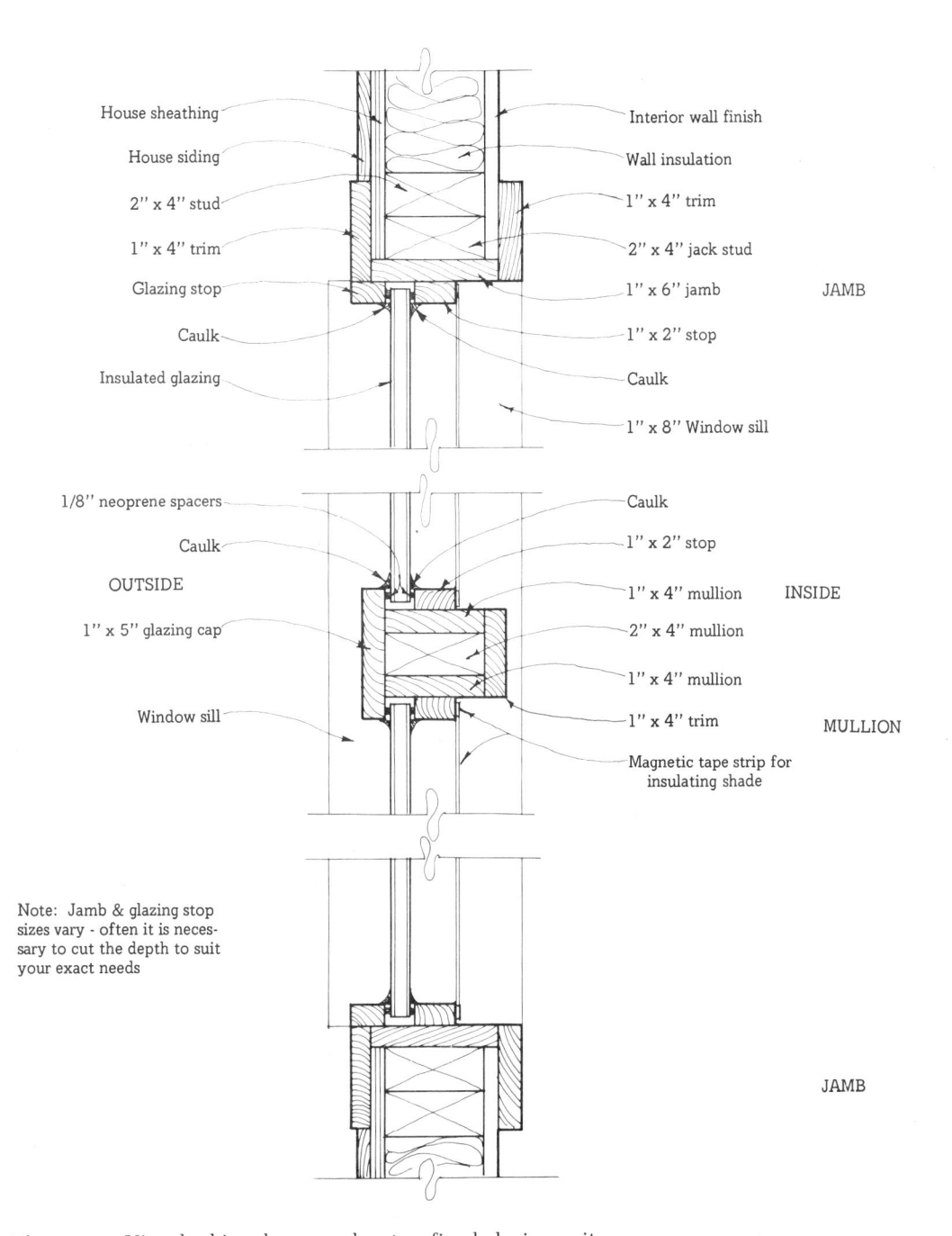

Fig. 2-12 View looking downward on two fixed glazing units

square. Check the rough opening dimensions. *Always insulate between studs.*
8. Cut the saw kerf and bevel the edge of 1 in. × 8 in. sill. Determine the length and width of the sill; cut, then nail it into place.
9. Measure the length and width of the jambs, 1 in. × 5 in. head and mullions. Cut and nail these pieces into place. For fixed glazing, the height and width of the opening should now be 1/2 in. larger than the glazing.

Note: Mullions are constructed of several pieces of wood laminated (glued and nailed) together to minimize warpage from continuous exposure to direct sunlight.

10. Calculate and mark the depth for the interior glazing stops. Allow a 1/8 in. space between the front and rear of the glass unit and the wood (1/4 in. overall). Cut lengths and nail the interior stops in place along the sill, jambs, and head. (When it is difficult to insert the glazing from the outside, the exterior stops should be nailed in place first so the glazing can be inserted from the inside.)
11. Cut lengths and nail the 1 in. × 4 in. interior and exterior trim in place.
12. Prime all wood, including the stops and glazing caps not yet installed.

Glass Installation

1. Set the neoprene setting blocks and spacers in place as shown. The setting blocks must be wide enough to support both sheets of glass. Use a dab of caulk as the adhesive.
2. Install the glazing unit. Two people can handle a 34 in. × 76 in. unit.
3. Nail the exterior stops and glazing caps in place. Insert the exterior neoprene spaces. Caulk the glazing, then paint the interior and exterior frames. Exterior latex caulk should be painted.
4. Clean the glazing. A razor blade is good for removing paint from glass.

Note: Painting the frame around the glazing a light color increases reflected light into the house and reduces the heat stress on the wood frame.

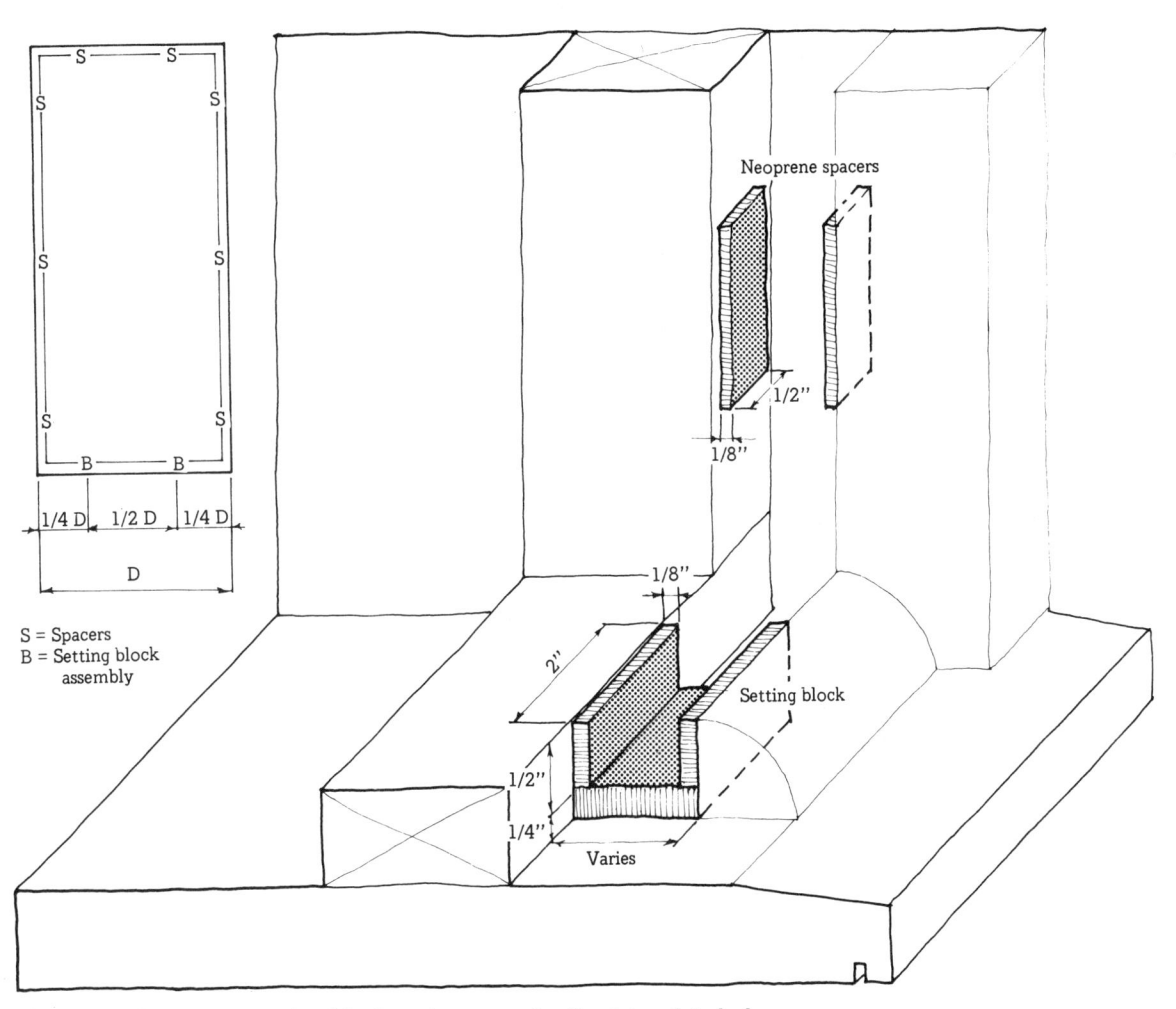

Fig. 2–13 Neoprene setting block and spacers for fixed insulated glass unit. Place ¼-in. diameter polyethylene rope between the end of the insulated glass unit and the wood frame. The rope provides a surface to caulk against, making an excellent seal with less caulk. (This detail applies to installation of glass in each of the four retrofit systems.)

Insulating Shades

For maximum efficiency, Direct Gain glazing must be covered at night with insulating window shades which reduce both convective and conductive/radiant heat loss. The shade must not only be an good insulator, but must also fit tightly around the glazing's perimeter. A shade with good conductive/radiant insulating properties, but poor perimeter seals will encourage reverse thermosiphoning of house air: cold air next to the glazing enters the room and is replaced by heated house air, which creates cold drafts along the window area.

I have used two types of insulating shades which are effective, easily built, and low-cost: spring-loaded roller shades and roll-down shades. Either can be appropriate for your Direct Gain or Solar Greenhouse system. Many other effective insulating shades and shutters are available—from do-it-yourself kits to completely installed units. For a complete analysis of these, see William Shurcliff's *Thermal Shutters and Shades* (1980, Brick House Publishing).

By the way, once you have constructed shades for your new solar system, you should construct them for the other windows in your house as well. On windows that aren't south-facing, where you don't have to leave shades open all day for heat gain, you can gain additional savings by leaving insulating shades drawn for part of the day.

Note: Insulating shades may create condensation on windows. You can keep water from the windowsill by placing foam weatherstripping along the bottom of the glass. The foam absorbs the water and allows it to evaporate.

Window shade materials

1. Aluminized shade material, such as "Astrolon," available from Shelter Institute, Bath, Maine; or "Foylon" available from S.U.N., Box 306, Bascom, OH 44809 (Tel. 800-537-0985).
   Cost: approximately $2 per sq. yd.
   Note: It is important that the surface of the shade facing the glazing be reflective to infrared (heat) radiation.
2. Adhesive-backed magnetic tape, 1/2 in. × .03 in., available from Permag Northeast Corp., 10 Fortune Drive, Billerica, Massachusetts 01865 or S.U.N., Box 306, Bascom, OH 44809.
   Cost: approximately 35¢ per lin. ft.
3. For roll-down shade unit: 1¼ in. dowel, 3 pulleys or 1/2 in. screw eyes, rope cleat, and 1/8 in. nylon cord.

For spring-loaded roller shade unit: spring loaded roller with wall mounts (available at hardware store).

Note: I do not recommend using "Astrolon" shades for summer shading because they break down from long exposure to direct sunlight. Hopefully, other more durable reflective materials will soon be available to provide a year-round insulated shading device.

The insulating roll-down shade

Roll-down shades are ideal for large Direct Gain and Solar Greenhouse glazing areas. The shade can be constructed of a single or double layer of aluminized material. The double layer adds to the shade's insulating value, but the bulk of two layers makes the shade somewhat more difficult to operate. If you use two layers, make several small holes at the top of the layer that is closer to the window. The holes allow air to enter and escape from between the layers as the shade is lowered and raised. You can apply fabric to dress up the inside of the shade. Patterned fabrics are recommended to hide wrinkles.

The four edges of the shade are sealed airtight in different ways. The top edge is permanently secured to the top of the window frame with a piece of molding. When the shade is lowered, the sides are sealed to the frame with magnetic tape. The bottom is sealed either by magnetic tape or by the weight of the shade roller on the window sill or floor. The larger the shade, the fewer shades you'll need, and the fewer edges you'll have to seal. Sixteen-foot wide shades work well.

Construction of insulating roll-down shades is a good one-day project. First, measure and cut the shade material wide enough to accommodate the side magnetic tape strips and long enough to extend 12 inches beyond the window opening. Leave a little extra width to allow for horizontal waves in the material. The extra length allows the top of the shade to be placed several inches above the top of the window and permits some shade material to remain on the roller when the shade is fully closed. When the shade is fully raised it should not block the top of the glazing. For double layered shades, be sure to double the amount of material ordered. The two layers can be sewn together using a zigzag stitch, with few stitches to the inch.

Direct Gain

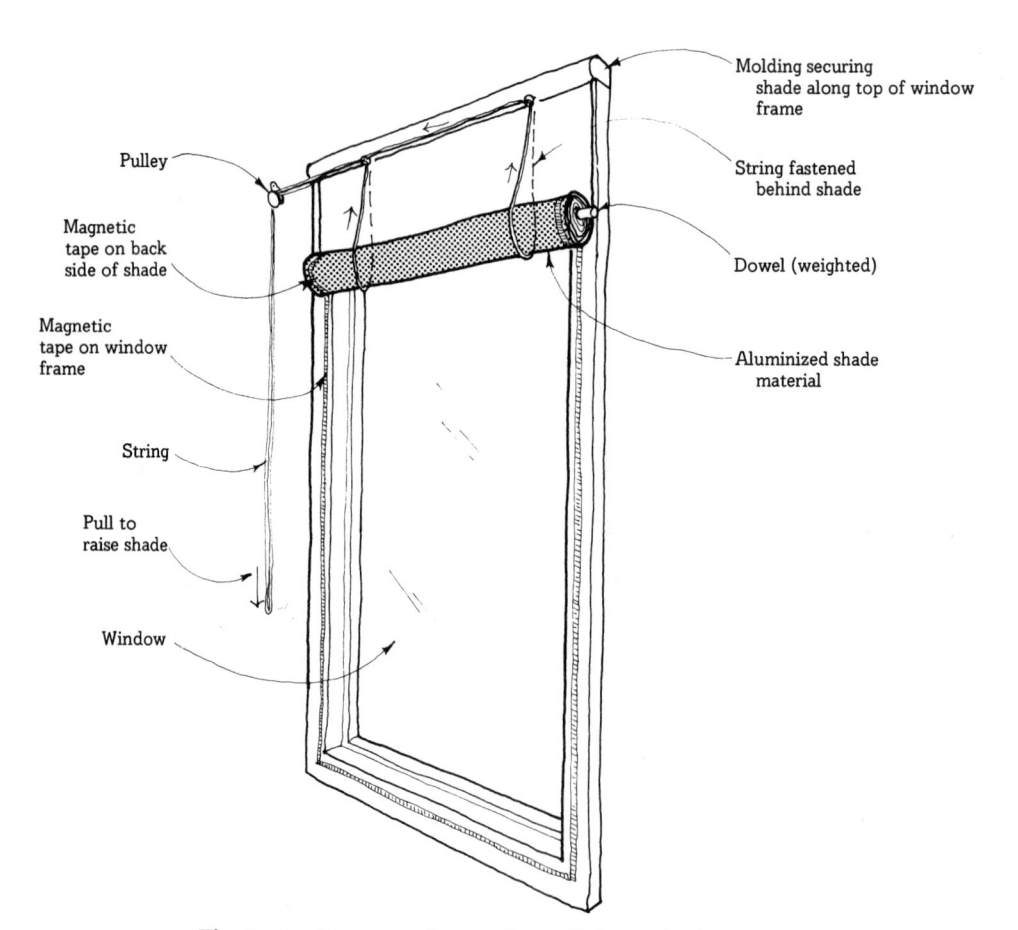

Fig. 2-14 Diagram of insulating roll down shade

Cut the roller several inches larger than the width of the material. For small shades a heavy dowel works best. If the shade does not roll up properly because the dowel is too light, weight the dowel by wrapping lead flashing around it. Staple the material to the dowel, and then mount the hardware as shown.

Temporarily mount the shade in place by tacking the top edge of the shade material to the window trim and installing the guide ropes. Test the shade's operation by rolling it up and down several times.

You are now ready to mount the magnetic tape strips. First, secure the tape strips to the window frame.

Note: The magnetic tape on the window frame must be mounted with reverse polarity to the tape on the shade. The reversal of magnetic poles causes the tapes to self-align when the shade is lowered.

Next, align and mount the magnetic tape on the shade. The tape will fasten better if you remove the shade from the window. Making shallow cuts every 1/4 inch on the non-adhesive side of the shade's tape makes the tape roll more easily.

Refasten the shade material to the window by nailing the molding over the shade and across the top of the window trim, and your shade is operational!

For greenhouses, the roll-down shade design works well with the addition of support wires or 3/4 inch pipe, and flat, wooden, horizontal battens. The support wires make the shade material conform to the slope of the glazing and the battens, similar to sail battens, give the shade horizontal rigidity. The side edges of the sloped shades can be sealed with magnetic tape or long zippers. You may need to fuss with the magnetic seals on these shades occasionally because of their tendency to pull away from the side edges. Fuller Moore, designer of this magnetic perimeter seal system, has constructed a 12-foot high by 26-foot wide greenhouse shade with a 60° slope.

The insulating spring-loaded roller shade

This shade's design makes it ideal for average size windows. The spring-loaded roller design is impractical for large windows because the shade's width is limited by available roller sizes, and because spring-loaded shades are difficult to operate if they are large and bulky.

Construction of a spring-loaded roller shade is similar to that of a roll-down shade. The shade material should be cut several inches longer than the length of the window and wide enough to extend 1/2 inch beyond the magnetic tape strip along each side. Staple the aluminized shade material to the roller. (When purchasing the roller, be sure it is wide enough to allow for the magnetic tape strips.) Then fasten the roller to the wall.

Fig. 2–15 Insulated roll down shade (Photo by Nancy Hazard)

Attach magnetic tape strips to both the sides and bottom of the window frame. Be sure the tape along the bottom of the window is in the same plane as the tape on the sides. If your existing windowsill extends too far into the room to allow this, add a 3/4 inch piece of molding to the sill. Then align the magnetic tape on the shade with the tape on the window frame, and attach it to the shade.

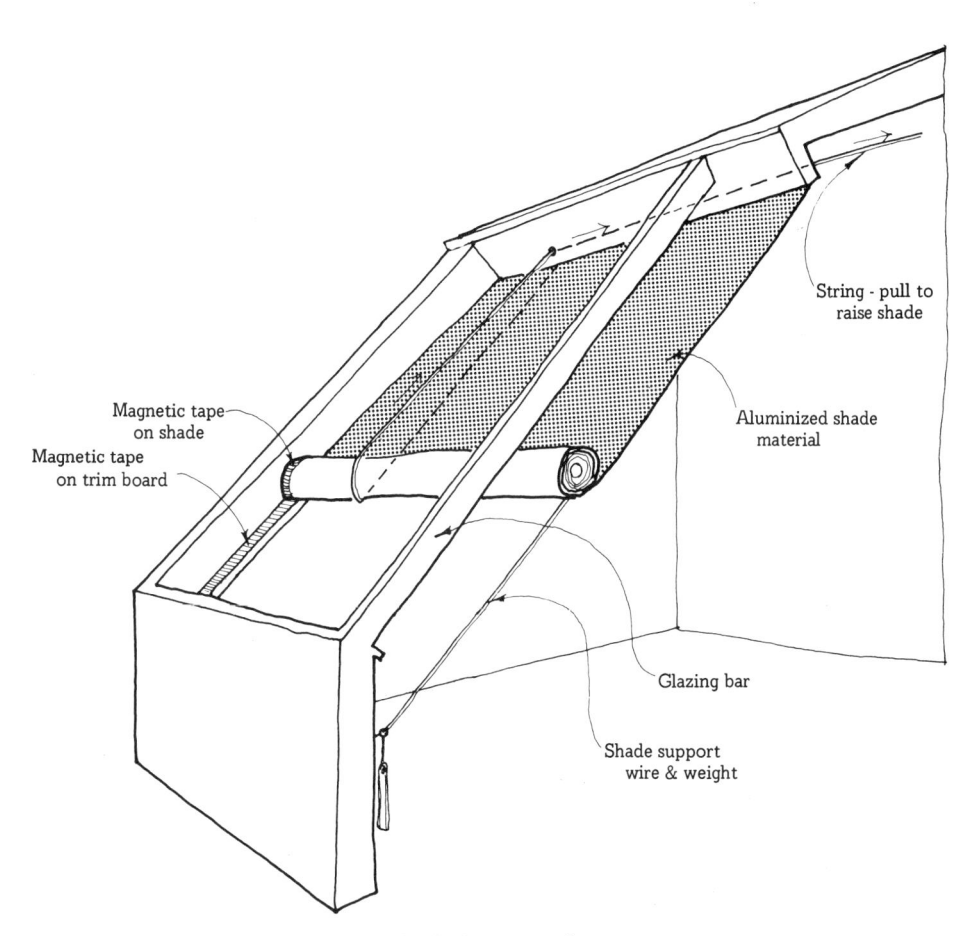

Fig. 2–16 Diagram of roll down shade for a greenhouse

To lower the shade, pull it down and away from the window. Pulling the shade away from the window prevents the magnetic tape from sealing until the shade is in the desired position. The spring-loaded roller locks the shade in the lowered position. To raise the shade, "peel" it free, and pull it to activate the roller's return spring.

Direct Gain solar heating requires daily attention to insulating shades. Shades should be fully opened each morning and tightly closed each evening. All shade edges must be airtight!

Maintenance

54 Direct Gain

Fig. 2–17 Insulated roll down greenhouse shade (Fuller Moore designer, photo by Fuller Moore)

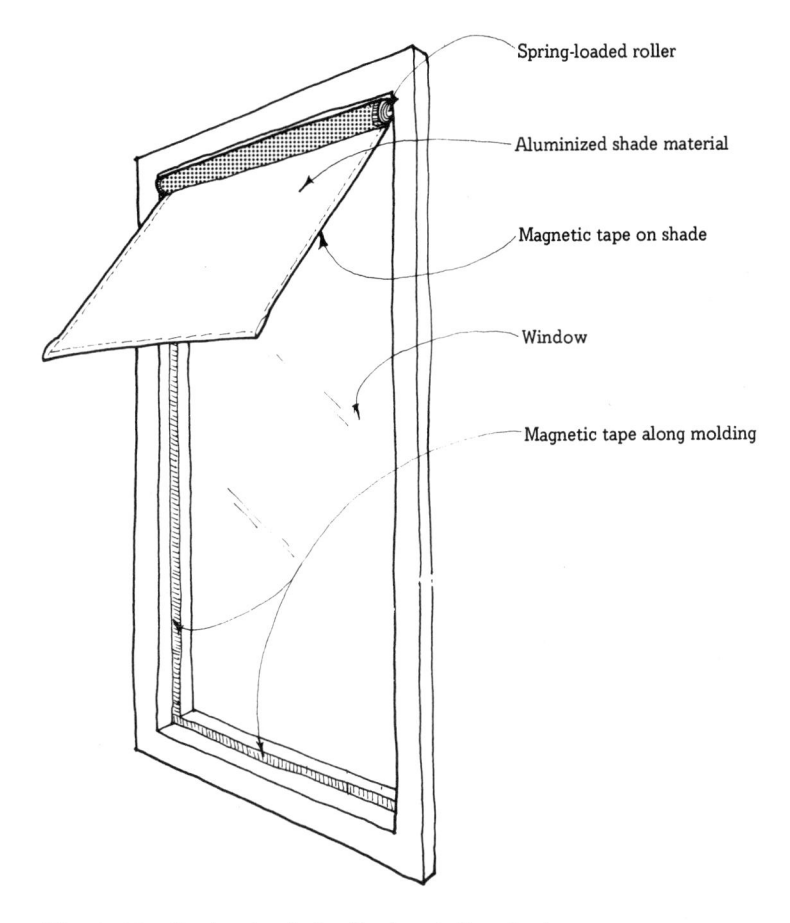

Fig. 2-18 Spring-loaded roller insulating shade

Air leakage causes a continuous thermosiphoning flow which creates cool drafts. Be sure to open both shades and drapes *completely* on south windows to receive the full benefit from every square foot of glazing.

Your Direct Gain heating system should be maintained along with the rest of your house. Periodically clean the glazing, especially at the start of the heating season. Remember, plastic glazings may need special treatment, so check the manufacturer's recommendations. Also, check caulking and weatherstripping annually and repair as necessary, to prevent air infiltration along the seams. Finally, prune any new plant growth that shades your south glazing.

Direct Gain

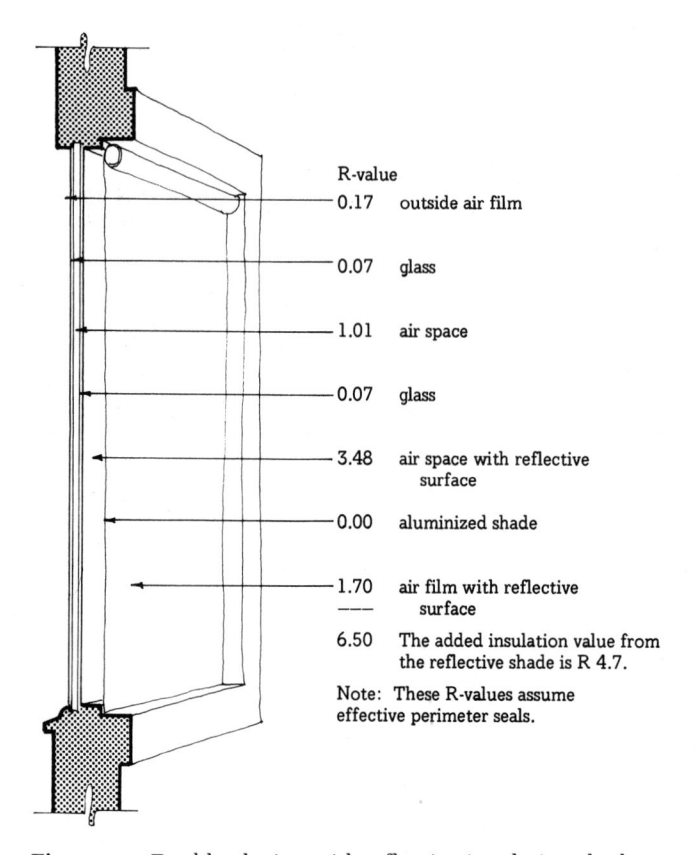

Fig. 2–19 Double glazing with reflective insulating shade

R-value
- 0.17 outside air film
- 0.07 glass
- 1.01 air space
- 0.07 glass
- 3.48 air space with reflective surface
- 0.00 aluminized shade
- 1.70 air film with reflective surface
- 6.50 The added insulation value from the reflective shade is R 4.7.

Note: These R-values assume effective perimeter seals.

Reference

1. D. Lewis and W. Fuller, Total Environmental Action, Inc., Harrisville, N.H., *Solar Age*, December, 1979.

3

THE THERMO-SIPHONING AIR PANEL (TAP)

A Thermosiphoning Air Panel (TAP) system, like Direct Gain, uses insulated glass. The TAP, however, is more sophisticated, because it uses an absorber plate to convert the sun's energy to heat, and moves the heated air into the house by natural means. Basically, the TAP consists of insulated glazing, a black aluminum absorber plate, and wood frame on the outside of the house and two air vents on the inside.

How It Works

TAPs operate on the principle that warm air rises. Sunlight penetrates the insulated glass unit on the outside of the TAP and strikes the black aluminum absorber plate. The absorber plate converts the sunlight to heat and reaches temperatures above 100°F. As the absorber plate becomes hot, it in turn heats the air around it. Behind the absorber plate there is an air passage which is connected to the house by the upper and lower vents (see illustration). When the air behind the absorber plate is sufficiently hot, it naturally rises and enters the room through the top vent. As the warm air enters the house through the upper vent, cool air along the floor is drawn into the bottom vent to replace it. *This air movement is a natural energy flow.*

The Thermosiphoning Air Panel (TAP)

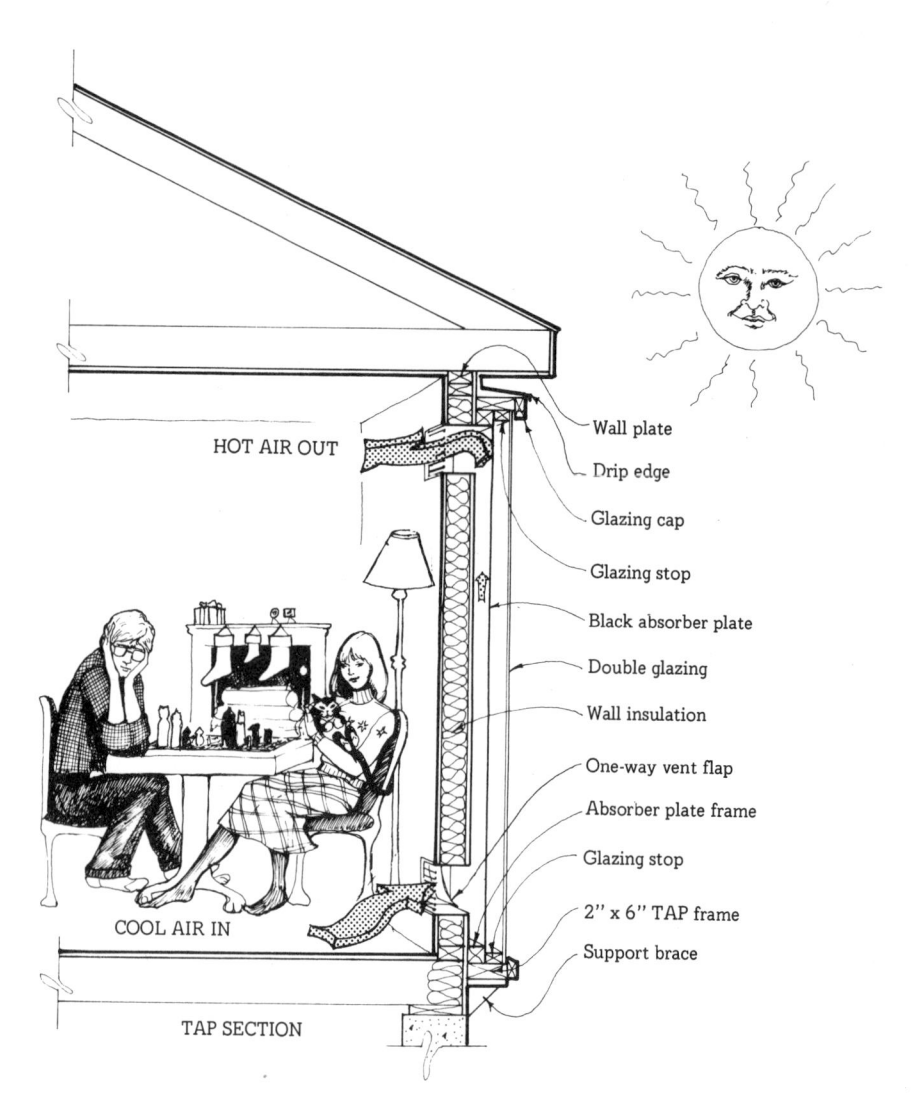

Fig. 3–1

The TAP is designed to provide solar heat to your home during daylight hours. At night the automatic one-way vent flap in the lower vent prevents cold air in the TAP from entering the house.

The Thermosiphoning Air Panel (TAP)

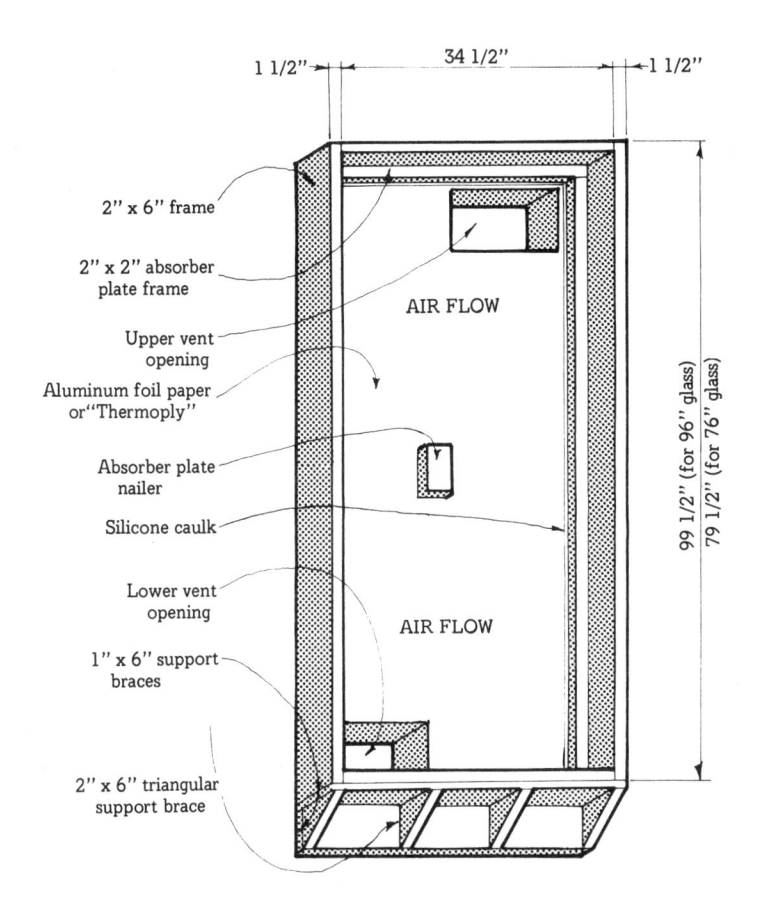

Fig. 3–2 TAP: Air flow behind the absorber plate

Thermosiphoning air panels are ideal for a home with good southern exposure, where the rooms adjacent to the south wall are used during the day. On sunny winter days, the TAP delivers solar heated air to the room directly behind it. Since TAPs have limited heat storage capacity, they are most appropriate in cool and cold climates where daytime heating is needed for several months.

Any unobstructed southern wall space 3 feet, 1½ inches wide and 7 feet, 2 inches high (for a 34-inch by 76-inch glass panel) or 8 feet, 10 inches high (for a 34-inch by 96-inch glass

System Strategies

Fig. 3-3 Thermosiphoning Air Panels

panel) is a potential TAP space. Where possible, you should group TAPs together in large, continuous units of two, three, four, or more modules. Connected TAP modules maximize absorber plate size, simplify construction, and increase efficiency by reducing edge heat losses.

Material costs for construction of the TAP are approximately $180 per panel, or $8 per square foot of collector surface. A weekend builder with one assistant can build three or four TAPs in two or three weekends. TAPs are a low-cost way to use solar energy. If you have a limited amount of money to spend, you can build one or two, and add more later.

Note: This solar heating system will heat the house wall behind the collector to higher than normal temperatures. Therefore, I do not recommend placing this collector on any wall containing inflammable insulation or other material.

The Thermosiphoning Air Panel (TAP)

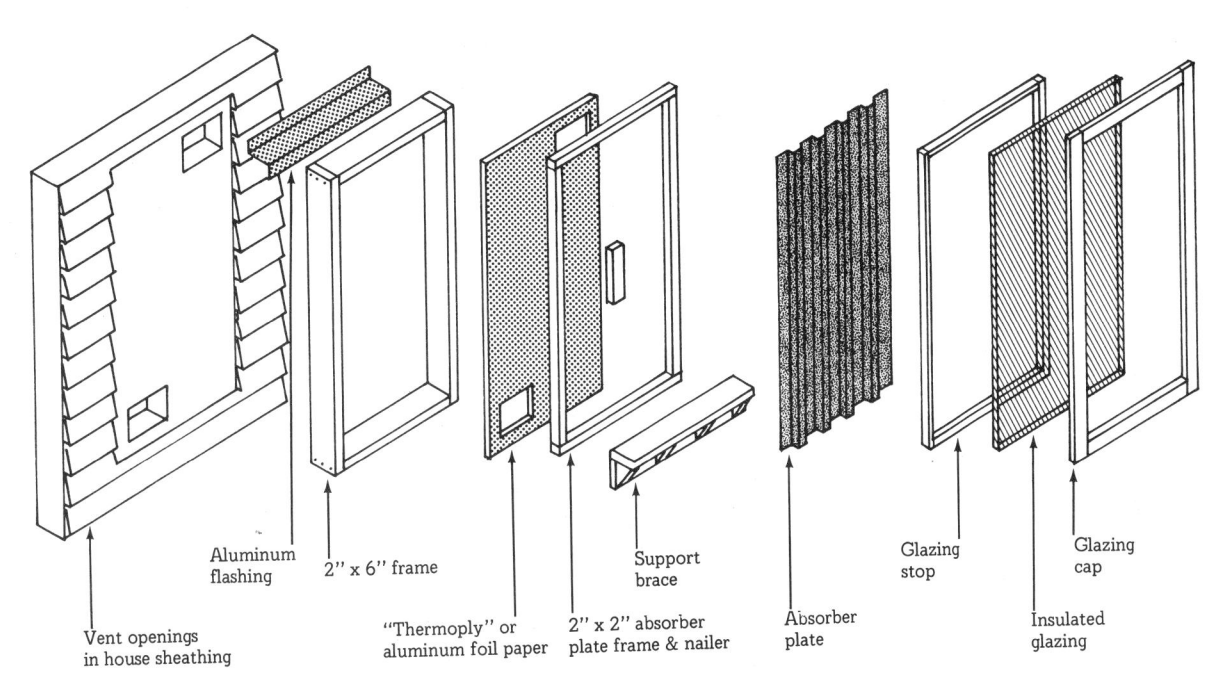

Fig. 3–4 TAP components

Materials

Materials used in TAPs must be able to withstand extreme temperature fluctuations. On an unusually warm, sunny November day, when the sun is low in the sky and the TAP vents are shut tight to avoid overheating the house, the inside of the system can reach temperatures above 200°F. On sunny winter days the temperature of the absorber plate can reach 120°F at solar noon and then be cooled to below zero that night. These temperature extremes can have devastating effects on building materials.

An 8-foot length of aluminum expands and contracts over 1/8 inch when its temperature changes by 150°F. Glass under similar circumstances expands and contracts less than 1/10 inch. To allow for expansion and contraction and still keep your TAP weathertight, careful detailing and material selection are essential. Any variations from the recommended materials or procedures should be analyzed in regard to the daily thermal shock your TAP will undergo.

Absorber plate

The absorber plate converts the sunlight that passes through the glazing to heat. For high collector efficiency the absorber must be painted flat black. The absorber plate should be approximately .02 inch in thickness for rapid transfer of heat to the air behind it.

The daytime temperature of the absorber is often above 100°F. At night, the absorber cools to the outside temperature. The severe temperature variation places thermal stress on the absorber's painted surface, and on the connection between the absorber plate and its frame. Aluminum can withstand these extreme temperature fluctuations.

Carefully follow the manufacturer's instructions for degreasing the metal absorber plate surface, removing the degreasing agent, and applying flat black, high-temperature paint (barbecue black or woodstove paint can be used). Factory baked-on painted finishes are ideal, but not readily available in flat black. The absorber plate should be cut to size before being painted.

To prevent paint outgasing from accumulating on the glazing, allow the paint to dry at least two days before installing the glazing over the absorber plate.

Note: Paint application is critical for high performance. If the paint peels, the glazing will have to be removed to recondition the absorber plate.

To improve the transfer of heat from the absorber plate to the air that flows to the house, the interior surface of the plate should be lightly textured. Non-textured surfaces slightly reduce collector efficiency. Corrugated aluminum sheets are recommended for absorber plates and are available at lumber yards and building material suppliers for metal roofing.

Aluminum foil paper (or "Thermoply")

This material seals the existing building sheathing to prevent hot air from the collector from entering into the stud wall cavity. Heating of the sheathing causes heat stress and heats the wall, which results in heat waste. Aluminum reduces heat absorption, and prevents these problems.

"Thermoply," a foil-faced cardboard sheathing material, should be used when available. Thermoply is manufactured by Simplex Product Group, 3000 W. Beecher Road, Adrian, Michigan 49221 and is available at some lumber yards.

Heavy grade aluminum foil paper is also good. Aluminum foil paper with tar backing should not be used because the tar releases noxious gases when exposed to high temperatures.

Caulk

The collector must be well caulked to ensure good performance. All seams should have a continuous bead of caulk. Clear silicone caulk is recommended for use inside the collector because of its ability to withstand high temperatures. Silicone caulk is flexible and waterproof, and will not degrade when subjected to ultraviolet light.

Glazing

The glazing is exposed to daily temperature fluctuations of 100°F. Because glass expands and contracts less than 1/10 inch under these conditions, it is the best glazing material for TAPs. Plastics are not recommended for TAP glazing because they expand and contract as much as 1/2 inch with the same temperature variations. It is difficult to maintain weather tightness and a quality appearance with this much movement.

Ideally, the glass should be double-glazed, tempered, low-iron, and sealed with a flexible double layer of silicone and polybutyl. Low-iron glass allows 10 percent more light to pass through it and therefore has a higher efficiency than ordinary glass. It appears clear when viewed on its edge, while ordinary glass appears green in comparison. Low iron glass is generally available only with textured surfaces.

Sliding glass door replacement panels are an inexpensive, readily available alternative for TAP glazing. They are available at lumber yards and glaziers for about $60 for a 34-inch by 76-inch double-glazed unit. Although these units are not low-iron, nor are they double-sealed with silicone and polybutyl, they have been used with satisfactory results. When using glass door panels, be sure that the seals are flexible and not welded.

Wood

All framing must be done to a tolerance of 1/16 inch. To insure this accuracy all wood must be straight and true.

Pine should not be used for glazing stops because it outgases when exposed to high temperatures. These outgases condense on the inside of the glazing and reduce the amount of light entering the TAP. Fir or spruce (spruce flooring) can be used.

Tap materials list

These materials make one 96 in. × 34 in. double-glazed unit. For 76 in. × 34 in. double-glazed unit use the 79½ in. frame and 76½ in. absorber plate frame and glazing caps.

Part	Dimensions	Quantity	Notes
frame	2″ × 6″ × 99½″	2	
	2″ × 6″ × 34½″	2	
absorber plate frame	2″ × 2″ × 96½″	2	
	2″ × 2″ × 31½″	2	
glazing stops	1″ × 4″ × 96½″	2	
	1″ × 4″ × 33″	2	
brace	1″ × 6″ × 37½″	2	
triangular support braces	2″ × 6″ × 5½″	4	
glazing caps	1″ × 3″ × 96½″	2	
	1″ × 3″ × 37½″	2	
absorber plate nailer	2″ × 6″ × 12″	1	
aluminum foil paper	3′ × 9′		or one 4′ × 8′ sheet of "Thermoply"
nails	10d galv./1 lb.		
	16d galv./1 lb.		
	8d finishing/1 lb.		
	10d aluminum/¼ lb.		
duct tape	2″	1 roll	
clear silicone caulk		3 tubes	
latex caulk		1 tube	
flashing	12″	4′ (drip edge)	
		8′ (vent boots)	
vent registers	8″ × 14″	1 with fixed louvers	
		1 with operable louvers	

The Thermosiphoning Air Panel (TAP)

Part	Dimensions	Quantity	Notes
vent flap	13½" × 7½"	1	Use thin, nonadhesive "Frisket paper," available at local art supply stores or Dick Blick, Inc., P.O. Box 1267, Galesburg, Ill. 61401 (Tel. 1-800-447-8192).
neoprene setting blocks	1/4" thick × 1" × 2"	2	
neoprene spacing blocks	1/8" thick × ½" × 2"	20	Available at glazier
absorber plate	33½" × 95½"	1	If not factory painted, paint with high temperature, flat, black paint.
"inside" end closure strips		2	For corrugated absorber plate, use 2 end closure strips. Unpainted, corrugated absorber plates and end closure strips are available through Sears' catalog.
glazing	34" × 96"	1	Tempered, double-glazed glass unit with 1/2" air space; flexible sealed with silicone and polybutyl (double sealed). Cost $2.50–$4.00/sq. ft.

Layout

On the exterior of the south wall of your house determine all unshaded, flat wall areas large enough for one or more TAP units. Look for obstructions such as chimneys, utility meters, drain pipes, and wiring. In some cases these can be moved clear of the TAP location.

Visualize where the upper and lower vent registers will be placed on the interior of the south wall. Note any potential obstructions such as cabinets, electrical outlets, appliances, and plumbing lines. Most obstructions can be managed, but each should be studied to simplify installation. Any heat

Construction

The Thermosiphoning Air Panel (TAP)

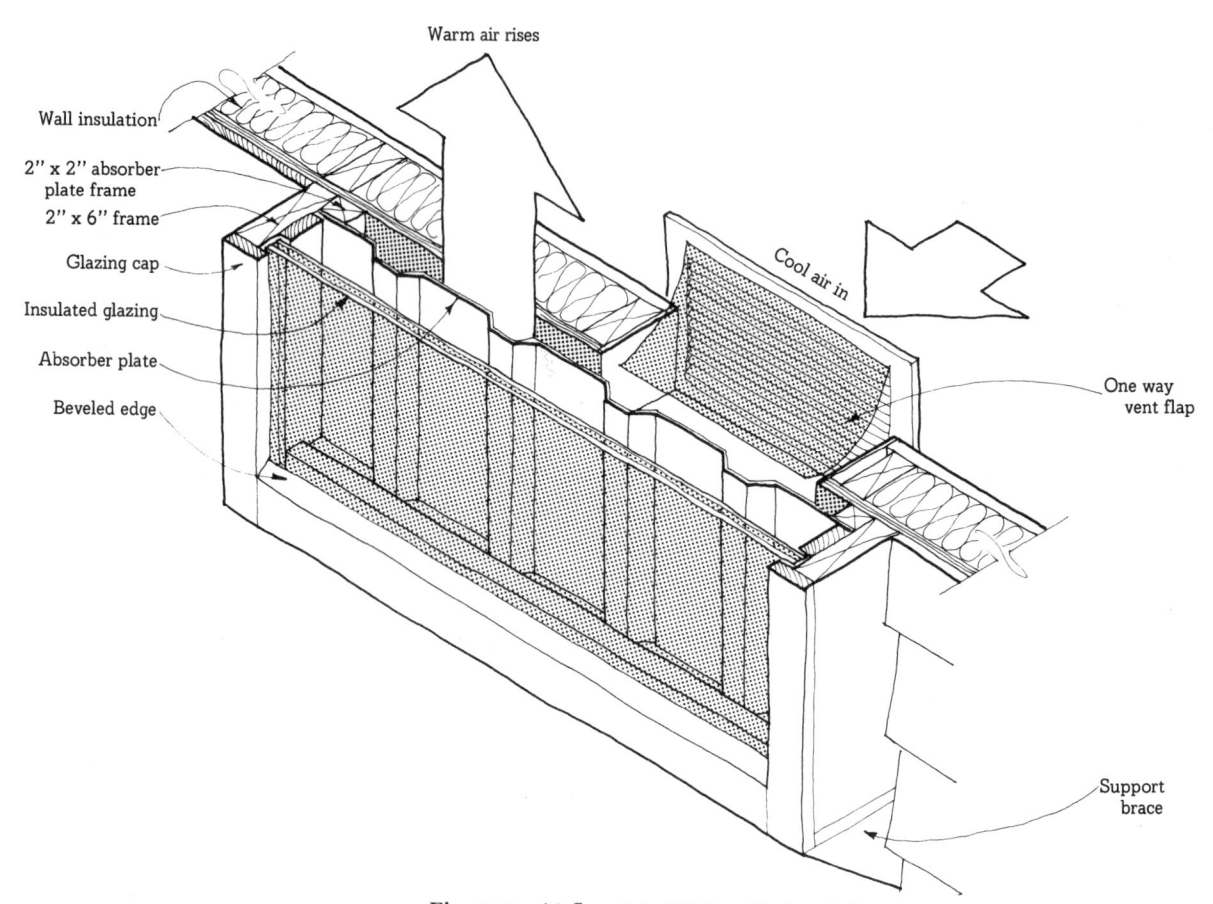

Fig. 3–5 Airflow into TAP and behind absorber panel

source located beneath the TAP intake register will reduce the efficiency of the collector and should be avoided. Vent placement can be unique in each installation.

Using a windowsill as a reference point, determine where the interior floor and ceiling lines are located on the exterior wall. First, measure the distances from the inside windowsill to the ceiling and floor. Then through the open window, mark the height of the inside windowsill on the exterior wall. Using this mark as a reference point, mark the locations of the ceiling and floor on the exterior to indicate the maximum high and low positions for your vents.

Note: Place the vents as high and low as possible to increase the natural thermosiphoning effect. But do not cut the top or bottom wall plates (horizontal 2 × 4s located at the top and bottom of the house wall studs) to further increase the distance between the vents. The top of the upper vent should be within one inch of the inside top edge (the absorber plate frame) of the TAP. The bottom of the lower vent can be several inches above the bottom of the TAP frame.

Procedure

Note: Before cutting, make certain the glass size you need for your TAP is available.

Preparing the absorber plate

Prepare the absorber plate before TAP construction, allowing adequate time for the paint to dry.

1. Cut the absorber plate to proper size.
2. Degrease the absorber plate with solvent, following the manufacturer's instructions. Remove the degreasing agent.
3. Paint the absorber plate with high-temperature (300+°F), flat black paint (barbecue black or woodstove paint).

Framing, Vents, and Absorber Plate

1. Mark the dimensions of the TAP plus support braces on the exterior wall of the house, allowing 1/4 in. overall clearance.
2. Remove the siding down to the sheathing. Set depth of circular saw blade to the thickness of the siding and use a straight piece of wood as a cutting guide.
3. Locate both sides of the wall studs by probing the sheathing with a nail, and draw the location of the upper and lower vents.
4. Prefabricate the 2 in. × 6 in. frame on level ground. Glue and nail each corner. The wood must be straight and true.

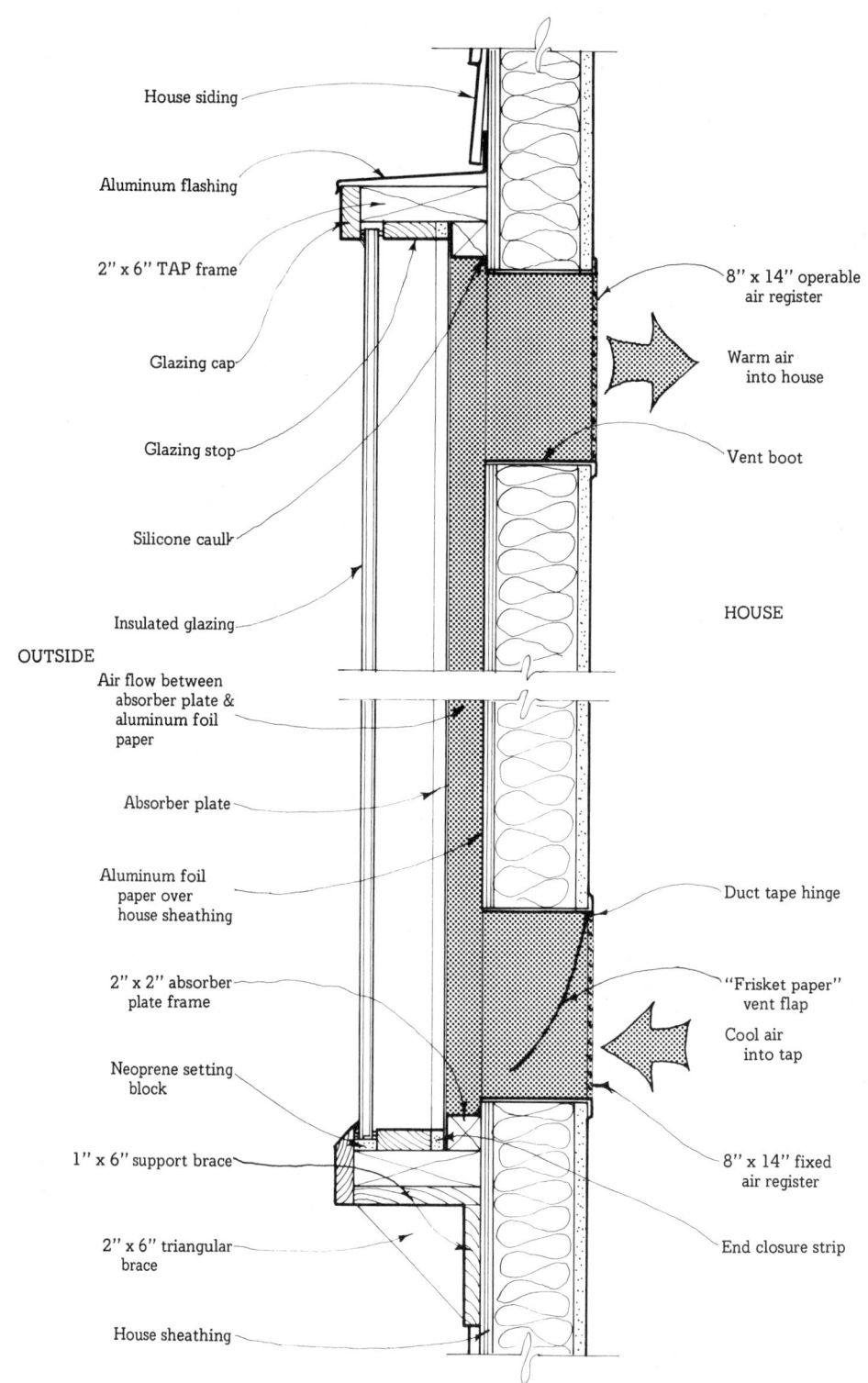

Fig. 3–6 TAP vertical section

The Thermosiphoning Air Panel (TAP)

Fig. 3-7 Cutting an upper vent in the sheathing

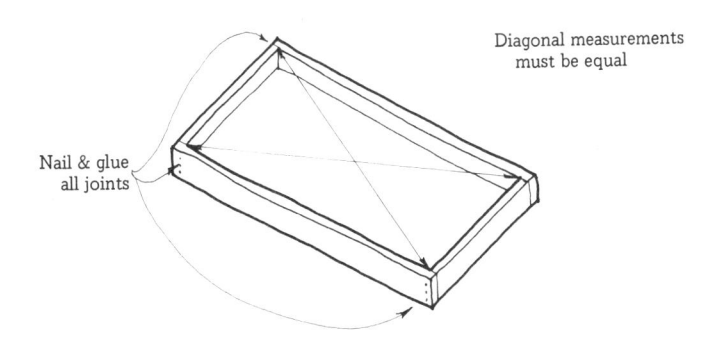

Fig. 3-8 Prefabricated 2 × 6-in. frame

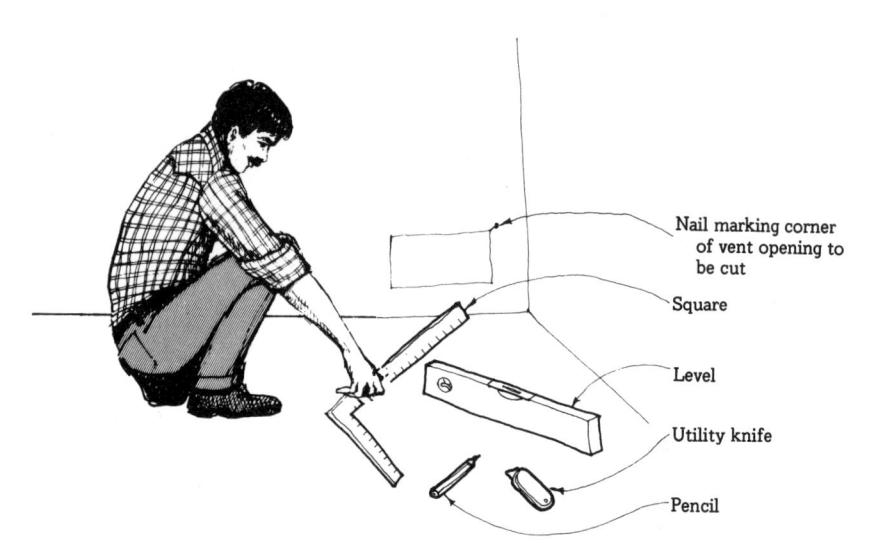

Fig. 3–9 Cutting vent opening in interior wall

Square the frame by making the diagonals equal and note the diagonal measurement for later use.

Note: All wood should be primed before installation.

5. Cut the upper and lower vent openings in the sheathing. A 14-in. opening should fit between a standard 16 in. on-center stud bay. Where possible, locate the vents in opposite corners of the TAP—but do not cut out studs to do so! The upper vent should be as high as possible within the TAP frame; *note where all the vents will be on the interior before making any cuts.*

6. Hammer a nail through one corner of each vent opening in the sheathing. When the nail penetrates the interior wall, use this point to mark and cut the vent openings in the interior wall.

Note: Double-check the location and size of the interior vent openings before making any cuts. This precaution can save a lot of repair work later.

7. Staple the aluminum foil paper over the sheathing. Cut the foil away from the vent openings. Use "Thermoply" building sheathing if available instead of foil paper.

The Thermosiphoning Air Panel (TAP)

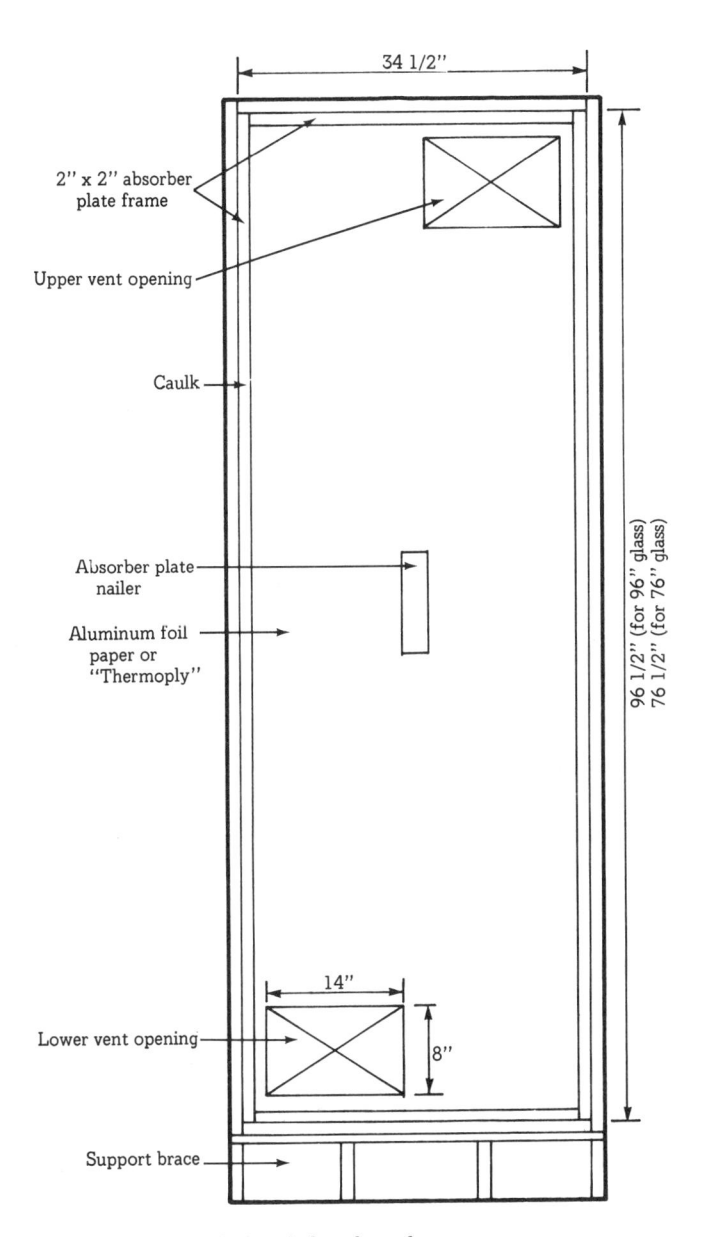

Fig. 3–10 Front view of TAP behind absorber plate

Locate "Thermoply" within the 2 in. × 6 in. frame and nail the Thermoply to the sheathing.

Fig. 3–11 Square the TAP frame by making the diagonal measurements equal.

8. Secure the aluminum flashing at the top of the TAP between the siding and the sheathing. Bend flashing so that it does not interfere with installation of the 2 in. × 6 in. frame.

The Thermosiphoning Air Panel (TAP)

9. Attach the 2 in. × 6 in. frame to the sheathing. Square the frame by making the diagonals equal.

10. Nail the 2 in. × 2 in. absorber plate frame securely to the sheathing, then to the 2 in. × 6 in. frame. Any space between the 2 in. × 6 in. frame and the sheathing (caused by discrepancies in the house sheathing) should be covered by nailing the absorber plate frame tightly to the sheathing before nailing it to the 2 in. × 6 in. frame.

11. Nail the 1 in. × 6 in. support braces to the bottom of the TAP frame; then nail the other 1 in. × 6 in. brace to the house sheathing. Cut, nail, and glue the four triangular 2 in. × 6 in. support brackets to the 1 in. × 6 in. pieces.

12. A vent boot must be placed in both the upper and lower vent openings. The boots seal in the air passing to and from the back of the absorber plate and the house, preventing it from entering the wall cavity. The boots can be either factory-made 8 in. × 14 in. × 6 in. deep or site-made with aluminum flashing. Nail each vent boot to an adjacent wall stud. When additional support is needed to secure the vent boot, construct a wood frame in the wall cavity to which the boot can be nailed.

13. Install the upper and lower vent registers on the inside wall. Place the register with movable louvers in the upper vent opening. See the instructions for constructing a one-way vent flap for the lower, fixed-louver register. When the flap is installed, observe its functioning from the exterior to ensure free movement and return. If necessary, use foam or felt weatherstripping to make an airtight seal between the back of the lower register and the interior wall surface.

14. Caulk the 2 in. × 2 in. absorber plate frame to the foil paper or "Thermoply" to create an airtight seal.

15. Securely nail the absorber plate nailer to the sheathing in the center of the TAP opening.

16. Secure the painted absorber plate to the nailer and the 2 in. × 2 in. frame by nailing it to the frame every 3 inches, using nails of the same material as the absorber plate. (For an aluminum absorber plate, use aluminum nails.) When using a corrugated absorber plate, affix the end

Fig. 3–12 Secure the end closure strips to the absorber plate before fastening the absorber in place.

closure strips at the top and bottom of the absorber plate with silicone caulk before mounting it to the frame. The end closure strips should be able to withstand high temperatures.

Note: Leave a 1/4 in. space between each side of the absorber plate and the 2 in. × 6 in. frame, and a 1/2 in. space at the top and bottom to allow for expansion.

Fig. 3-13 Mount the absorber plate nailer in the center of the TAP.

The Thermosiphoning Air Panel (TAP)

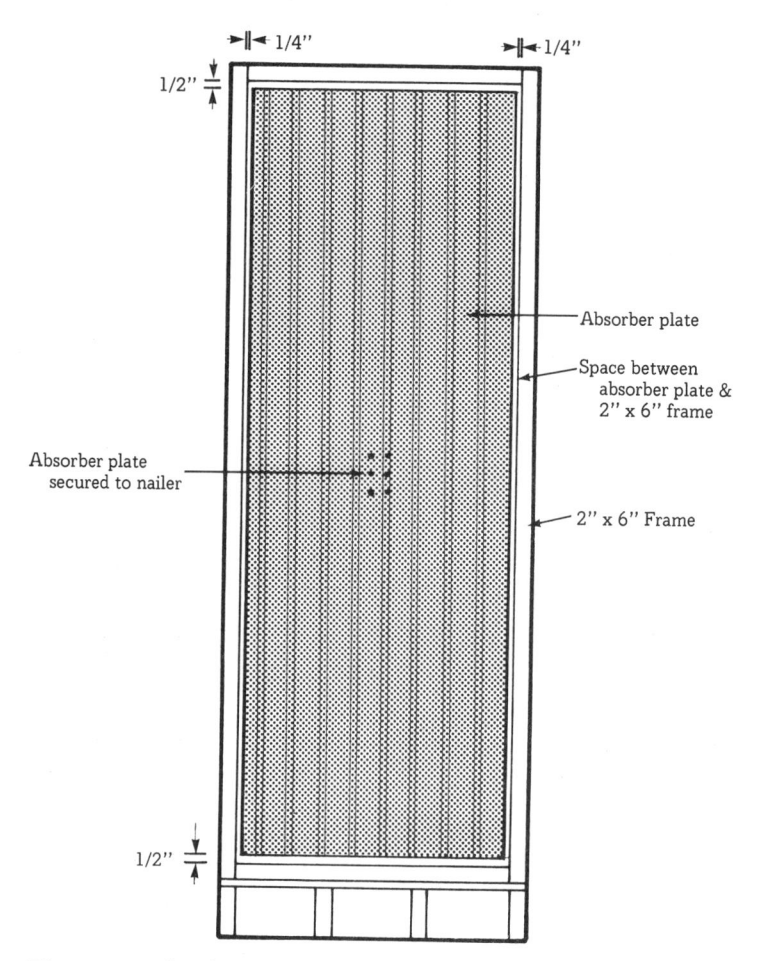

Fig. 3–14 Absorber plate spacing

One-way vent

The one-way vent flap on the lower vent register is the only moving part of the TAP. It controls the movement of air into the collector. When there is heat in the collector the flap will open to circulate the hot air into the room. At night the flap prevents the cold air in the collector from flowing into the house.

For proper operation, pay careful attention to detail when constructing the one-way vent. When closed, the flap must make an airtight seal with the inside of the vent register.

The Thermosiphoning Air Panel (TAP)

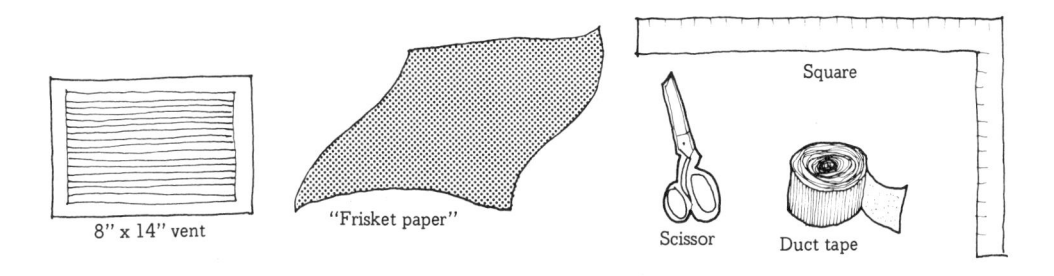

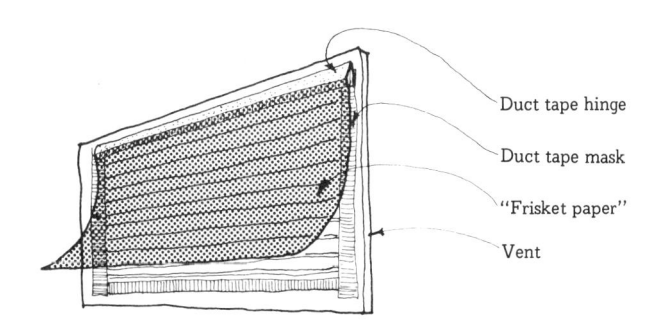

Fig. 3–15 Making a one-way vent

When installed, the flap must move freely within the vent boot without its edges catching on the sides of the boot.

MATERIALS

1. 8″ × 14″ vent register with fixed louvers.
2. 2″ duct tape
3. Vent flap material: 13½″ × 7½″ "Frisket paper" (thin, non-adhesive)—available at art supply stores.

TOOLS

1. Scissor
2. Tape measure
3. Triangle or square

CONSTRUCTION

1. Tear the 2 in. duct tape to 1 in. and use it on the absorber plate side (the backside) of the fixed-louver vent register

The Thermosiphoning Air Panel (TAP)

Fig. 3–16 One-way vent flap

    to seal all four raised edges along the perimeter of the louvers.
2. Place the 13½ in. × 7½ in. vent flap *squarely* on the taped louvers. (See illustration.) With an additional piece of duct tape, tape the flap along the top edge of the register. This tape makes a hinge for the vent to open and close.
3. Test the flap by moving the register to simulate air movement. The flap should open easily and completely. When closed, it should make an airtight seal with the duct tape.

Installing the glazing

1. To calculate the depth of the glazing stop, measure the distance between the absorber plate and the front edge of the 2 in. × 6 in. frame and subtract the glazing unit

The Thermosiphoning Air Panel (TAP)

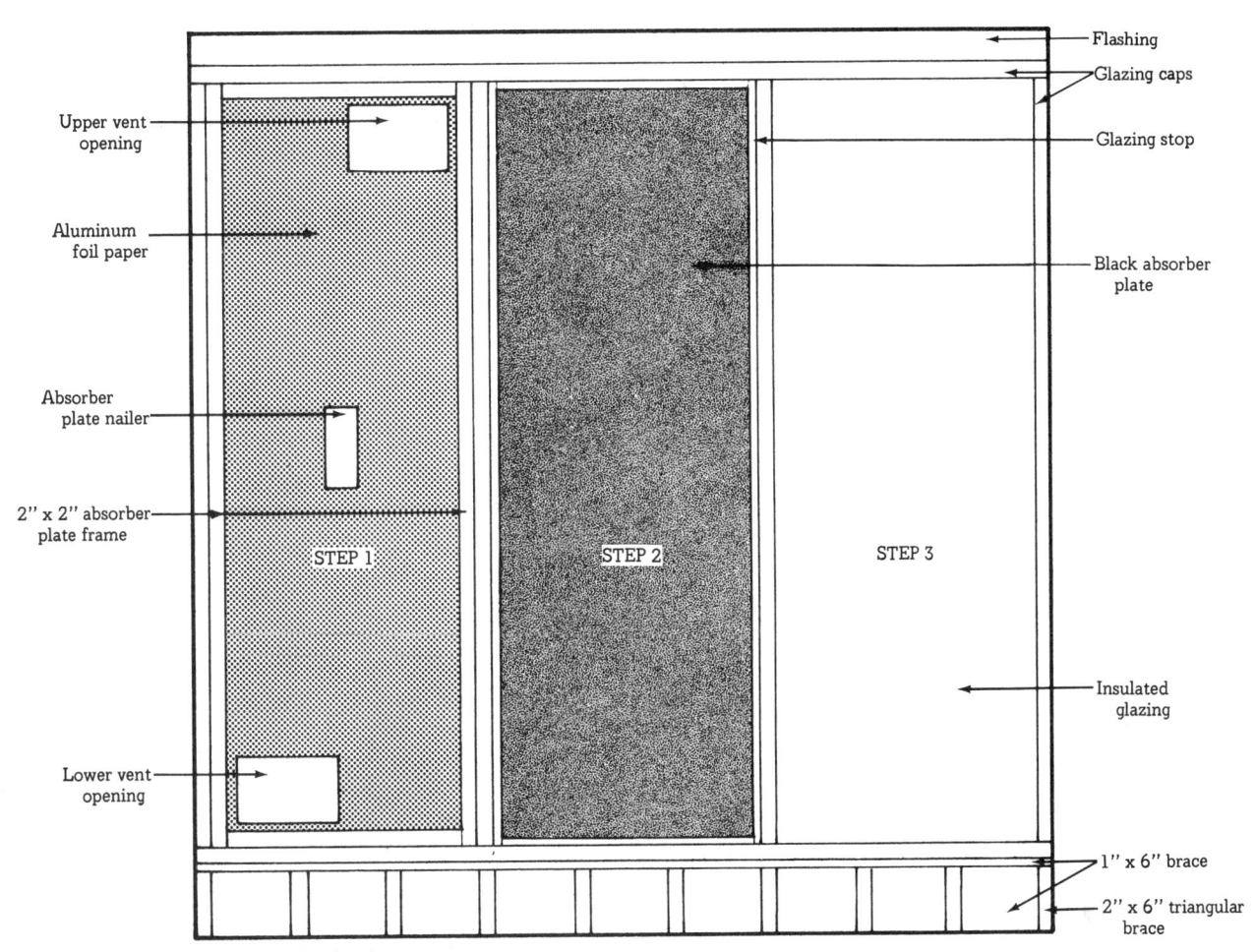

Fig. 3–17 Construction of a three-TAP unit

thickness, and 1/8 in. front and rear spacing. Cut the glazing stops to the calculated depth.

Note: To minimize outgasing, glazing stops should be constructed of spruce or fir (not pine) and be primed and painted a light color.)

2. Drill two 1/8 in. weep holes in the 2 in. × 6 in. frame. The holes allow moisture that accumulates beneath the glass unit to evaporate.

3. Set the neoprene spacers and setting blocks as shown in Fig. 2–13, with a dab of silicone caulk. For a 7/8 in. thick

glazing unit use 1/4 in. × 1 in. × 2 in. setting blocks at quarter points to set the glass on; and 1/8 in. neoprene spacing blocks.

Note: The setting blocks must support both sheets of glass.

4. Touch up the absorber plate paint where needed.
5. Thoroughly clean the back of the glass before putting it into the frame. Install the glass. You will need two people to lift the glass and a third person on a ladder to guide it from above.
6. Temporarily secure the glass. Silicone caulk between the edge of glass unit and the 2 in. × 6 in. frame.
7. Cut the glazing caps to 2¼ in. Bevel cut the bottom glazing cap to shed water. Install the glazing caps and set 1/8 in. neoprene spacing blocks between the glazing caps and the glass.
8. Paint all exterior wood.
9. Caulk between the glass and the glazing caps to form a double seal.
10. Clean the glass and go inside and test your collector!

Maintenance The thermosiphoning air panel is engineered for maximum efficiency and minimum maintenance. For continued high efficiency you should understand the TAP's operating principles and maintain it as needed.

Clean the outside of the glazing periodically, especially in the fall when the heating season begins. Also, in the fall, prune any new plant growth that shades your TAP and check to see if the TAP needs caulking and/or painting, which should be done as part of a general tightening up of your house for winter.

Check the TAP venting system periodically for proper operation. On a cold sunny day you should be able to feel continuous warm air coming from the upper vent. If you do not, make sure the upper vent control is in the *open* position. Open this vent once in the fall and close it in late spring to prevent overheating of your house. Another possible cause of reduced air flow through the upper vent is obstruction of the lower vent opening. Do not place any solid furniture piece within 3 inches of the front of either vent.

Fig. 3-18 Upper and lower TAP vents

Check occasionally at night to make sure no cold air is entering your house through the lower vent. If cold air is coming in, look into the lower vent with a flashlight. If the one-way vent flap is not flat against the backside of the vent register, or if the flap is bent, free it by blowing on it or pushing it with a flat, dull object such as a thin piece of cardboard.

If the flap is creased or will not return to a flat position it must be replaced. Reach the flap by removing several screws in the vent register, and follow the instructions in this chapter to make a replacement flap.

Performance

You can test TAP performance by using smoke to trace the intake-to-exhaust cycle. When strong sunlight is striking the collector surface, gently blow smoke into the lower vent opening of the TAP. Carefully count the number of seconds until the smoke scent is traced at the upper vent opening. For proper efficiency, the intake-to-exhaust cycle should be four seconds or less.

Calculation of heat from TAP

The total delivered heat can be calculated by multiplying the volume of air that passes through the TAP *times* the number of degrees that air is heated (the difference between the intake air temperature and the exhaust air temperature) *times* the heat capacity of air.

Total delivered heat =
 Volume of air × temperature difference × heat capacity of air

Volume of air

To calculate the volume of air that passes through the TAP you will need to determine both the cross sectional area of the air channel behind the absorber plate and the speed at which the air is moving through the TAP.

The cross sectional area of the air channel behind the absorber plate in our TAP design is 31¼ inches wide by 1½ inches deep.

$$31\frac{1}{4} \text{ in.} \times 1\frac{1}{2} \text{ in.} = 47 \text{ sq. in.}$$

To convert square inches to square feet, divide by 144 square inches.

$$\frac{47 \text{ sq. in.}}{144 \text{ sq. in.}} = \frac{1}{3} \text{ sq. ft.}$$

To determine the speed at which the air is moving through the TAP you will need to know the exact time for the intake-to-exhaust smoke cycle and the distance between the upper and lower vent openings. After you have timed the smoke cycle, measure the distance between the upper and lower vent openings. Add to this measurement the depth of both vent boots to determine the total distance the smoke traveled during the smoke test. To calculate the air speed through the TAP divide the total distance by the cycle time.

For example, if the intake-to-exhaust cycle is 4 seconds, and the total distance is 8 feet, then the air speed is 2 feet per second (ft./sec.).

$$\frac{8 \text{ ft.}}{4 \text{ sec.}} = 2 \text{ ft./sec.}$$

Now convert 2 ft./sec. to feet per minute by multiplying ft./sec. by 60 sec./min.

$$2 \text{ ft./sec} \times 60 \text{ sec./min.} = 120 \text{ ft./min.}$$

The volume of air that passes through the TAP equals the speed of the air times the cross sectional area.

In our example: 120 ft./min. × 1/3 sq. ft. = 40 cu. ft./min.

Temperature difference

To determine the number of degrees the air passing through the TAP is heated it is necessary to measure the temperatures of the air entering the lower vent opening and leaving through the upper vent opening. Subtract the temperature of the intake air from the temperature of the exhaust air. Solar engineers refer to this "temperature difference" as delta T (ΔT).

For example, if the intake air temperature is 60°F and the exhaust air temperature is 110°F, then the ΔT is 50°F.

Heat capacity of air

The last number needed to calculate the total delivered heat from the TAP is the heat capacity of air. The heat capacity of a material is defined as the number of Btus needed to raise the temperature of one cubic foot of the material 1°F. The heat capacity of air is 0.0182 Btu/cu. ft.·°F. The heat capacity of air is low because air is so light.

Using the example, where the volume of air passing through the TAP is 40 cu. ft./min. and the ΔT is 50°F, multiply these calculations times the heat capacity of air to determine the total heat delivered:

$$40 \times 50 \times 0.0182 = 36 \text{ Btu/min.}$$

To calculate the amount of heat delivered in one hour, multiply 36 Btu/min. times 60 minutes. The total heat delivered from the TAP per hour equals:

$$36 \text{ Btu/min.} \times 60 \text{ min.} = 2160 \text{ Btu/hr.}$$

4

ATTACHED SOLAR GREENHOUSE

The Attached Solar Greenhouse is a room designed to collect sunlight to grow plants and provide the adjoining house with supplementary solar heat.

How It Works The south wall of the Attached Solar Greenhouse is entirely double-glazed and oriented within 30° of solar south. Sunlight penetrates the double glazing, shining directly on plants and passive thermal storage within the greenhouse. The plants and storage absorb the sunlight and convert it into heat. Sunshine striking the interior, light-colored greenhouse walls is reflected to the thermal storage and the plants. The reflected light reduces the plants' tendency to grow directly toward the south facing glazing. On sunny days, the greenhouse quickly reaches temperatures above 75°F, even when the outside temperature is well below freezing.

Note: Solar Greenhouses *without* plants or thermal storage must have dark interior surfaces to absorb the sunlight and convert it to heat.

During the day, excess heat generated by the greenhouse is vented into the house to avoid overheating the plants—and, of course, to supplement house heating. Greenhouse air, moist and high in oxygen, is desirable in winter, especially in weathertight houses. Greenhouse air is vented to the house

Fig. 4–1 An Attached Solar Greenhouse is ideal for growing plants as well as for providing solar heat.

Attached Solar Greenhouse

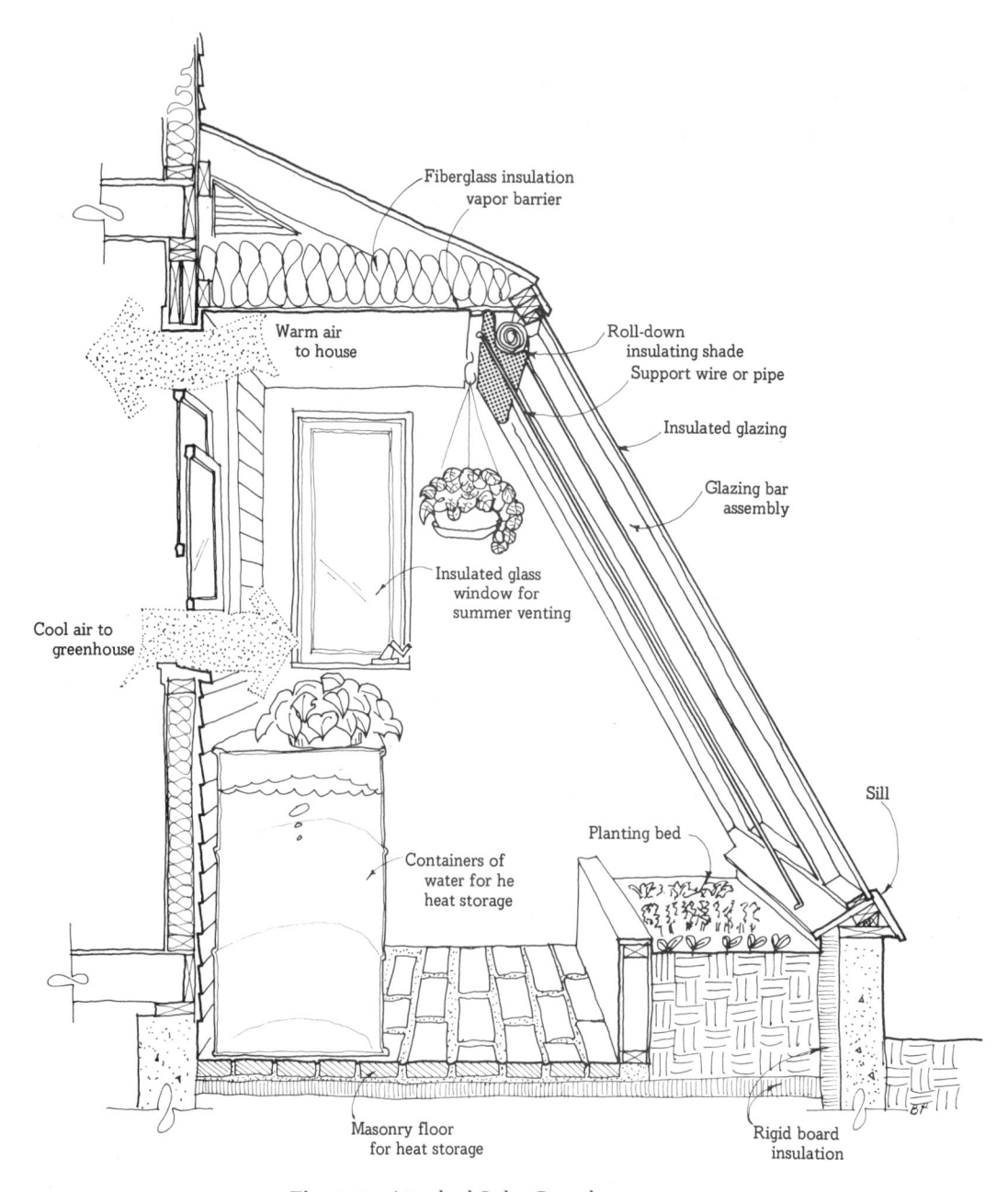

Fig. 4–2 Attached Solar Greenhouse

by natural thermosiphoning through an open door and/or window; or by a fan mounted on the wall between the greenhouse and the house.

Natural thermosiphoning is adequate only for moving small quantities of heat. To move additional heat to the house, a fan near the greenhouse ceiling blows the hottest greenhouse air into the house, and the cool air returns from the house through an adjoining doorway or low window opening.

System Strategies

The Attached Solar Greenhouse is ideal for year-round gardening, extending the growing season into the spring and fall, and for providing solar heat to your house during the day. The dollar value of the food you can grow in a well-maintained year-round greenhouse is even greater than the dollar value of the heat it supplies to your home. With or without plants, the Attached Solar Greenhouse is an ideal extension to your living area. In winter the greenhouse serves as a buffer between the house and the outdoors.

Solar collection in a greenhouse is a special case, because the south-facing glazing is tilted rather than vertical. A tilt of 45 to 70° from the horizon is ideal. In the winter when the sun is low, this angle allows plants to receive more sunlight, especially on cloudy days, than they would with vertical glazing.

On greenhouses oriented east or west of solar south, the side wall oriented closer to the south can also be glazed to increase the amount of sunlight on the plants. When the south wall is oriented *due* solar south, and *both* side walls are suitable for glazing, glaze the east wall to provide plants the morning sunshine they prefer. You may notice some retardation of plant growth in December and January, even though the greenhouse temperature remains above freezing. This is often a result of diminished daylight rather than cold temperatures.

The Attached Solar Greenhouse, like other passive solar systems, is ideally constructed adjacent to south-facing rooms that are used during the day. The greenhouse's north wall, then, adjoins the house. It is possible to connect the east or

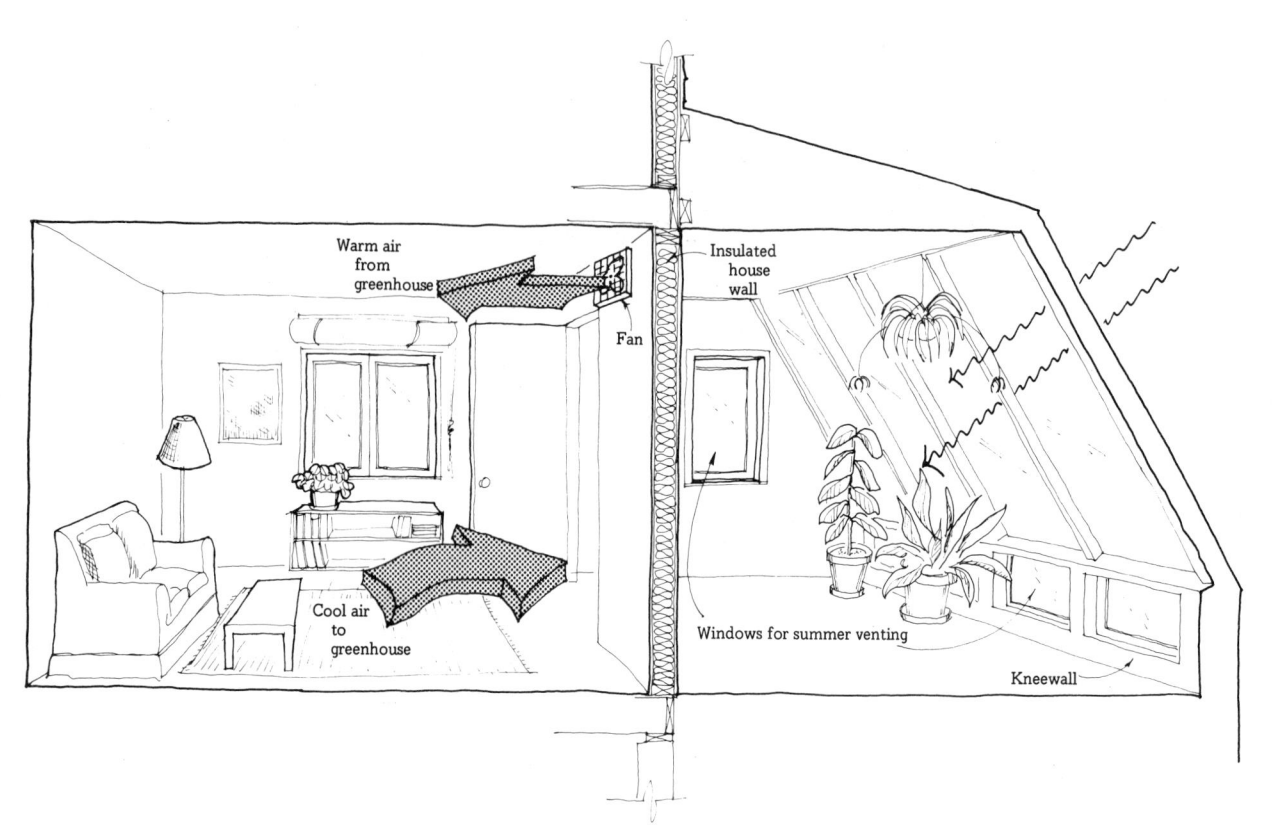

Fig. 4-3 Attached Solar Greenhouse without heat storage

west wall of the greenhouse to the house, but in these cases you'll need to carefully assess and compensate for shading of the greenhouse by the house and provide for adequate heat exchange between the two.

When it isn't possible to connect the greenhouse to a room used during the day, it can be usefully connected to any heated room. For heat exchange and easy entrance, a door and perhaps a window should be built into the wall between the house and the greenhouse.

The small amount of thermal storage needed in an Attached Solar Greenhouse can usually be integrated into the architecture of the greenhouse, in the form of masonry walls and floors, or containers for storing water. *These passive storage systems work only when the storage material is in direct sunlight.* The storage materials, therefore, compete

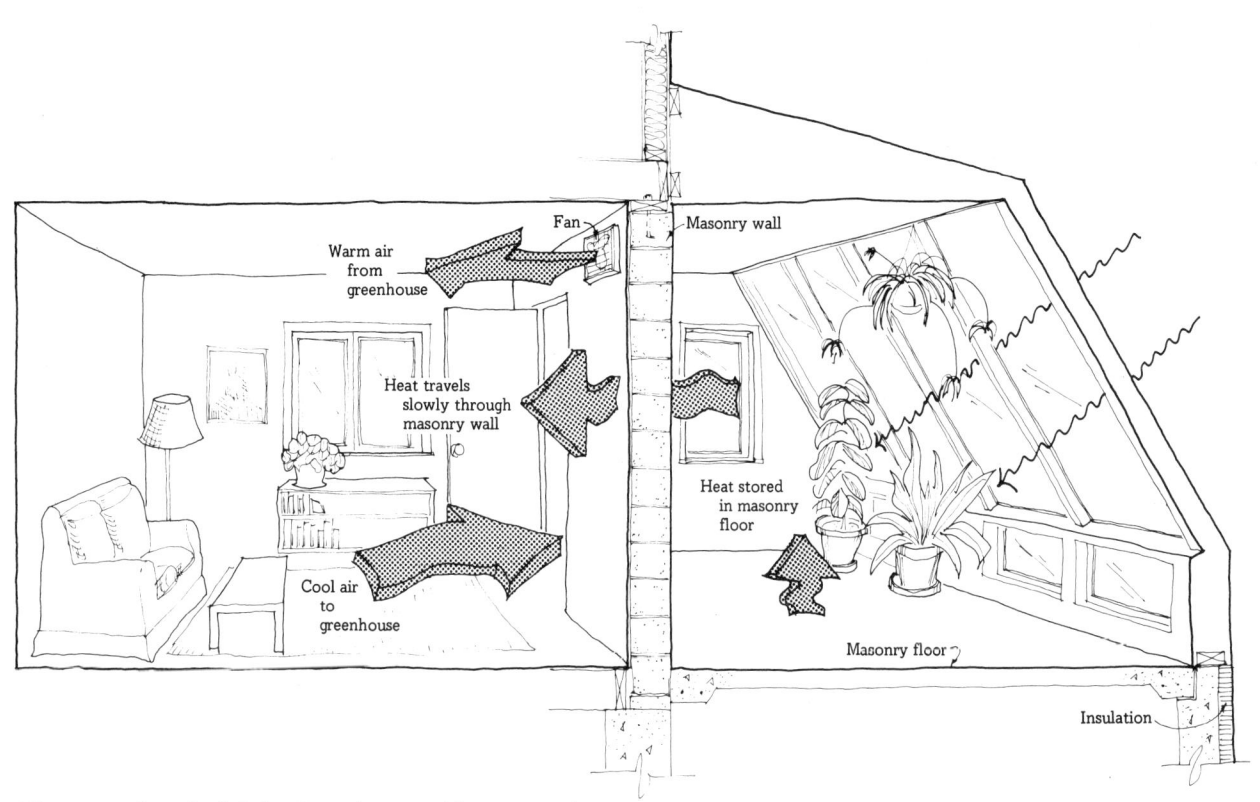

Fig. 4–4 Attached Solar Greenhouse with masonry heat storage

with the plants for direct sunlight. I recommend using two to four gallons of water for each square foot of south glazing.

Active rock bed thermal storage is an alternative to passive storage, but involves additional money and time to install a fan, thermostat, ductwork, and rock storage bin. With this system solar-heated air is blown through a large container of fist-size rocks. The rocks become warm and store the solar heat for later use.

Two potential problems of Solar Greenhouses are freezing in winter and overheating in summer. With proper construction and maintenance, however, these problems can be effectively avoided.

One important factor in maintaining above-freezing temperatures in the greenhouse is proper insulation, caulking, and weatherstripping of the roof, floor, walls, and glazing. A

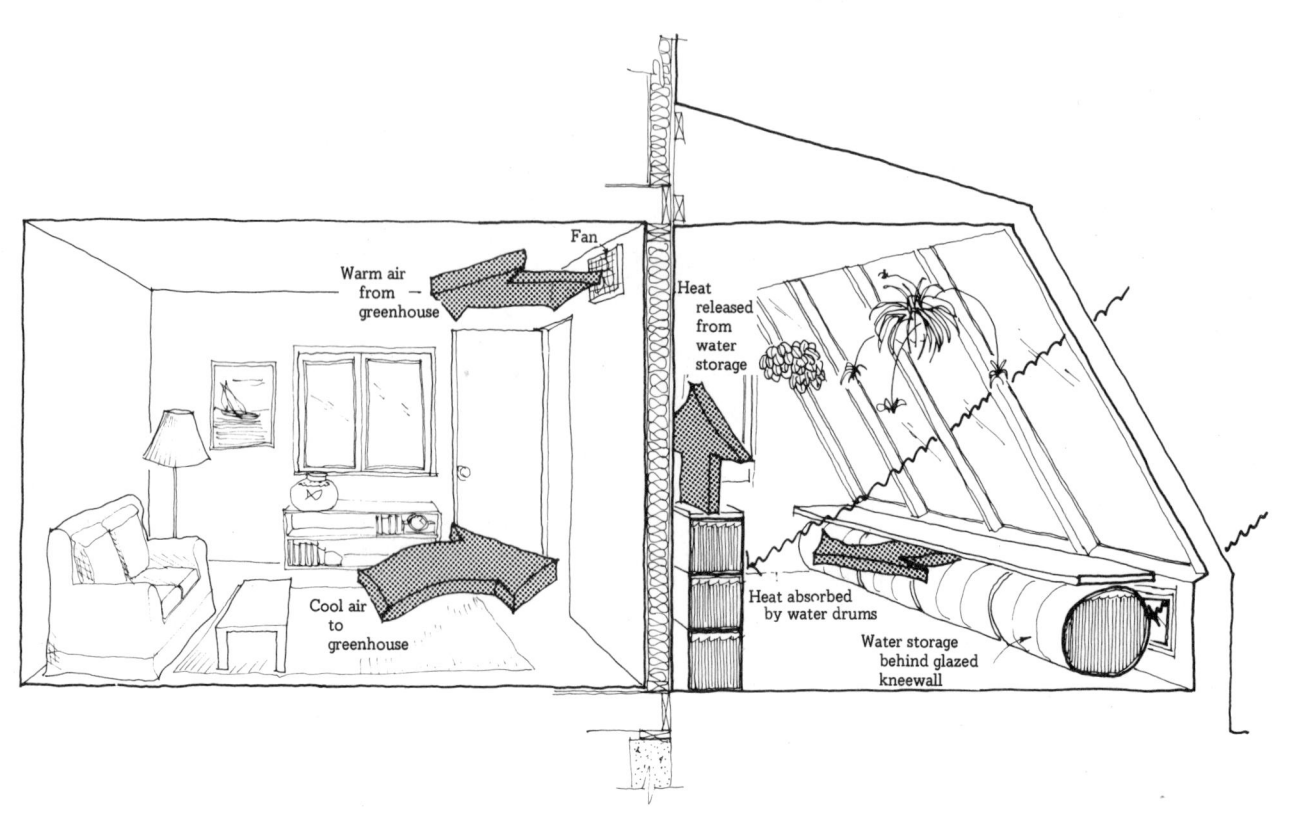

Fig. 4–5 Attached Solar Greenhouse with water heat storage

key part of greenhouse insulation is the use of insulating shades on glazed areas; the shades must be drawn every night, and they must fit snugly. See Chapter 2 for complete directions for constructing insulating shades.

On cold nights, leaving a door or window slightly open between the greenhouse and the house will help warm the greenhouse. The amount of heat needed from the house depends on two factors: the amount of thermal storage in the greenhouse and the severity of nighttime temperatures. Careful attention to weatherproofing, thermal storage, and heat transfer from the house to the greenhouse will prevent winter freezing problems.

In the summer, the greenhouse must be vented to the outside to minimize overheating. Locate vents both high and low in the greenhouse exterior walls to take advantage of

Fig. 4–6 Attached Solar Greenhouse: a) before construction; b) after construction

natural thermosiphoning and prevailing summer breezes. Exterior windows and doors are an excellent way to provide venting. Also, quick-growing plants such as sunflowers in front of the glazing make perfect natural shades.

The depth from the glazed wall to the north wall of the greenhouse should be between 8 and 12 feet. The length should be a minimum of 12 feet. Total material costs for a greenhouse with double glazing are approximatley $15 to $25 per square foot of greenhouse floor area.

A weekend builder with a helper can construct a 9 ft. × 12 ft. attached greenhouse in six or seven weekends. The work involves skills similar to those necessary for building a small cabin from foundation to roofing. An attached solar greenhouse is a beautiful addition to any home.

Design

The design of an Attached Solar Greenhouse is unique to each home. This system, more than the other three, requires many design decisions. The design process is exciting and should involve the whole family. Building a model of your greenhouse is a good first step. Of course, the south glazing must be carefully oriented, as with any solar system.

You will need to decide on the following: 1) the slope of the south glazing, 2) foundation type, flooring material, and height of the floor above ground, 3) whether to use side wall glazing, 4) window/vent size and location, 5) access to the house and the outside, 6) the arrangement and size of planting beds, and 7) and the design of thermal storage.

Slope of the south glazing

The glazing on solar greenhouses should slope away from the roof. Vertical glazing, although excellent for heat gain, does not provide the well-distributed light necessary for a greenhouse, especially for plants furthest from the glazing. *For maximum winter light and heat gain, the south wall glazing should form an angle with the ground equal to your latitude plus 20°.* The angle can be several degrees smaller in regions with cloudy winters, to allow more light inside the greenhouse. With lower angles, the plants "see" more of the sky. Actually, angles plus or minus 10° from the optimum function well. Remember, lower angles, while receiving more light, can cause some overheating.

Foundation and flooring

In most areas, local building codes specify foundation materials, minimum size, depth below ground level (to frost line), need for footing (which depends on the type of soil around your house), and other requirements. Foundations vary considerably in terms of material cost and labor requirements.

Fig. 4–7 Kneewall and side wall windows provide good summer venting. Acrylite is used to glaze the triangular sections of the side wall. (Terry Fenton, designer and builder)

In general, foundations must structurally support the sill to below the frost line, must keep nonpressure-treated preserved wood a minimum of 6 inches above ground level, and must form a continuous barrier against vermin from the sill to 2 feet below ground level.

Note: The earth around the foundation must shed water away from the greenhouse. This is usually not a problem since your house should already have adequate drainage.

Four foundation systems are: poured concrete, concrete block, concrete "sonotubes" (cylindrical cardboard tubes which are used as forms for pouring concrete posts), and pressure-treated wood posts. The latter two are generally less expensive and less time-consuming to construct.

The type of flooring you select for your greenhouse-earth, concrete slab, or wood—influences your foundation selection. With a raised wooden floor, concrete or wooden posts are appropriate. For a concrete slab floor, poured concrete or concrete block foundation is best.

Note: The floor will have to support the weight of the planting soil and heat storage materials.

When designing the foundation, consider the height of the kneewall and whether it should be glazed. (The kneewall is a low wall that raises the bottom of the south glazing above the foundation.) This elevation not only provides a place for snow sliding down the south wall to accumulate, but also increases utilization of space under the sloped glazing. The kneewall should raise the greenhouse ceiling high enough to allow ample headroom for the doorway adjoining the house.

Side wall glazing

The east/west (of solar south) orientation of your site will greatly influence the design of the greenhouse side walls.

If your site is 10 to 30° east or west of solar south, then the side wall nearest south can include some glazing to increase the amount of light on your plants. The side wall glazing usually creates a net heat loss, but is necessary for good growing. On sites oriented within less than 10° of solar south, the side walls can be built without glazing, or with some easterly glazing. Plants prefer morning (eastern) light to afternoon light.

"Acrylite" is excellent material for fixed side wall insulated glazing. It can be site cut to any shape with a fine tooth circular saw blade and is aesthetically pleasing. (See "Glazing" for specifications and availability.) Sliding glass doors meet both access and glazing needs.

Window/vent size and location

Greenhouse air must be vented to the outdoors in summer and to the house in winter.

For summer venting the total area of vents to the outdoors should be no less than 1/6 the greenhouse floor area. One

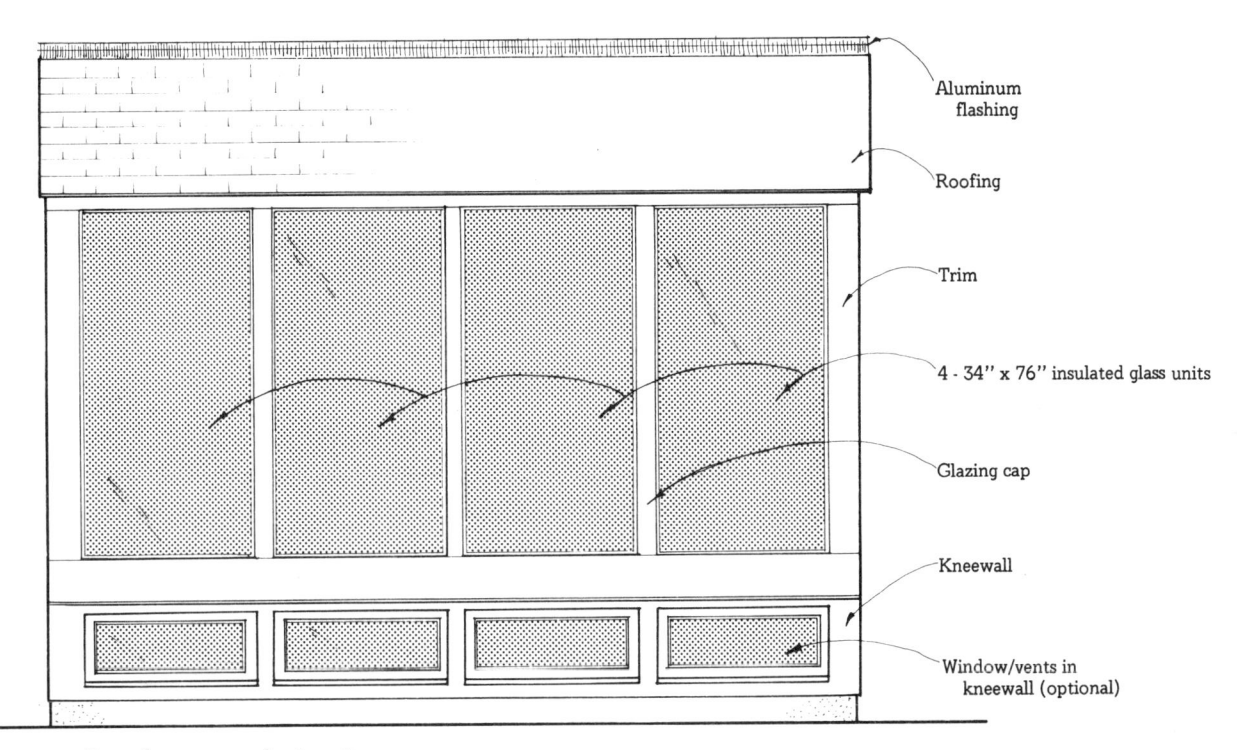

Fig. 4–8 Greenhouse, south elevation

exterior screen door and one or more windows provide adequate venting for moderate size greenhouses. These vents should be located on opposite or adjacent walls.

When there is no exterior door, windows should be placed both high and low to increase natural thermosiphoning. The upper windows should be 1/3 larger than the lower windows. They can be placed in a south-facing kneewall or in either side wall. It is generally much easier to install a factory-made window unit than to construct a weathertight operable vent. Pivoted windows should open out, and all windows must be double-glazed. Whenever possible, locate vents to take advantage of prevailing summer breezes.

To circulate warm air from the greenhouse to the house during cold months, use a fan as well as natural means. The warmest air is near the greenhouse ceiling. This air should be vented to the house. The coolest air—along the house floor—should be returned to the greenhouse.

Be careful to protect plants from extremely high temperatures which can occur on sunny winter days in an inadequately vented greenhouse. Plants accustomed to moderate temperatures can be badly damaged when exposed to 100°F for several hours. To minimize the chance of overheating, a greenhouse fan to the house can be thermostatically controlled, or a window vent can be equipped with an automatic thermostatically controlled opener.

Access to the house and outdoors

Your greenhouse can have a doorway to the house, to the outside, or to both.

Connected to the house, the greenhouse becomes an added room. You can enter the greenhouse through the house, without letting cold outside air in. When designing the greenhouse access, check the height of the exterior grade (ground level) relative to the height of your house floor. If the exterior grade is a different level than the house floor, a stairway must be provided or the greenhouse floor must be constructed at the level of the house floor. Where steps are constructed, be sure to design a headroom clearance of at least 6½ feet.

An outside door is desirable for a gardening greenhouse, where you need to move plants, earth, and other materials back and forth from the greenhouse to the outdoors. With an exterior door and no door between the house and the greenhouse, you can build an airlock vestibule to minimize heat loss when the door is opened. With both interior and exterior doors, the greenhouse serves as an air lock entryway for the house.

Note: The exterior door should be either foam core insulated or insulated glass. You need a screen for summer venting. If you intend to move a wheelbarrow in and out, be sure the opening is large enough.

Arrangement and size of planting beds

For maximum food and/or flower growth in a limited space, planting areas must be carefully designed. Planting can be done in pots on benches, shelves, or hangers, or directly in the ground. Planting benches and shelves should provide for drainage and have a 2-inch lip to prevent pots from falling off. The east and west sides of the greenhouse are good places for plants on stakes and strings. The planting areas should be approximately 3 feet wide for comfortable reaching. Walkways between the areas should be 18 in. wide and must allow for drainage.

Concrete, gravel and wood slats are suitable flooring materials. Dirt floors do not drain well. The soil depth necessary for growing plants varies, with 12 to 18 inches adequate for most. When plants are grown directly in the ground, use 4 inches of 3/4 inch gravel under the soil to provide drainage. Sandy soil usually does not need additional drainage.

Design of thermal storage system

Heat storage should be built into the greenhouse to reduce daily temperature swing, help prevent the greenhouse from freezing at night, and increase the amount of useful heat that can be transferred into the house. Heat can be stored in water, masonry, and rock beds. Passive water or masonry storage systems are best because of their simplicity, low cost, and design flexibility. Passive heat storage material must be painted a dark color and placed in direct sunlight.

Note: Dark blue absorbs only 3% less light than black—so you don't have to paint everything black.

If the adjoining south wall of your house is masonry, you have built-in thermal storage. Otherwise, 2 to 4 gallons of water for each square foot of south glazing is recommended. 55-gallon drums and 5-gallon metal tins make good water containers. Remember to leave space for water expansion. Place these containers along the adjoining wall of the house, or along a glazed kneewall.

Note: Planting soil also adds thermal storage to your greenhouse.

Active storage systems which involve mechanical movement of hot greenhouse air to the storage medium are generally unnecessary and expensive.

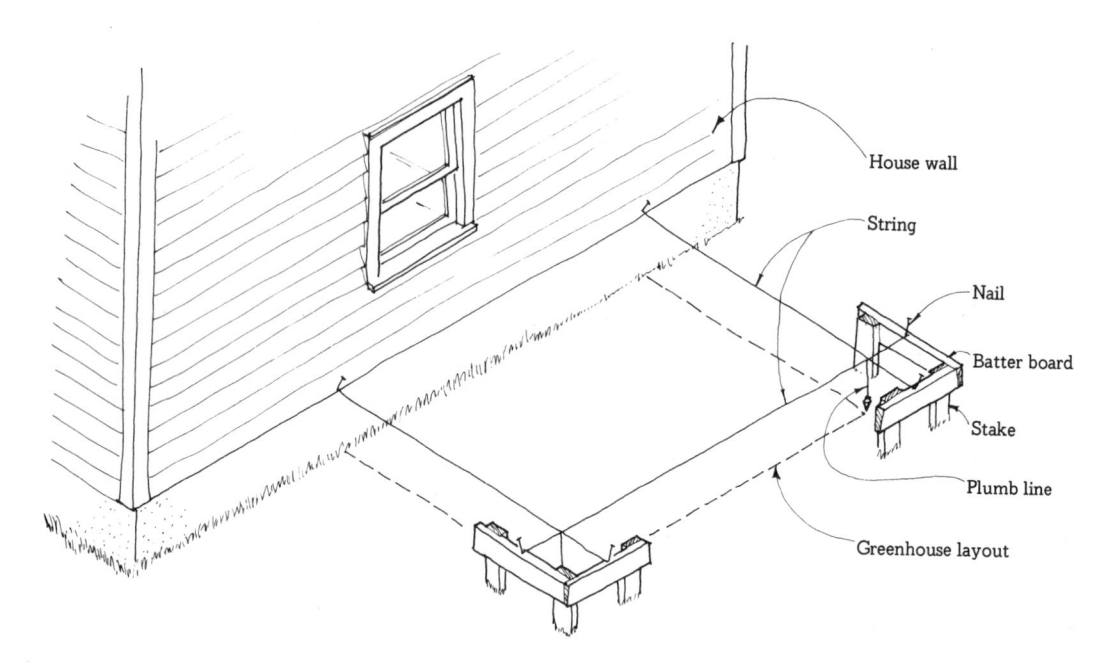

Fig. 4–9 Greenhouse foundation layout

This chapter discusses materials and construction details for a moderate cost, high-quality greenhouse suitable for most homes. Other greenhouses can be built at a substantially higher or lower cost. The size of your greenhouse and the interior detailing greatly influence the total cost of the project.

Materials The interior of a solar greenhouse is subjected to constant high moisture. This is the most crucial factor in the selection of greenhouse materials.

Wood

Be sure to treat all greenhouse wood with copper napthenate. (Creosote and pentachloraphene preservatives are not suitable.) Although redwood and cedar are naturally resistant to decay, one coat of preservative is still recommended. Apply preservatives and allow them to dry *before* planting.

Paint with primer can be applied over treated wood. Paint the greenhouse interior and glazing frames a light color to reflect more light onto the plants.

Glazing

Greenhouse glazing can be transparent or translucent. Although transparent glazing may be more aesthetically pleasing, translucent glazing provides more uniform light so the plants are less likely to grow directly toward the low winter sun.

"Acrylite" and fiberglass-reinforced plastics such as "Filon," "Lascolite," and "Kalwall" are good translucent glazing materials. Because they can be site cut to any shape, they are excellent for glazing triangular portions of the east and west side walls. Be sure to double or triple-glaze all east and west windows.

A major drawback of plastic glazings is that their appearance often deteriorates after several years. Cleaning and wear can cause surface scratches on rigid plastic sheets, especially transparent plastics. Flexible plastic sheets can become wavy in appearance after years of daily expansion and contraction.

Insulated glass is available in both translucent and transparent units. Glass is recommended for the south wall and other large glazed areas because it is attractive and wear-resistant. Low-iron glass (which appears clear, not green, when viewed on its edge) has a higher solar transmittance and is usually translucent. Transparent glass is available in large, insulated sliding glass door replacement panels from lumber yards and glaziers for approximately $60 for a 34 inch by 76 inch unit.

Note: Glass prices can vary more than 100 percent, so comparison shop. Also, low-iron glass and panels larger than 34 inches by 76 inches may be difficult to locate and expensive in small quantities. One potential source of low-iron glass is a solar collector manufacturer or distributor.

Insulation

The greenhouse walls and ceiling can be insulated with fiberglass, a moderately priced material with good insulating properties. A vapor barrier of 4 mil. polyethylene must be applied on the *interior* side of the insulation to prevent moisture from entering the wall and ceiling cavities.

Dow "Styrofoam" rigid board is recommended for all below grade insulation. Most other rigid insulation boards absorb water which significantly reduces their insulation value.

Soil

Greenhouse soil must be lighter and richer than garden soil. Light soil is necessary for good drainage. To lighten the soil, mix in coarse, washed horticultural-grade sand or perlite. Peat moss and vermiculite are excellent for retaining moisture, as well as lightening the soil. Remember, frequent watering tends to pack the soil.

Enrich the soil with manure and/or compost. Be sure that manure is well rotted. Chicken manure should be composted before using it on plants. As in all gardening, compost is an excellent and inexpensive fertilizer.

Fan and thermostat

The size of the fan for moving greenhouse air into your house will depend on the severity of your climate and the amount of heat you are storing in the greenhouse. Fan sizes are measured in CFM (cubic feet of air per minute). For each square foot of south glazing you need between 2 and 4 CFM. Variable speed fans are ideal, but are more expensive. When buying a fan, consider noise level. Kitchen exhaust fans and room-to-room fans, available from wood stove dealers, are recommended.

A thermostat that controls fan operation eliminates the need for daily greenhouse temperature monitoring and prevents overheating of your plants when you are away. You need a *cooling thermostat*, such as an attic fan thermostat, which turns the fan ON when the temperature is above the set point. These thermostats are available from heating and air conditioning suppliers.

Note: All electrical installations must be done according to local building codes.

Materials list

Note: Greenhouse design varies considerably according to your needs, site, and budget. Use this list as a *guide* in determining your exact material needs.

Part	Dimension	Quantity	Notes
Foundation:			
poured concrete:			
concrete			
concrete forms			
rigid insulation board			Dow's "Styrofoam" recommended for use below ground level.
8″ anchor bolts, washers, and nuts			
concrete block:			
concrete block			
mortar			
rigid insulation board			
12″ anchor bolts, washers, and nuts			
concrete "sonotubes":			
"sonotube" forms			
concrete			
header	2″ × 6″	4	
vermin barrier			aluminum flashing, asbestos board, or troweled on cement coating (i.e., "Dryvit")
rigid insulation board			
12″ anchor bolts, washers, and nuts			
wood posts:			
wood posts			pressure treated with wood preservative
header	2″ × 6″	4	
vermin barrier			
rigid insulation board			
Floor:			
concrete:			
concrete			
concrete forms			
wood:			
wood flooring			Apply 4 mil. polyethylene under flooring. Staple 1″ wire mesh to the underside of insulation to protect it from vermin.
floor joists			
fiberglass insulation under flooring (optional)			
Sill:			
sill			
cant strip	2″ × 4″		
sill sealer			

Part	Dimension	Quantity	Notes
Side walls:			
door			
windows			
studs			
plate			
header			
nailer	2" × 4"		
trim			
corner trim board			
sheathing			
siding			
1/4" AC plywood or waterproof sheetrock			
insulation			
South wall:			
glazing bars	2" × 4"		
glazing stops	1" × 3"		
trim board			
glazing caps	1" × 4"		
double top and bottom plate	2" × 4"		
Adjoining wall:			
fan and thermostat			
door			
windows			
trim			
Roof:			
plywood sheathing	4' × 8'		
15 lb. felt	3' roll		A standard roll covers 432 sq. ft.
shingles			
8" drip edge (3 sides)			
roofing tar			
flashing			
rafters			
collar ties	2" × 4"		
ledger	2" × 4"		
nailer	2" × 4"		
Ceiling:			
insulation			8"–10" fiberglass insulation recommended
ceiling—1/4" AC plywood or waterproof sheetrock			
Miscellaneous:			
nails	10d galv. box	5 lbs.	
	16d galv.	5 lbs.	
	6d galv. finishing	3 lbs.	
	8d galv. finishing	3 lbs.	

Part	Dimension	Quantity	Notes
nails *(Continued)*	16d galv. casing	1 lbs.	
	roofing nails	10 lbs.	
	sheetrock or 4d galv. finishing		
wood screws			
caulk			
paint			
primer			
glue (exterior grade)			
insulated glazing			
1/8" neoprene spacers		20 per glazing unit	available from glazier
1/4" neoprene setting blocks		2 per glazing unit	available from glazier
fiberglass insulation			
lag bolts	4"		for ledger
polyethylene vapor barrier	4 mil		
fan			
thermostat (optional)			

Glazing materials for solar greenhouses and collectors

Type of Material	Brand Name and Manufacturer	Use	Solar Transmittance for Double Layer (%)	Max. Temp. (°F)	Estimated Life (in Years)	Cost $/sq. ft. Double Glazing	Notes
Glass	(1) "Sunadex",* AFG Industries, Box 929, Kingsport, TN 37662	Excellent for all systems	83			$2.50 to $7.00 depending on quantity and source.	Excellent aesthetic quality; large double glazed sheets are heavy, but otherwise easy to install.
	(2) "Solatex",* AFG Industries, Box 929, Kingsport, TN 37662		81	400	Very long		
	(3) Standard float glass (i.e., sliding glass door panel)		71			$2.80	*
Acrylic	(1) "Plexiglas," Rohm & Haas Co., Independence Mall W., Philadelphia, PA 19105	Greenhouses & Direct Gain systems	86	180	20		Large thermal expansion makes weatherizing difficult.

Type of Material	Brand Name and Manufacturer	Use	Solar Transmittance for Double Layer (%)	Max. Temp. (°F)	Estimated Life (in Years)	Cost $/sq. ft. Double Glazing	Notes
Acrylic (Cont.)	(2) "Acrylite",* Cyro Industries, 897 Route 46, Clifton, NJ 07015 (Also referred to as Exolite)	Greenhouses & Direct Gain systems	86	180	—	$2.50	Double skinned, translucent sheet, 5/8" thick. Available in 4'×8', 4'×10', 4'×12' sheets. Cyro Industries' aluminum glazing caps are recommended for sealing the edges of rigid plastic glazings with large thermal expansion.
Polycarbonate	(1) "Tuffak Twin-wall," Rohm & Haas Co., Independence Mall W., Philadelphia, PA 19105	Greenhouses & Direct Gain systems	77	190	5	$1.25	High impact strength. Large thermal expansion makes weatherizing difficult.
	(2) "Lexan",* General Electric					$5.50	
Fiberglass Reinforced plastic	(1) "Sun-lite," available in factory made panels and 4' and 5' wide rolls, Kalwall Corporation, Solar Components Div., Box 237, Manchester, NH 03105	All systems	77	225	20	$2.50 factory-made panels, $1.20 on rolls	Must be treated with chemicals every few years. Large thermal expansion makes material from rolls difficult to apply tightly. Panel sizes 4'×8', 4'×10', 4'×12', 4'×14'.
	(2) "Filon",* Vistron Corporation		74	225	—	$2.00	
Films	(1) "Tedlar", Dupont, CSC Chestnut Run, Wilmington, DE 19898	Greenhouses & Inner collector glazing	86	150	4	$0.60	Low cost.
	(2) "Teflon," Dupont, CSC Chestnut Run, Wilmington, DE 19898		92	300	—	$1.10	

*Translucent.

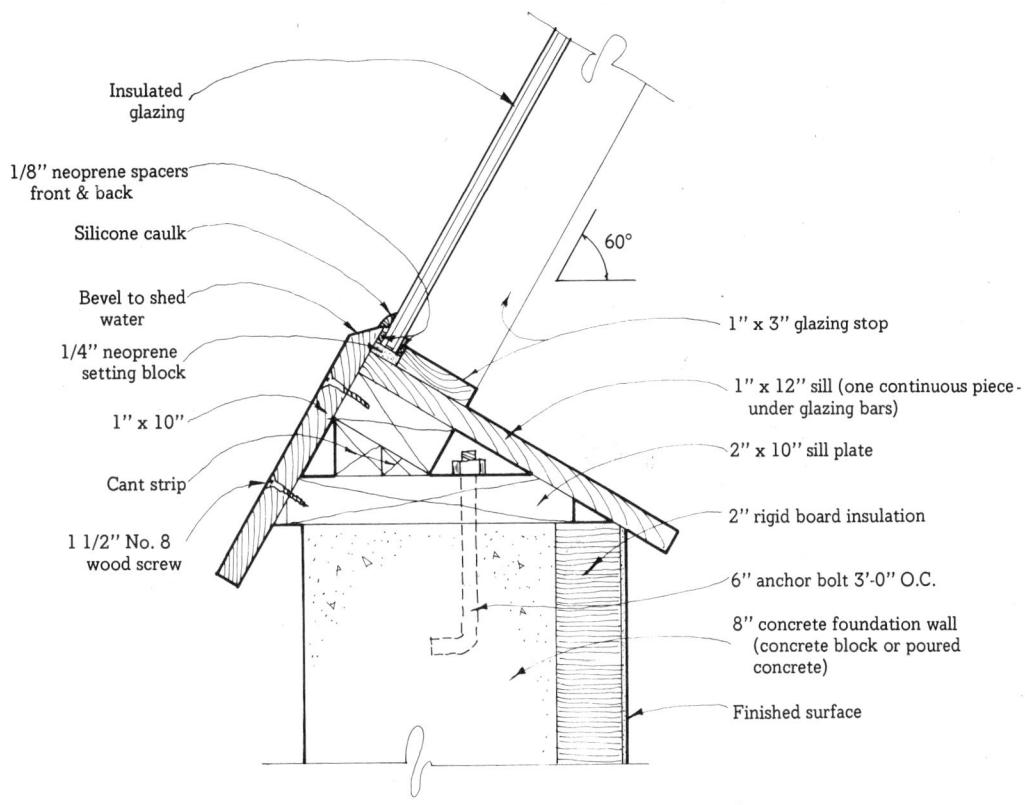

Fig. 4–10 Greenhouse south wall sill detail for a continuous foundation wall

Layout

Determine the exact location and size for your Attached Solar Greenhouse, based on architectural and budget requirements. Check the height of the greenhouse floor for compatibility with the height of the house floor. Are steps needed to go from one to the other? Look for roof or other projections which might interfere with construction of the greenhouse adjoining the house wall.

Use stakes, batter boards, and string to lay out the greenhouse foundation. The string should mark the top of the foundation wall. Level the string using a line level. Check the squareness of the layout by making sure diagonal measurements are equal.

Construction

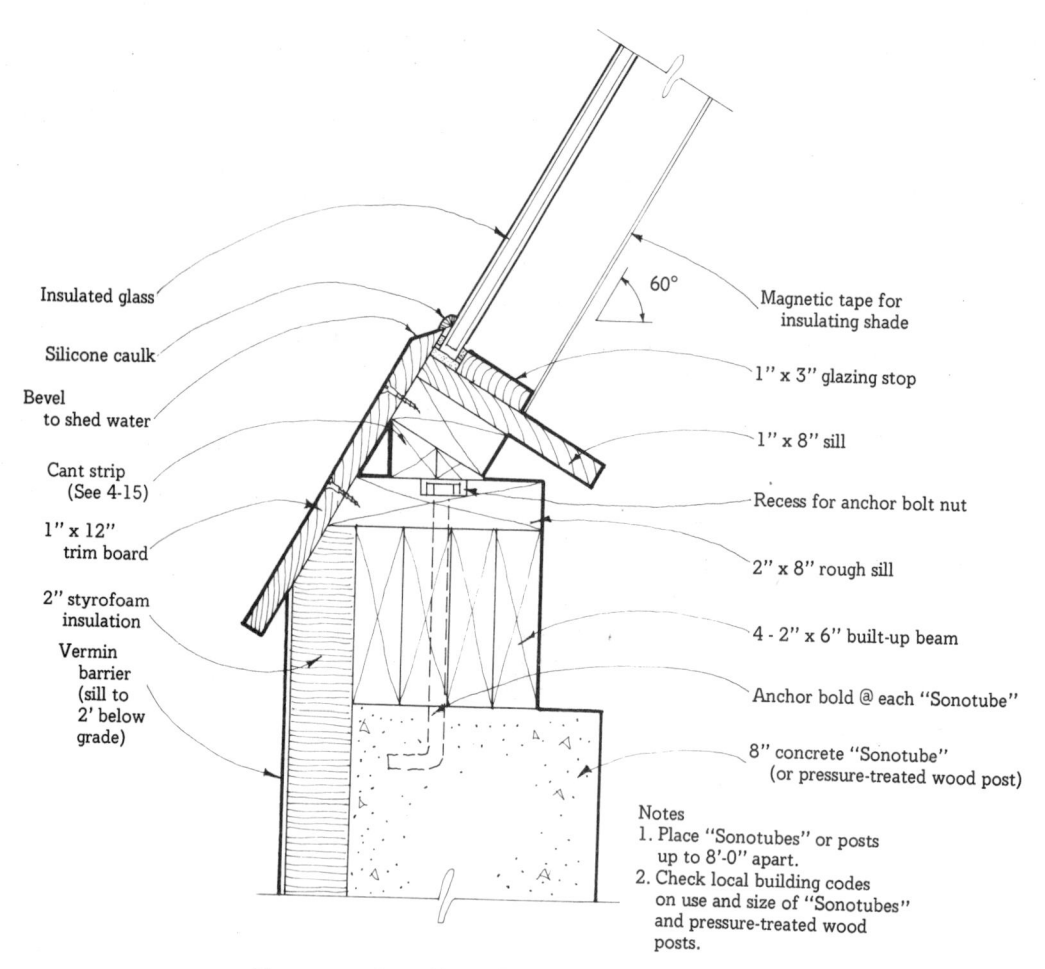

Fig. 4-11 Greenhouse south wall sill detail for "Sonotube" or post foundation

Foundation

The depth and width of the foundation trench are determined by the depth of the frost line and the type of foundation. Trenches for concrete block and poured concrete foundations have to be wide enough to provide ample working room. Trenches for concrete and wood post foundations need be only large enough for lowering in materials.

In two work days, using hand tools or four hours with a backhoe (at about $25 per hour), you can dig a 4-foot deep

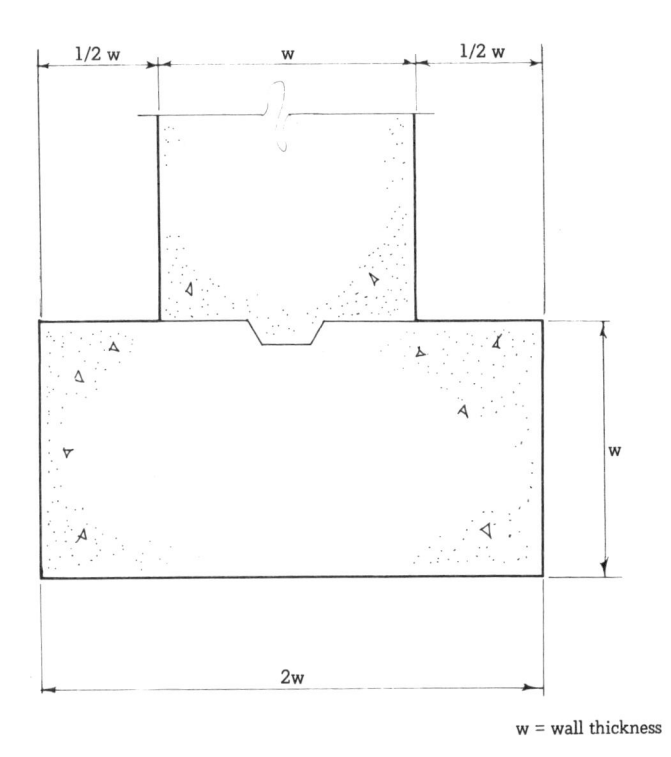

Fig. 4-12 Poured concrete footing detail

trench for a moderate size greenhouse. Use a plumb bob to keep the trench in line with the layout string.

Note: Take caution to avoid damaging underground utility lines. Check the location of service lines before digging.

Local building codes and soil conditions will determine if a footing is needed for your foundation wall. The footing spreads the weight load of the greenhouse wall and roof over a sufficient area to prevent settling. Load-bearing capabilities of soil vary greatly, but since the weight of the greenhouse is minimal, a footing twice as wide as the foundation wall is generally sufficient. For concrete or wood posts a footing 16 in. × 16 in. × 8 in. deep is usually adequate. (See illustration for details.)

To minimize lifting of the foundation wall by frost action, the wall surface should be smooth. When the ground freezes it rises several inches. If the foundation is rough, the rising

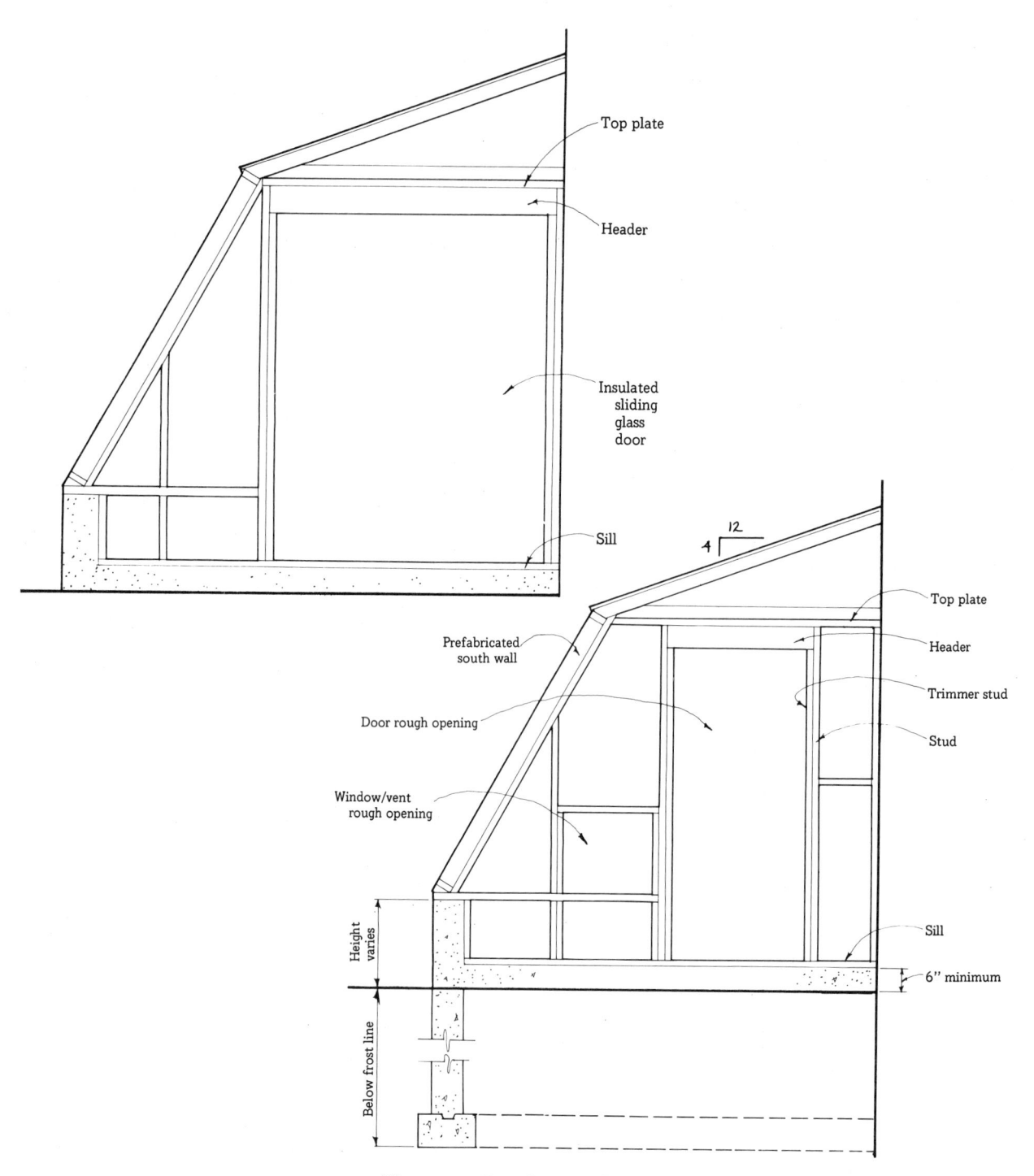

Fig. 4–13 Greenhouse side elevation, two views

earth will grab it and lift the greenhouse wall. Frost action will not raise a smooth foundation wall.

Place anchor bolts in the wet concrete at foundation wall corners and every three feet along the length of the walls. Check the sill detail illustration for anchor bolt location and height above the top of the foundation.

Note: There should be two anchor bolts at each corner where the sills meet. Do not place stress on the concrete until it thoroughly hardens.

For greenhouses with floors at ground level, insulation is needed along the foundation wall to reduce heat loss to the ground. Perimeter insulation should extend from the sill to below the frost line. If the foundation wall is poured concrete or concrete block, place the insulation on the inside of the wall where it is protected from physical damage. Construction adhesive can hold the insulation in place until backfilling is complete. The interior surface of the insulation should be covered to protect it from damage. For post foundations, the insulation board must be protected on the exterior from vermin. Sheets of .025 inch thick aluminum, asbestos board, or troweled-on cement coatings work well.

To further reduce heat loss to the ground, insulation can be installed beneath the floor. Although the temperature of the earth under the greenhouse is milder than the outside air temperature, it is still well below the average indoor greenhouse temperature.

Greenhouses with raised floors should, of course, be heavily insulated between the floor joists. Use fiberglass insulation with 1 in. wire mesh below it to protect insulation from vermin.

East and west walls

Remove the house siding down to the sheathing where the side walls will adjoin the house. Allow room for the studs, sheathing, interior finish, and interior and exterior corner trim boards. Also, remove the siding where the greenhouse roof construction will attach to the house.

Construct framing for the side walls and the kneewall, if any. Leave rough openings for windows and doors. ("Rough

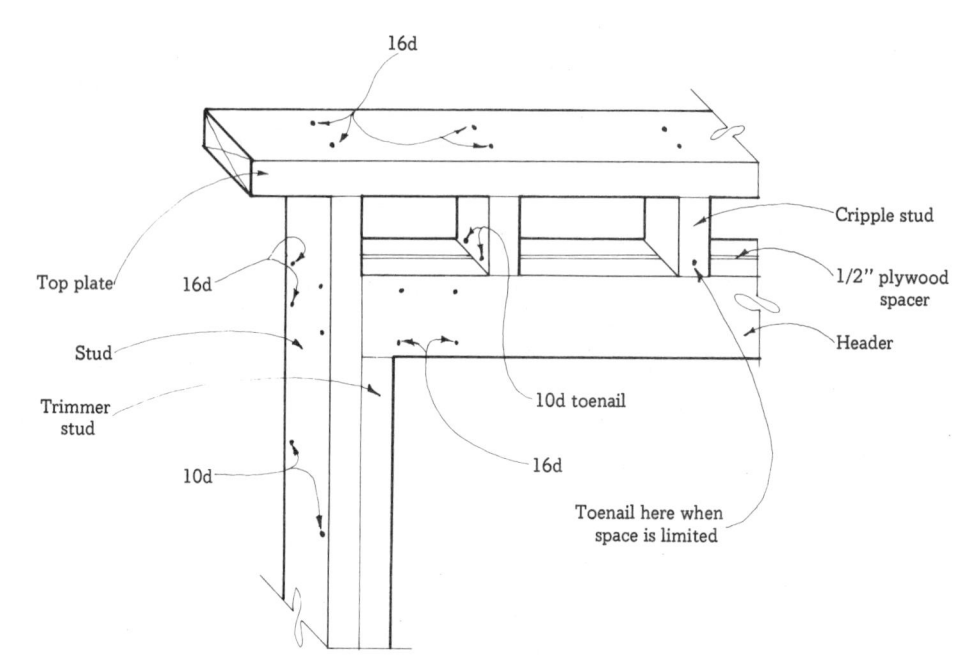

Fig. 4-14 Window and door framing and nailing

openings" are given by the window or door manufacturer.) Because it provides added insulation potential, 2 in. × 6 in. framing is recommended. But where a door and windows make up a large portion of the side wall, 2 in. × 4 in. construction is generally preferred. Most prehung windows and doors are made for 2 in. × 4 in. framing, and the additional work to convert them for 2 in. × 6 in. walls is often not justified by the increased R-value you will gain from such a small amount of additional insulation.

Note: Do not add sheathing or interior surface to the side walls until the south wall is constructed.

When the side wall framing is complete, brace it for temporary support.

South wall

The entire south wall must be carefully constructed within 1/16 inch tolerances. Inspect the end grain of the rough sill and place it as shown in the illustration to minimize move-

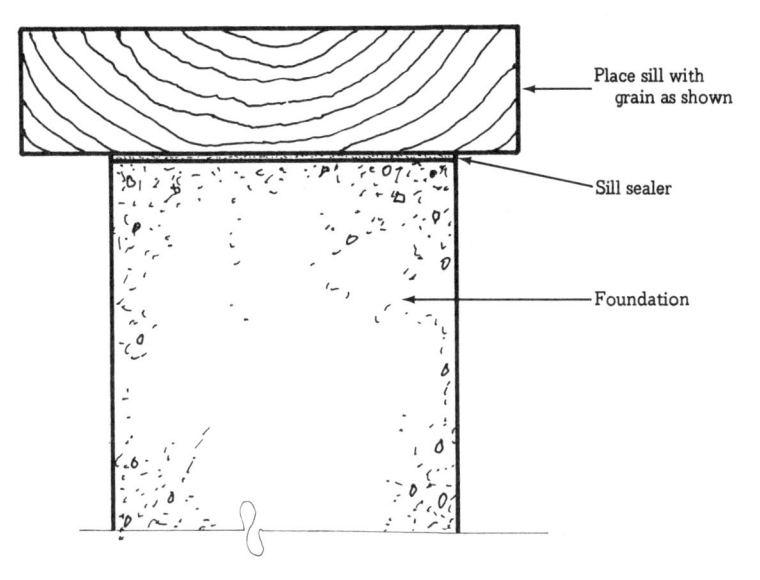

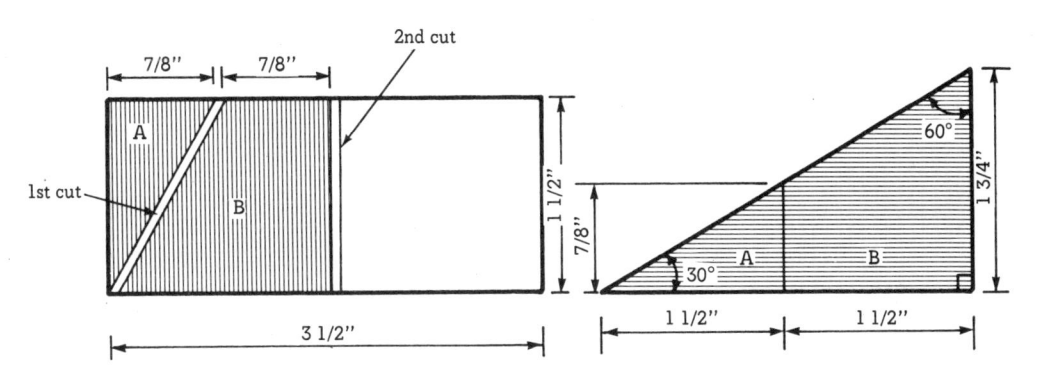

Fig. 4–15 Cant strip cut from 2 by 4 for 60-degree glazing slope

ment of the sill from shrinkage. Drill holes in the sill to allow placement over the anchor bolts. Sill sealer should be used to minimize air infiltration between the foundation and the sill. Secure the sill in place with washers and nuts. Do not stress the anchor bolts until the concrete has set for several days.

The cant strip can be cut from a single 2 in. × 4 in. or 4 in. × 4 in. piece of wood. This wood must be straight and true. Determine the angle of the cut from the slope of your south glazing. To cut both pieces from the same 2 in. by 4 in. piece, be sure to allow for the thickness of the saw blade before

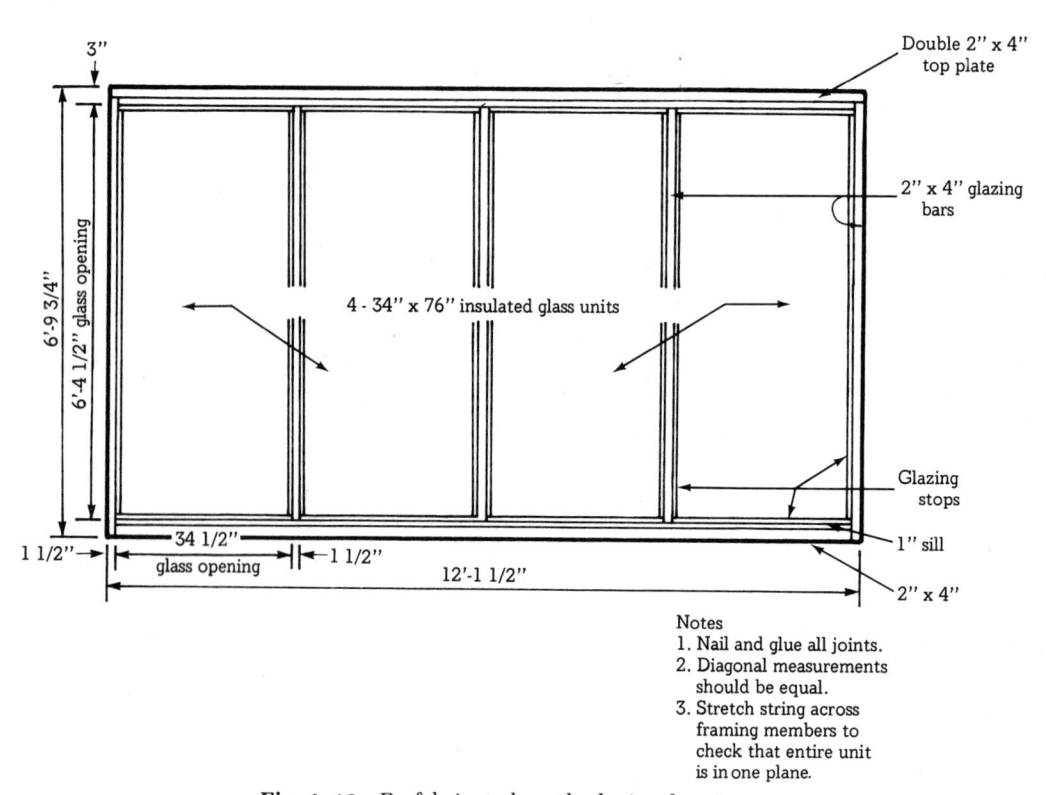

Fig. 4–16 Prefabricated south glazing framing

making your second cut. (See illustration.) To cut a 4 in. × 4 in. piece on an angle, you will need a table saw.

Nail and glue the cant strip securely in place.

The glazed south wall must be constructed flat and square. It should be constructed as one prefabricated piece. Carefully select each piece of wood.

To keep the frame square, check all diagonal measurements to be sure they are equal. Construct the unit on flat ground and use string tightly stretched across the entire frame to ensure that all pieces are in the same plane.

Note: For a 34 in. × 76 in. glass unit, the rough opening is 34½ in. × 76½ in. The 1 in. sill is one continuous piece beneath the glazing bars. From the front surface of the glazing bars, the glazing stops are set in 1/4 in. plus the thickness of the glazing unit. The 1/4 in. is for the 1/8 in. neoprene spacers on both sides of the glazing. The glazing bars should not be

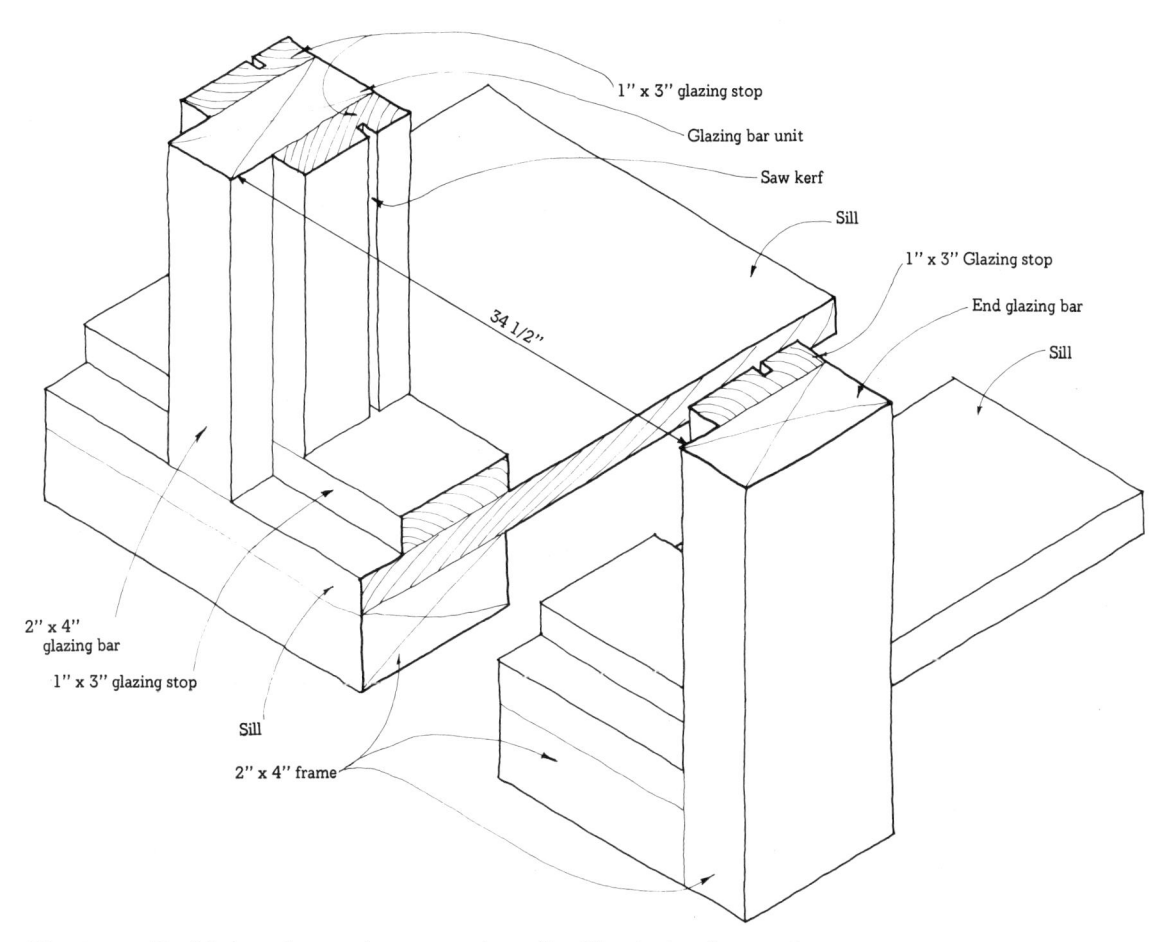

Fig. 4–17 Prefabricated greenhouse south wall: sill, glazing bar, and corner detail

deeper than 3½ in.—2 in. × 6 in. glazing bars will increase shading on plants significantly.

Set the prefabricated south wall in place. It should sit firmly on the cant strip and both side walls. If necessary, adjust or shim the side walls so that the south wall is level, square, and flat. Check the diagonal measurements and stretch a string across the south wall members. When everything looks good, nail the south wall securely in place. Now nail the exterior sheathing on the side walls to stabilize the wall construction.

114

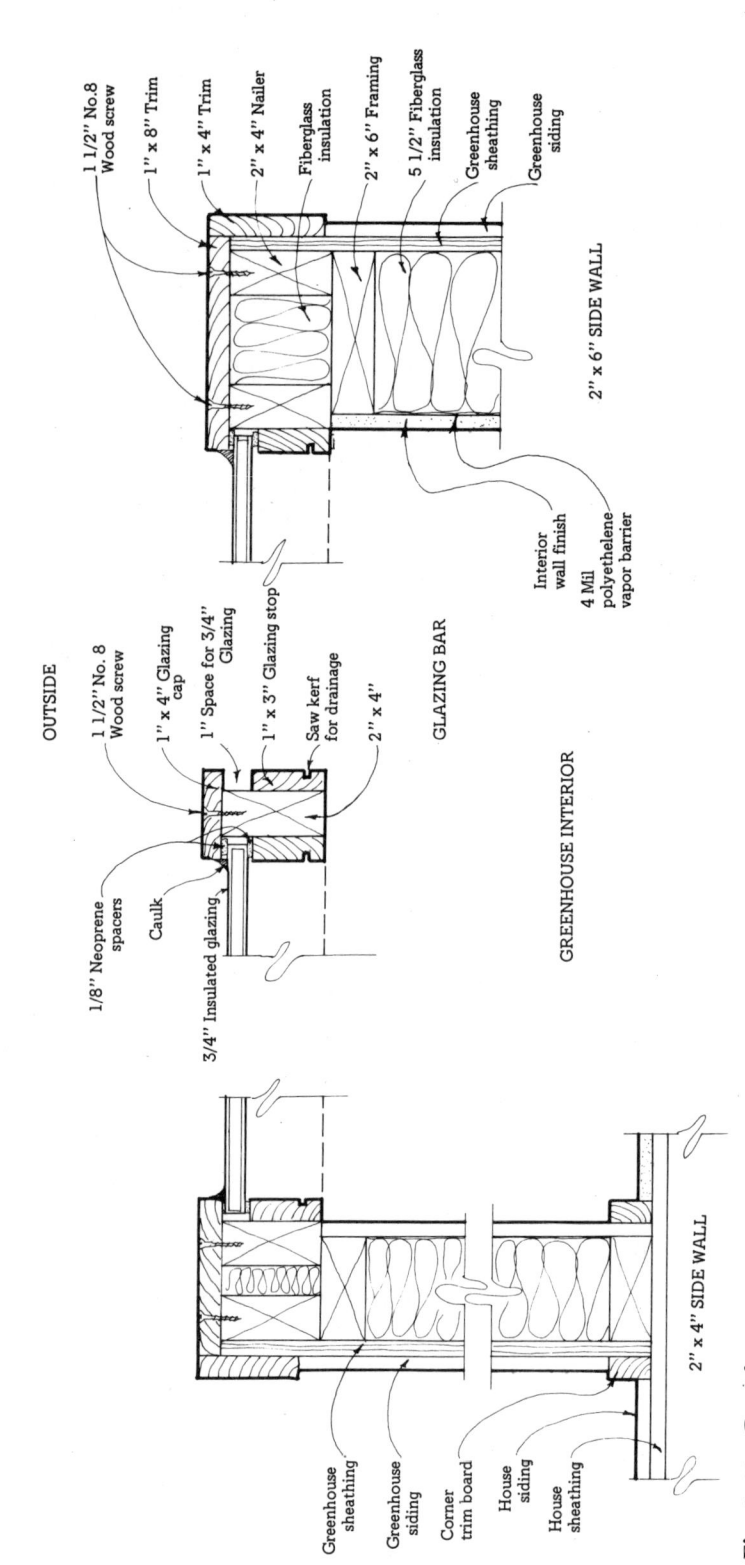

Fig. 4-18 Greenhouse interior

Fig. 4–19 Construction of greenhouse frame

Roof

Secure the 2 in. × 4 in. ledger into the house studs. The ledger can be beveled. For more support, leave the ledger square and cut a "bird's mouth" into each rafter. Cut the rafters to size and nail them into the ledger and double top plate of the south wall. Place rafters every 16 inches.

    Secure the 2 in. × 4 in. nailer by nailing it into the house studs. The nailer provides a firm anchoring for the collar ties and an edge along which to secure the greenhouse ceiling. If

Attached Solar Greenhouse

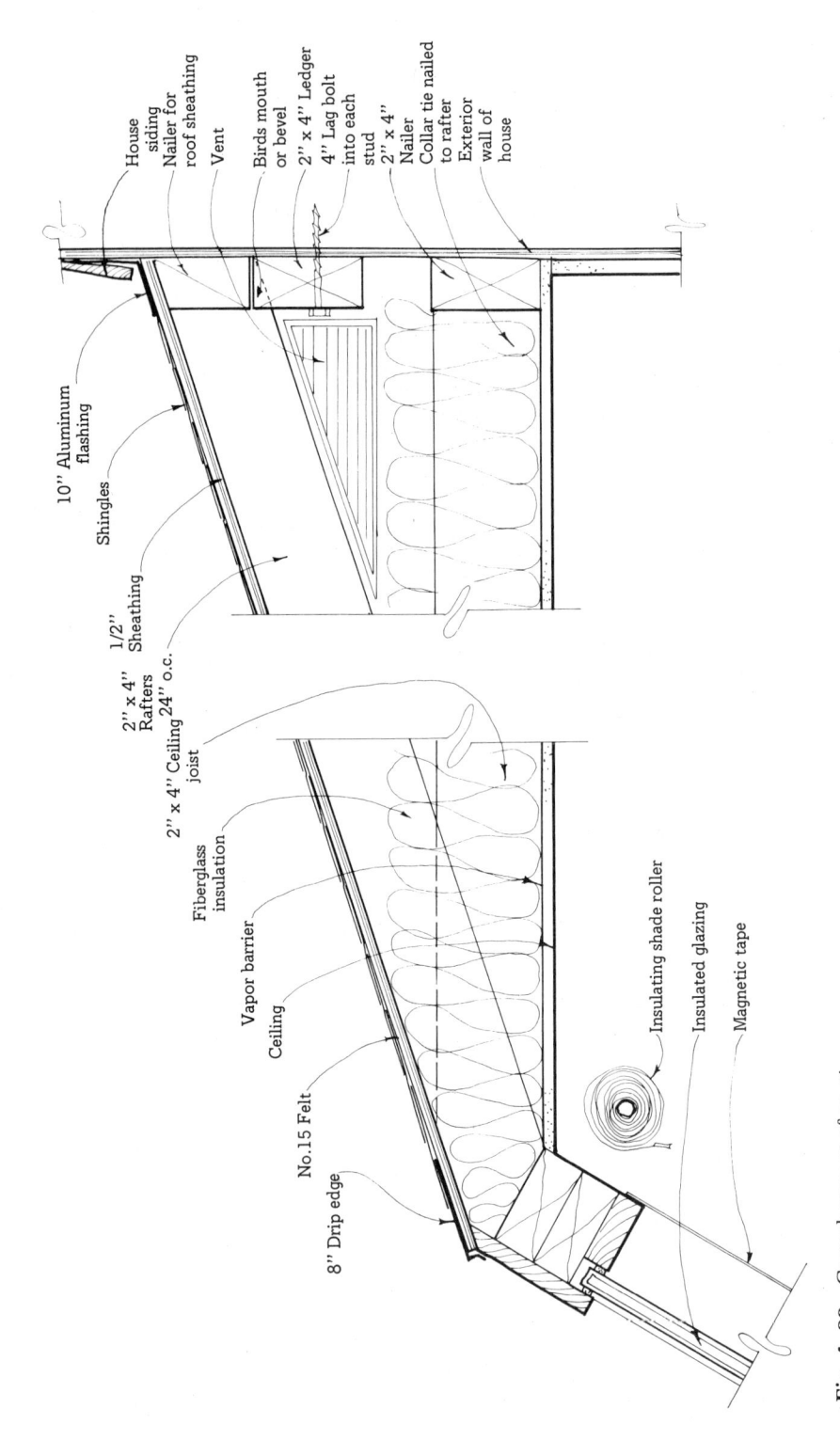

Fig. 4–20 Greenhouse roof section

Attached Solar Greenhouse

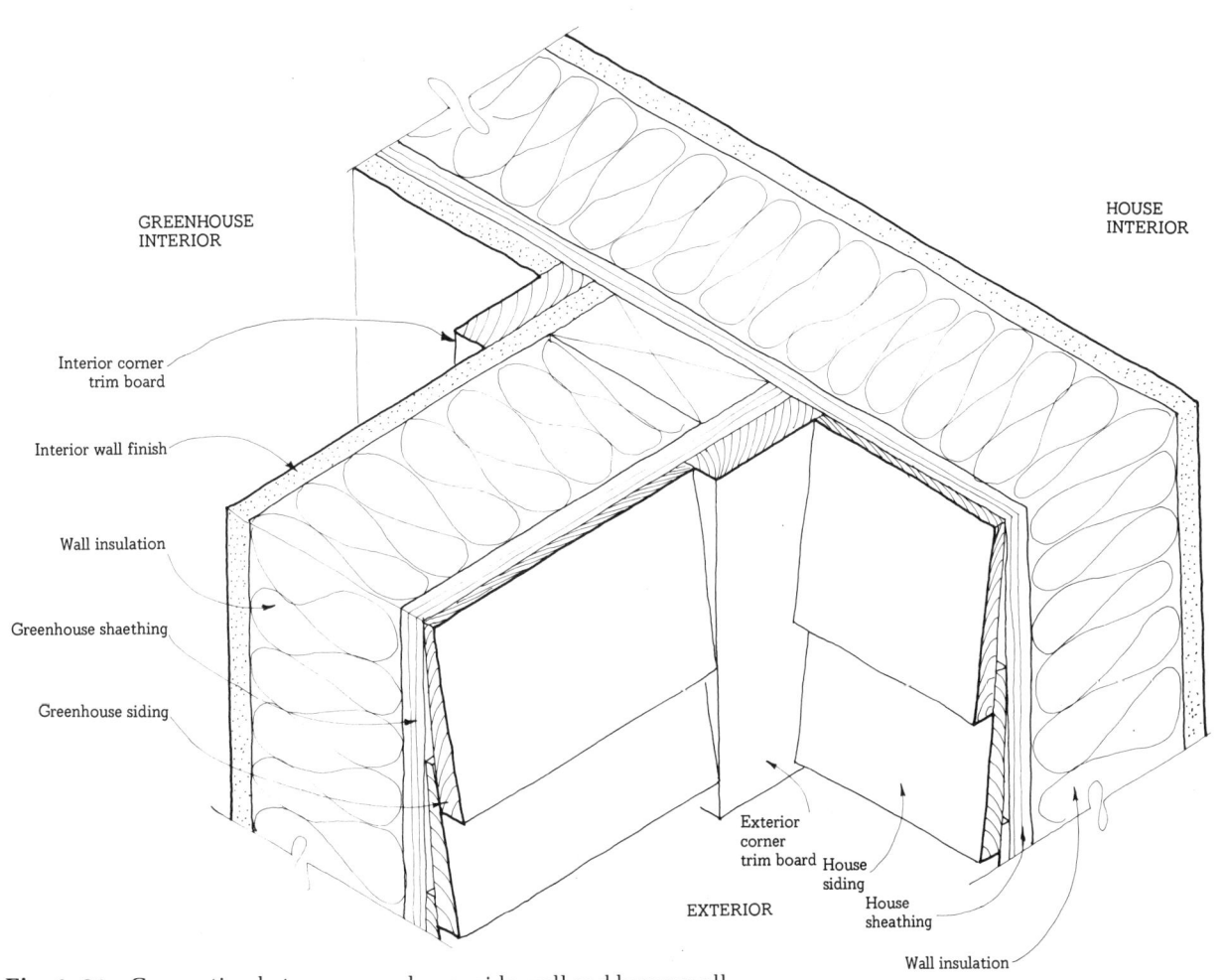

Fig. 4–21 Connection between greenhouse side wall and house wall

and an edge along which to secure the greenhouse ceiling. If the greenhouse ceiling must be raised at one point to provide clearance for a door to the house, arrange the nailer and collar ties accordingly. The collar ties, also called ceiling joists, can be nailed to the rafters or to the double top plate of the south wall.

Nail 1/2 in. plywood sheathing to the rafters. The roof sheathing provides rigidity to the entire greenhouse structure.

Staple #15 felt over the roof sheathing.

Nail the drip edge along the bottom and sides of the roof. Tar the drip edge to adhere the perimeter shingles and prevent them from being lifted by the wind.

Shingle the roof according to the manufacturer's instructions.

Secure the top edge of the aluminum flashing under the siding. Nail the bottom of the flashing to the roof and tar over the nails. (Optional: use tar to adhere the final decorative course of half shingles over the bottom of the flashing.)

Walls and interior

Level, then nail door and window frames in place using 16d galvanized casing nails. Flash above the windows and doors. Install the exterior siding and trim.

Insulate the walls and ceiling, being certain to fill every space. Fiberglass has the lowest cost per R-value and has good insulating properties. Where insulating space is limited, for instance in a 3½ in. thick wall, higher cost/higher R-value per inch foam insulation may be justified. Ten inches of fiberglass insulation in the ceiling is *not* excessive!

On the interior side of the insulation, a good vapor barrier is needed to keep moisture from entering the wall and ceiling cavities. Moisture can drastically reduce insulating values and also contributes to decay of the wood framing. To make a vapor barrier staple 4 mil. polyethylene in place, overlapping each seam one entire stud or joist bay.

The greenhouse interior is subjected to constant high humidity. Waterproof sheetrock and painted 1/4 in. AC plywood have both been used effectively for walls and ceiling. Paint these walls and ceiling a light color to reflect sunlight to plants and to the thermal storage.

Installing south glazing

Install the insulated glass units from the outside. Use neoprene setting blocks and spacers as shown in the glazing detail illustration (Fig. 2–13). Caulk between the glazing and glazing bars.

Note: The setting blocks must be wide enough to support both sheets of glass.

Fig. 4-22 Installing greenhouse insulated glass glazing

Cut the 1 in. × 4 in. glazing caps to 3 in. wide. This narrowing slightly increases the exposed glazing area and every bit counts. Bevel the lower glazing cap to prevent water from accumulating at the bottom of the glazing. The bottom of the vertical glazing caps will have to be cut to meet the beveled edge. Screw all glazing caps in place and caulk between the glazing caps and the glass.

Note: Manufacturers recommend that some types of caulk be applied to primed wood surfaces. Check the directions.

Maintenance Your attached solar greenhouse requires both daily and seasonal maintenance. On cold nights, draw insulating shades over all the glazed areas. Insulating shades can cut total night heat loss by half. When plants are endangered by extreme cold at night, be sure to allow some house heated air into the greenhouse by leaving an adjoining window or door slightly open.

On sunny winter days, you will have to control the flow of heat from the greenhouse to the house to ensure maximum heat gain to your house and reduce the chance of damaging plants from excessive heat. A thermostatically controlled fan is ideal for controlling this flow.

In snowy climates you may occasionally have to remove accumulated snow if it is blocking the glazing.

Each year check all caulking and replace where needed. If you have plastic glazing, follow the manufacturer's recommendations for cleaning and care. Otherwise, maintain your greenhouse as part of your house.

Your greenhouse can be used for winter growing, starting plants for outdoors in the early spring, and growing warm season crops in the summer. A few tips on winter growing:

Grow cool season crops such as cabbage, lettuce, and broccoli. These plants prefer temperatures between 45 and 75°F. The growth and quality of the plants will be greatly diminished if temperatures are allowed to fluctuate significantly beyond these extremes. Extreme temperatures also lead to disease, insect problems, and deformed growth. Begin these crops in September and October to establish good roots before entering winter with its reduced temperature and lighting levels. "Cold hardy" and "early" varieties of warm season crops can also be grown in winter, but with reduced yields. Do not be afraid to experiment—let your experience be your guide.

5

THE HORIZONTAL AIR FLOW ACTIVE COLLECTOR

Up to this point, the systems discussed in this book have been *passive* solar systems. The Horizontal Air Flow Collector is an *active* system—that is, mechanical means are used to move the solar-heated air into the house. Active solar systems offer the flexibility of thermostatically controlled heat delivery, thermal storage capacity, and separation between collector and heated space.

The Horizontal Air Flow Collector consists of insulated glazing, an absorber plate, and wood framing on the outside of the house, and a fan, thermostat, and heating ducts on the inside.

How It Works The Horizontal Air Flow Collector uses a thermostatically controlled fan to move heat from the collector to the house (or to thermal storage). During the day, sunlight passes through the double glazing and strikes the black absorber plate. The absorber plate becomes hot and heats the air in front of and behind it.

When the air behind the absorber plate reaches a temperature above the thermostat setting, the thermostat turns on the fan. The fan forces the hot air behind the absorber plate to move horizontally into the exhaust manifold at one end of

Fig. 5-1 Horizontal Air Flow Collector

the collector. The hot air then moves through ducts into the house or to storage.

Air from the house, or from storage, is pulled through other ducting into an intake manifold at the opposite end of the collector. This new, cooler air follows the same path behind the absorber plate, where it is heated, and then moves into the house or into storage.

The cycle continues until the absorber plate is cooled to the thermostat temperature setting. As long as the air temperature behind the absorber plate does not exceed the thermostat temperature setting, the fan remains off and no air is moved.

The Horizontal Air Flow Active Collector

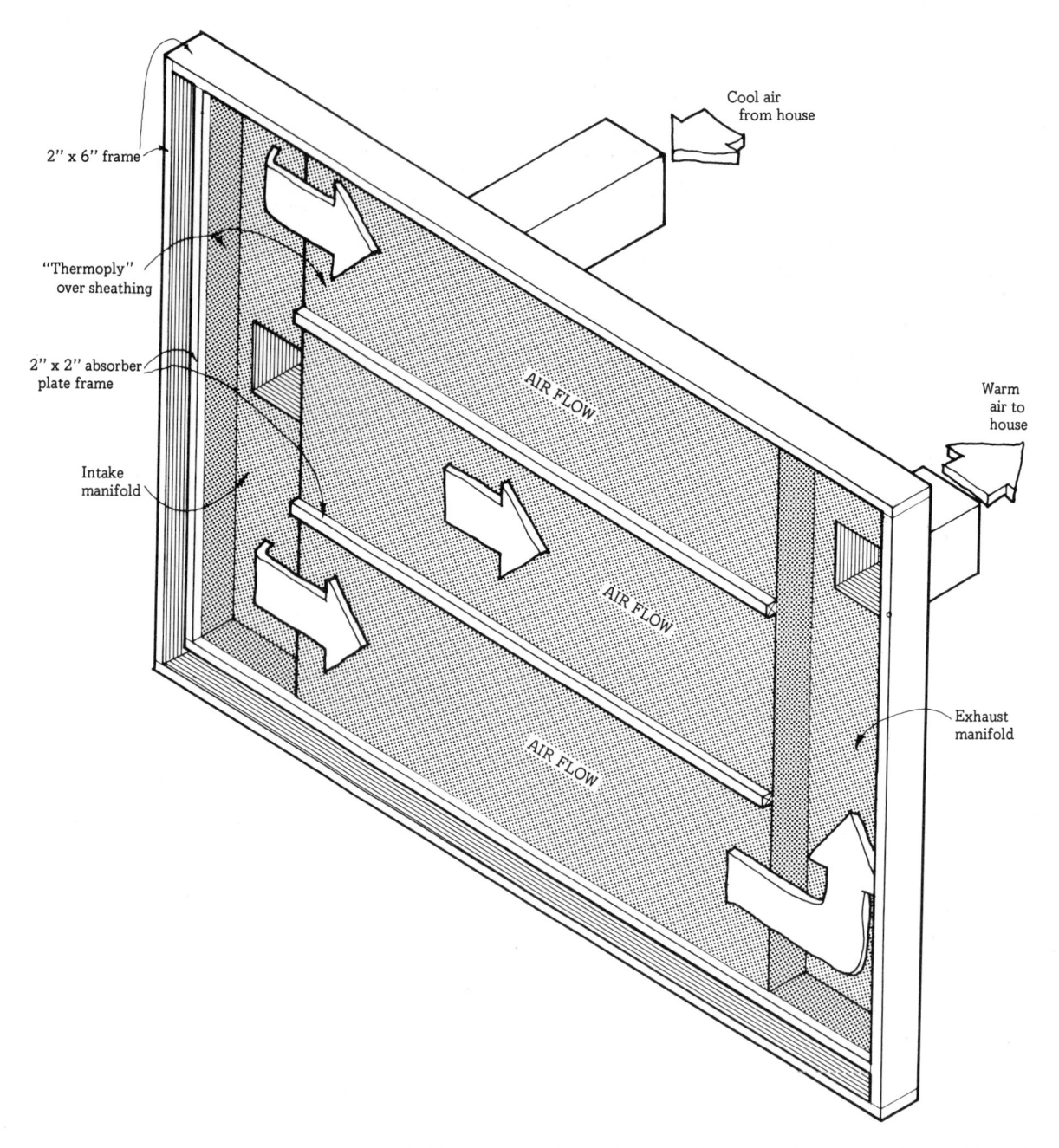

Fig. 5–2 Air flow behind absorber plate of Horizontal Air Flow Collector

At night and on cloudy days, manual or automatic dampers on the collector prevent cold air from entering the house or storage. When thermal storage is used, separate controls are needed to determine if stored heat is available and if it is needed in the house.

System Strategies

The Horizontal Air Flow Collector is designed to be incorporated into wood frame construction. The minimum recommended collector size is 7 feet 2 inches high × 14 feet 11 inches wide of flat, unobstructed south facing area. The system's construction is somewhat more complex than construction of Direct Gain or TAP solar heating systems.

Thermostatically controlled heat delivery provides available solar heat to the house as needed. The thermostat "knows" when heat is available in the collector; it also "knows" when to stop putting heat into the house (to prevent overheating). A system that includes thermal storage can be designed so that the thermostat "decides" whether available solar heat should go into the house or into storage for later use.

Thermal storage can be integrated into the Horizontal Air Flow Collector to achieve a higher solar heating fraction (the percentage of heating needs supplied by solar). With thermal storage, excess heat generated during the day can be saved and released into the house at night. When a high solar heating fraction is desired, thermal storage is needed because only 30 percent of a home's heat is used during the day.

It isn't *necessary* to add thermal storage with a Horizontal Air Flow Collector unless the collector produces so much heat that the house becomes too warm. For the average house in a cool or cold climate, up to 200 square feet of collector can be used before heat storage is needed. Beyond that size, storage is necessary or the house will probably overheat. (These numbers assume that the solar heat is distributed throughout the house. To avoid overheating in cases where the solar heat will be distributed to one or two rooms only, the collector size must be reduced by as much as 50 percent—or thermal storage must be added.)

With active air collectors, heat storage is best in rock beds or small containers of water. In many houses, thermal storage capacity is limited due to the excessive weight of the storage and lack of space. Thermal storage is more easily incorporated into new construction.

Unlike passive solar heaters, active collectors can be located away from the rooms to be heated. Active solar heating is ideal when the rooms to be heated are not located on the south side of the house, or when obstructions, shading, or other considerations rule out the use of the south wall as a collector surface. Heat from collectors located on a garage wall can be ducted to the house. Collectors mounted on exterior bedroom walls can heat other rooms used during the day.

The Horizontal Air Flow Collector described here is designed to provide economical, effective solar heating. Material costs for a 110 square foot active collector without thermal storage are approximately $1000, or $9 per square foot. An experienced builder and a helper can construct this system in three or four weekends.

Note: This solar heating system will heat the house wall behind the collector to above-normal temperatures. Therefore, I do not recommend placing this collector on any wall containing inflammable insulation or other material.

Materials

The design of the Horizontal Air Flow Collector is similar to that of the TAP. The components of both systems are exposed to extreme heat and cold. Therefore, the materials and detailing for this active system must meet the specifications noted in the chapter on TAP.

The fan, thermostat and electrical wiring of the Horizontal Air Flow Collector must also be rated for high temperature use.

Fan

Select a fan that delivers approximately 3 CFM (cubic feet of air per minute) for each square foot of collector area. A 100 square foot collector would need a fan moving 300 CFM at the static pressure (SP) of your system. Static pressure is the resistance to air movement through the collector and ducting.

Air speed and duct design determine the static pressure. Systems with few bends and short duct lengths have less air resistance.

Centrifugal blowers, also called squirrel cage fans, are recommended for most collectors. They are available in many sizes and are rated in CFM at a given static pressure. These fans can be installed on either the intake or exhaust side of the collector.

Despite their low cost, propeller fans are not generally recommended for active solar collectors, because they work well only where resistance to air flow is minimal as in small collectors with little duct work. With greater air resistance, the amount of air delivered will be drastically reduced. For moderate sized to large collectors, propeller fans are inadequate.

If you use a propeller fan, install it on the exhaust side of the collector. To maximize performance, mount an egg crate grill or short length of duct on the exhaust side of the fan. Since the fan motor will be directly in the air stream, the motor must be rated for high temperature use.

Thermostat

A *cooling thermostat* with a temperature probe that can withstand temperatures above 200°F must be used to control fan operation. The "Hawthorne 1503-A" differential thermostat is recommended for its performance and ease of installation. Its two probes allow it to sense both house and collector temperatures. When the collector temperature is 16°F higher than the house temperature, the thermostat turns the fan on. With the standard thermostat the fan remains on until the collector air is cooled to within 3°F of the house temperature.

Note: With this standard 3°F fan-OFF differential, air that is somewhat cool will be blown into your house. When ordering your thermostat, specify a fan-OFF differential of approximately 10°F. The Hawthorne 1503-A thermostat is available from Hawthorne Industries Inc., Solar Energy Division, 1501 South Dixie Highway, West Palm Beach, FL 33401.

The Hawthorne 1503-A can be plugged directly into a 120V, three-prong wall receptacle. The fan is then plugged

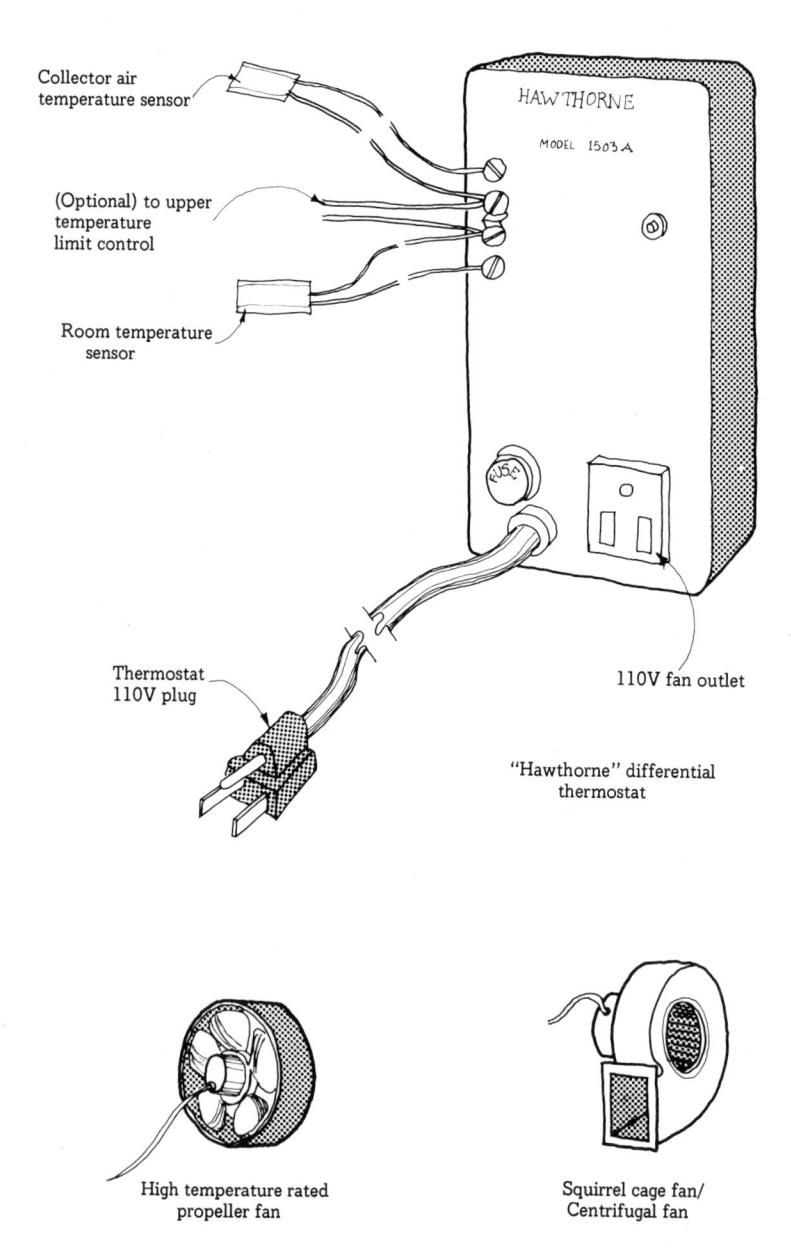

Fig. 5-3 Differential thermostat and fan components

into the 120V receptacle on the face of the thermostat. Since the temperature sensors are low voltage, they can be easily installed.

Another nice feature of the Hawthorne 1503-A thermostat is that a low-voltage heating thermostat can be used with it as an upper limit temperature control. This control prevents house overheating by turning off the fan when the house reaches the maximum desired temperature.

Note: Ducts, fans and thermostats are available from heating/cooling suppliers and contractors.

Materials list

Complete the quantity and size column of this material list according to the size of your collector and glazing units.

Part of collector	Dimension	Quantity/Size	Notes
frame	2″ × 6″		
absorber plate frame	2″ × 2″		
absorber plate support	2″ × 2″		
glazing stops	1″ × 4″		
mullions	1″ × 5″		
brace	1″ × 6″		
triangular braces	2″ × 6″		
glazing caps	1″ × 3″		
"Thermoply"			available at lumber yards. Manufactured by Simplex Product Group, 3000 W. Beecher Road, Adrian, Michigan 49221
nails	10d galv. 16d galv. 8d finishing 10d aluminum		
duct tape	2″		
clear silicone caulk			
latex caulk			
flashing			
neoprene setting blocks	1/4″ × 1″ × 2″		available at glazier
neoprene spacers	1/8″ × 1/2″ × 2″		available at glazier
absorber plate			If not factory painted, paint with high temperature flat, black paint.
end closure strips			For corrugated absorber plates, use inside end closure strips on top and bottom.
glazing			
fan			
thermostat			
ductwork			

Construction Layout

Exterior

Determine the exact height and width of your collector. The collector height equals:

> glazing unit height *plus* 1/4 in. spacing on top and bottom of glazing (1/2 in. total spacing);

plus top and bottom frame with flashing (3¼ in.);

plus lower support bracket (6¼ in.);

plus 1/8 in. top and bottom clearance (1/4 in. overall).

Thus, the total height equals the glazing height plus 10¼ in. The collector width equals:

> glazing unit width *plus* 1/4 in. spacing on each side (1/2 in. total spacing) *times* the number of glazing units;

plus number of mullions *times* 3/4 in. (the number of mullions is one less than the number of glazing units);

plus frame (3 in.);

plus 1/8 in. clearance on each side (1/4 in. overall).

The entire collector area must be on one flat wall with no obstructions. The collector must be placed so that the sides of the frame will allow the intake and exhaust manifolds to freely exchange air behind the absorber plate (see construction details). This can usually be accomplished by positioning the sides of the collector on or near wall studs. *The end stud bays must be at least 14 inches wide for proper manifold operation.* Wall stud spacing can be found from the interior of the house.

After determining the best location on the south wall for your collector, use nails to mark the four corners. Then, with a chalk line, mark the top, bottom, and sides. To ensure squareness, check to make sure diagonal measurements are equal.

Interior

Air to and from the intake and exhaust manifolds must come either directly through the interior walls—a convenient solu-

The Horizontal Air Flow Active Collector

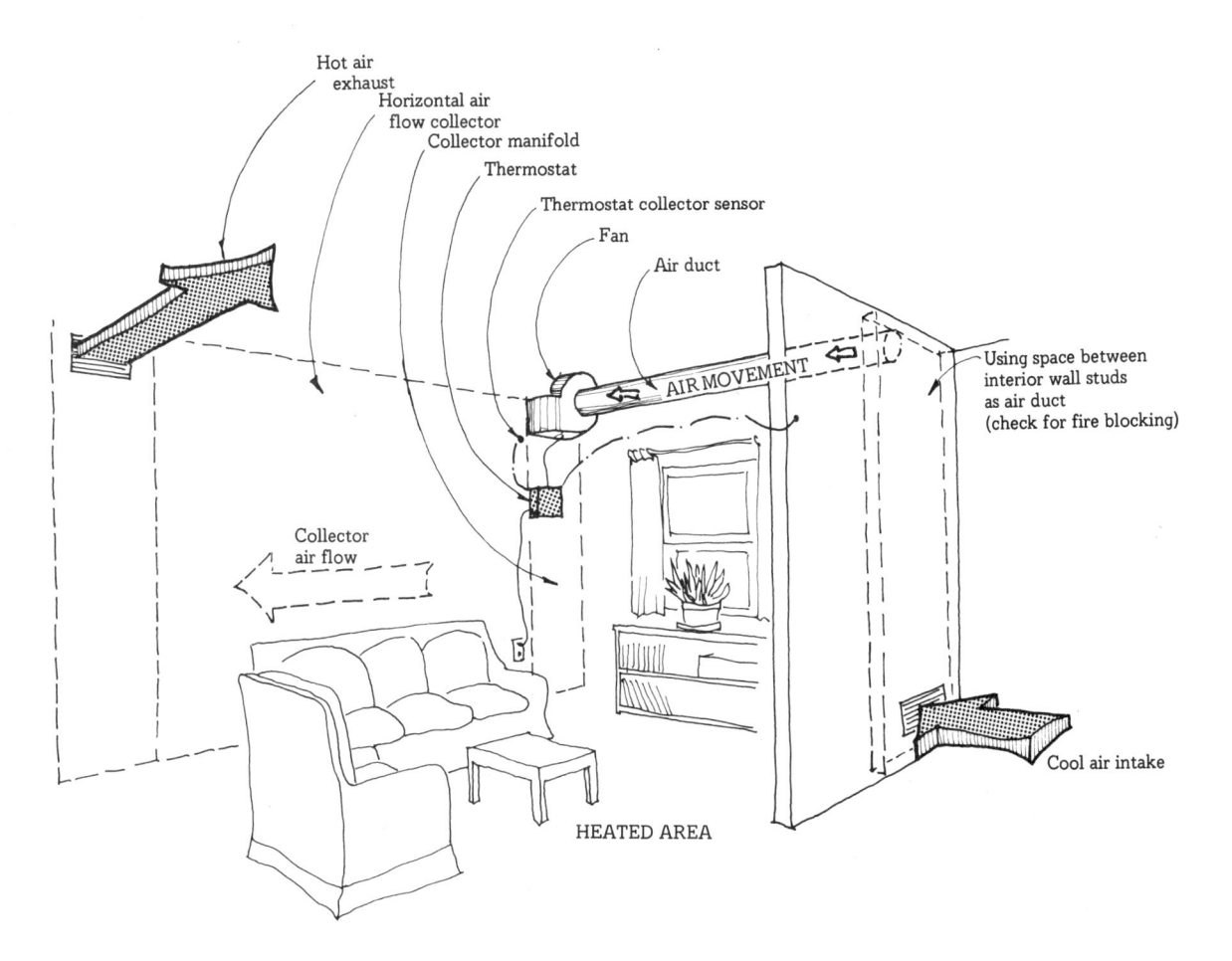

Fig. 5–4 Horizontal Air Flow System without heat storage

tion—or be ducted to the manifolds. A fan unit is needed to move the air along this route. the thermostat controlling the fan must be positioned to monitor both collector and house temperatures.

Visualize the air flow from the collector exhaust manifold, through the house interior, and back to the intake manifold. The path that the air travels is important for optimum collector performance and heat distribution.

Note: Construction details in this chapter do not include information about thermal storage because in most cases, the

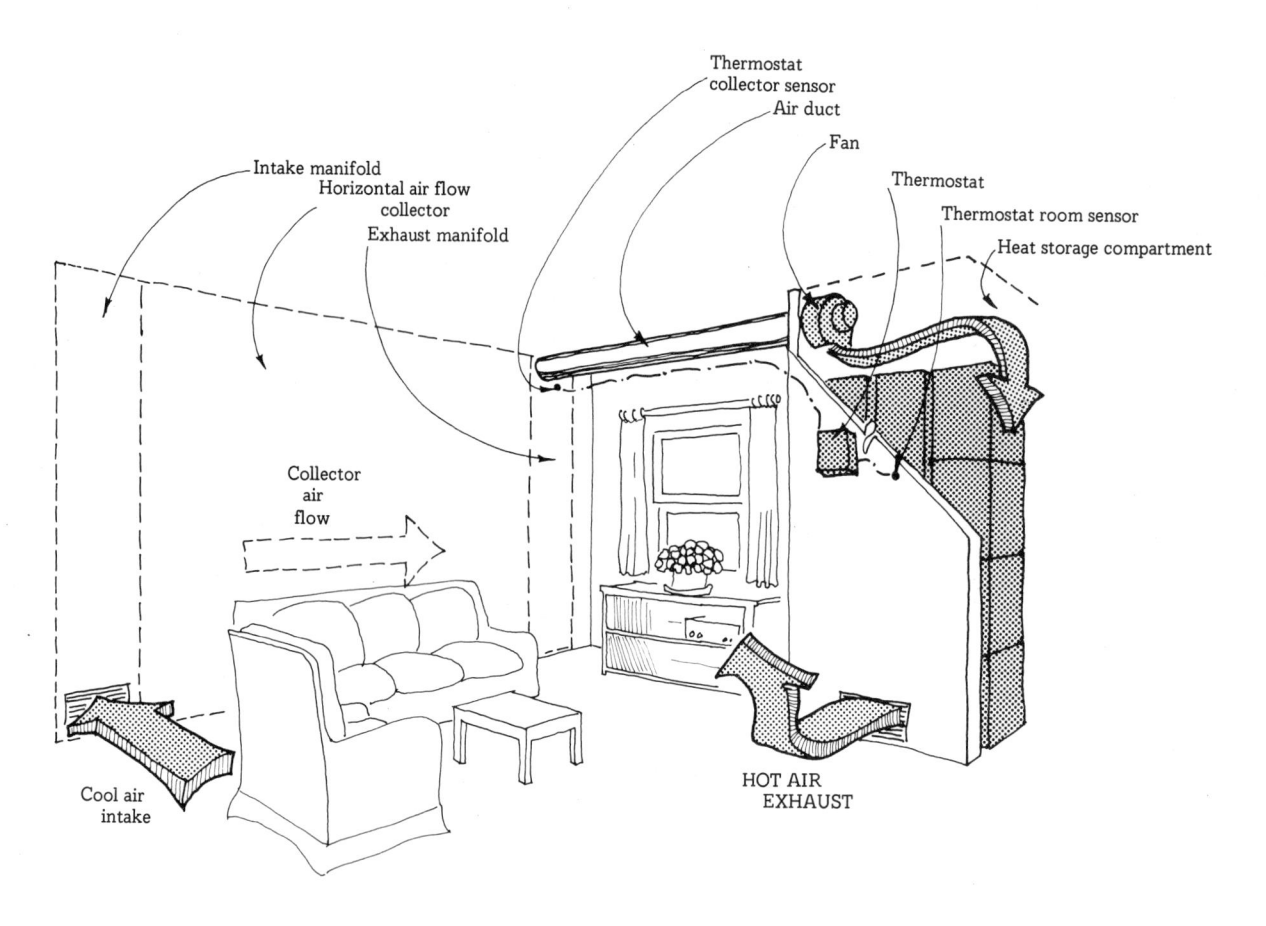

The Horizontal Air Flow Active Collector

Note:
Heat can be stored in small containers of water with air spaces around them for circulation. At night heat in storage can be recovered by thermosiphoning heated air into the adjacent rooms or with an independent fan system

Fig. 5-5 Horizontal Air Flow System with heat storage

architectural features of the house limit collector size so that most of the solar heat collected can be used immediately. Also, thermal storage systems are so unique to each retrofit that it is impossible to provide universal instructions. Chapter 7 includes general guidelines for thermal storage.

Warm air entering the house through the exhaust vent register will follow the shortest route—the path of least resistance—to the intake vent register. The house area between the exhaust and intake registers receives solar heat from this flow of air. If the registers are close together, only a small portion of a room will be heated. On the other hand, if the registers are rooms apart, the solar heat will be widely distributed. Depending on the size of your collector, however, heating efficiency may be decreased by dispersing solar heat to many rooms. See "Getting the Most from Your Solar Heating System" in Chapter 1.

The intake vent register should be located near the floor, preferably in a cold area in one of the rooms you are solar heating. Supplying the collector with colder air will take more heat from the absorber plate, and thus increase overall efficiency.

The design of air passages to and from the collector has led to some ingenious solutions. Try to keep ducting simple and direct. Duct sizes should be approximately 8 to 10 inches round (for long ducts), 4 in. × 14 in. (above hung ceilings), or 8 inches square. The larger the ducts, the less air resistance. Be sure to eliminate unnecessary bends in your ductwork, because they greatly increase air resistance. Also, extra long ducts must be a larger size.

Some innovative arrangements include using interior wall stud bays for vertical ducting, and using floor and ceiling joist bays for horizontal runs. While cool intake air can pass safely through wood ducting, hot exhaust air must pass through approved heat ducting materials.

Positioning of the fan unit should be determined by allowable space and *noise conditions*. Remember that the fan will be on most of the day, so noise is a major consideration. Install the fan where it can be easily serviced, yet safe for children. The thermostat can be mounted next to the fan and housed with it in one unit.

Note: All electrical work must meet local building codes.

Procedure

Preparing the absorber plate

Note: Prepare the absorber plates, allowing adequate drying time before installation.

134   **The Horizontal Air Flow Active Collector**

Fig. 5–6 Collector frame before installation of the absorber plate. Note the air manifolds at each end and the three horizontal air flow channels across the collector.

1. Cut the absorber plates to size.
2. Degrease the absorber plates with solvent, following the manufacturer's instructions. Remove the degreasing agent.
3. Paint the absorber plates with high-temperature (300+°F), flat black paint.

Preparing the exterior wall

1. Remove the siding down to the sheathing.

    Note: First remove the siding to within approximately one foot of each end. Then, after noting the end stud locations and determining the exact position for the collector, remove the remaining siding as necessary.

2. Locate all wall studs by probing the sheathing with a nail. Then mark the stud locations on the wall above and below where the siding was removed.
3. Confirm that the end stud bays are a minimum of 14 in. wide. Remove the sheathing *at each end stud bay only!* Leave all other sheathing intact.

    Note: Leave the sheathing on all studs.

4. Cut holes in the interior wall for ducting to the manifolds. The intake and exhaust air manifolds are the spaces made by removing the building sheathing. The back of the manifolds is the interior wall of the building, and the two sides of each manifold are the adjacent wall studs. The manifolds evenly distribute the air from the ducts to the horizontal air flow spaces behind the absorber plate.
5. Cover the sheathing and manifolds with "Thermoply." The foil surface must make an airtight seal over wall cavities. Locate it within the 2 in. × 6 in. frame.

Framing

Note: Prime all wood before installation.

1. Nail the 2 in. × 6 in. frame in place. Check the squareness by making diagonals equal.
2. Nail the 2 in. × 2 in. absorber plate frame to the sheathing and wall studs. Any space between the 2 in. × 6 in. frame

Fig. 5-7 Prime all wood before installation.

and the sheathing caused by discrepancies in the sheathing should be covered by nailing the 2 in. × 2 in. frame tightly to the sheathing before nailing it to the 2 in. × 6 in. frame. Use silicone caulk to seal the perimeter of 2 in. × 2 in. frame to the "Thermoply." Nail two 2x2s horizontally, forming three equal size air channels. The air behind the absorber plate will flow across the collector in these channels. The 2×2s must be nailed securely into the studs and sheathing.

The Horizontal Air Flow Active Collector

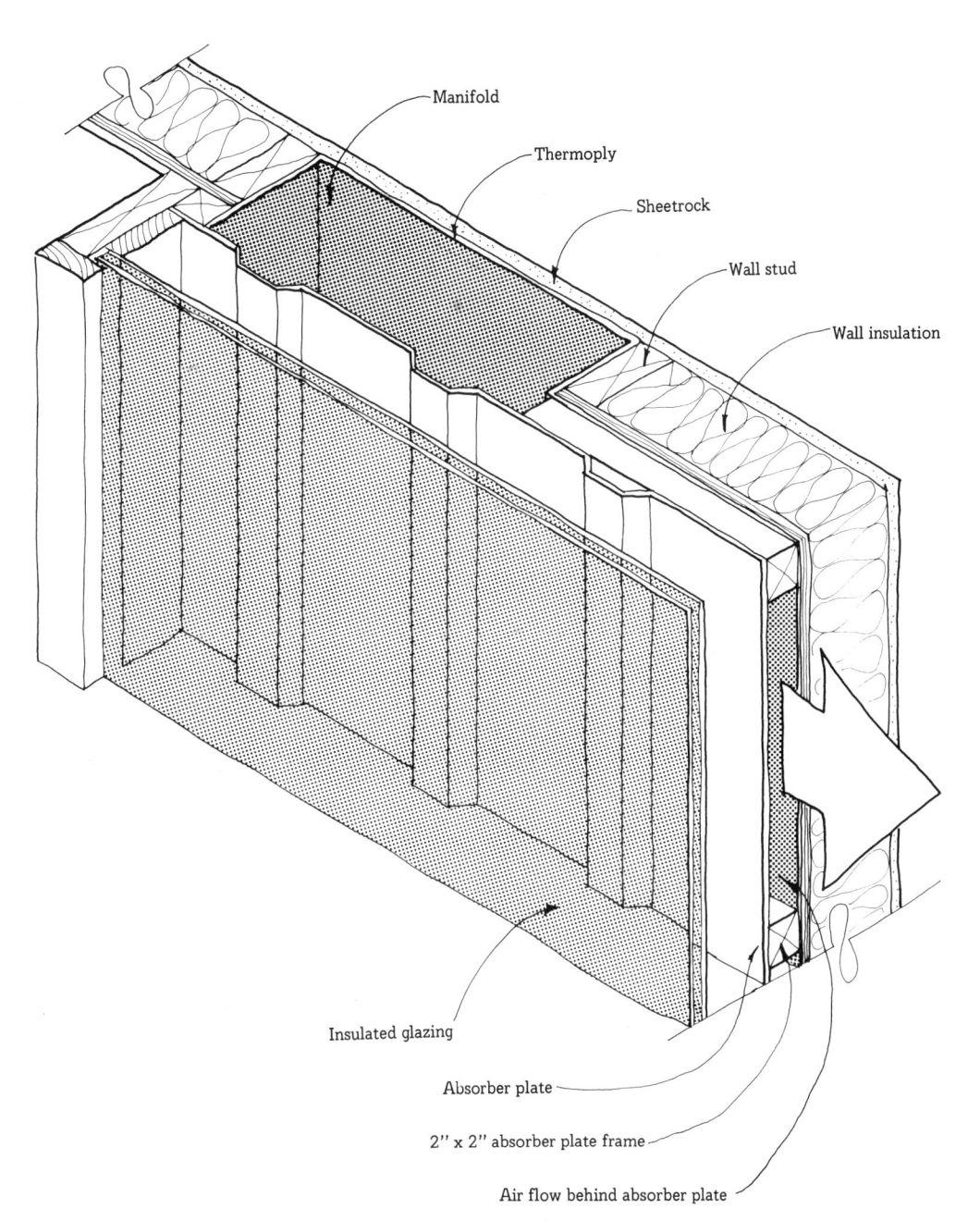

Fig. 5–8 Air flow through the manifold and behind the absorber plate

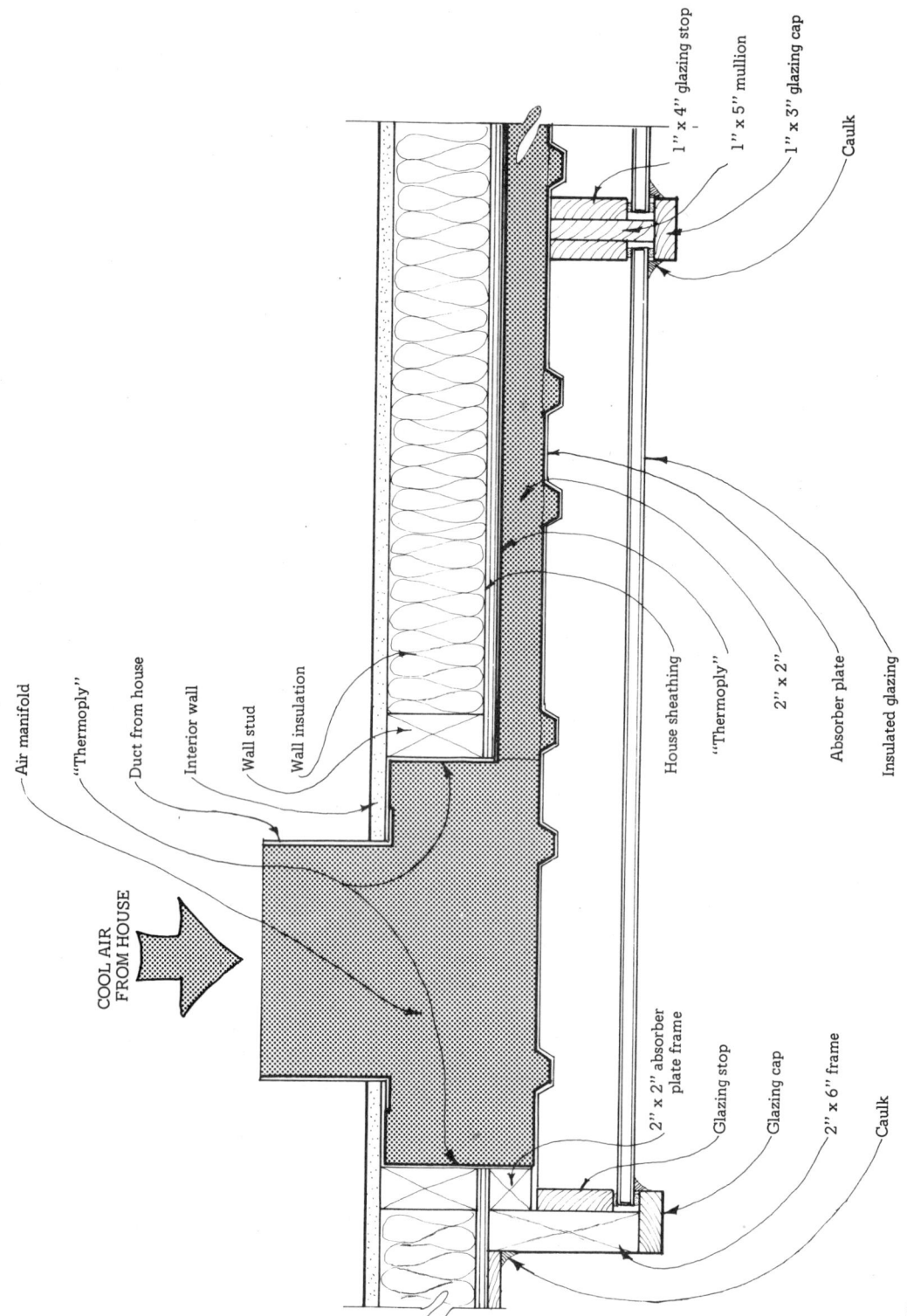

Fig. 5–9 Horizontal section through the air manifold and collector

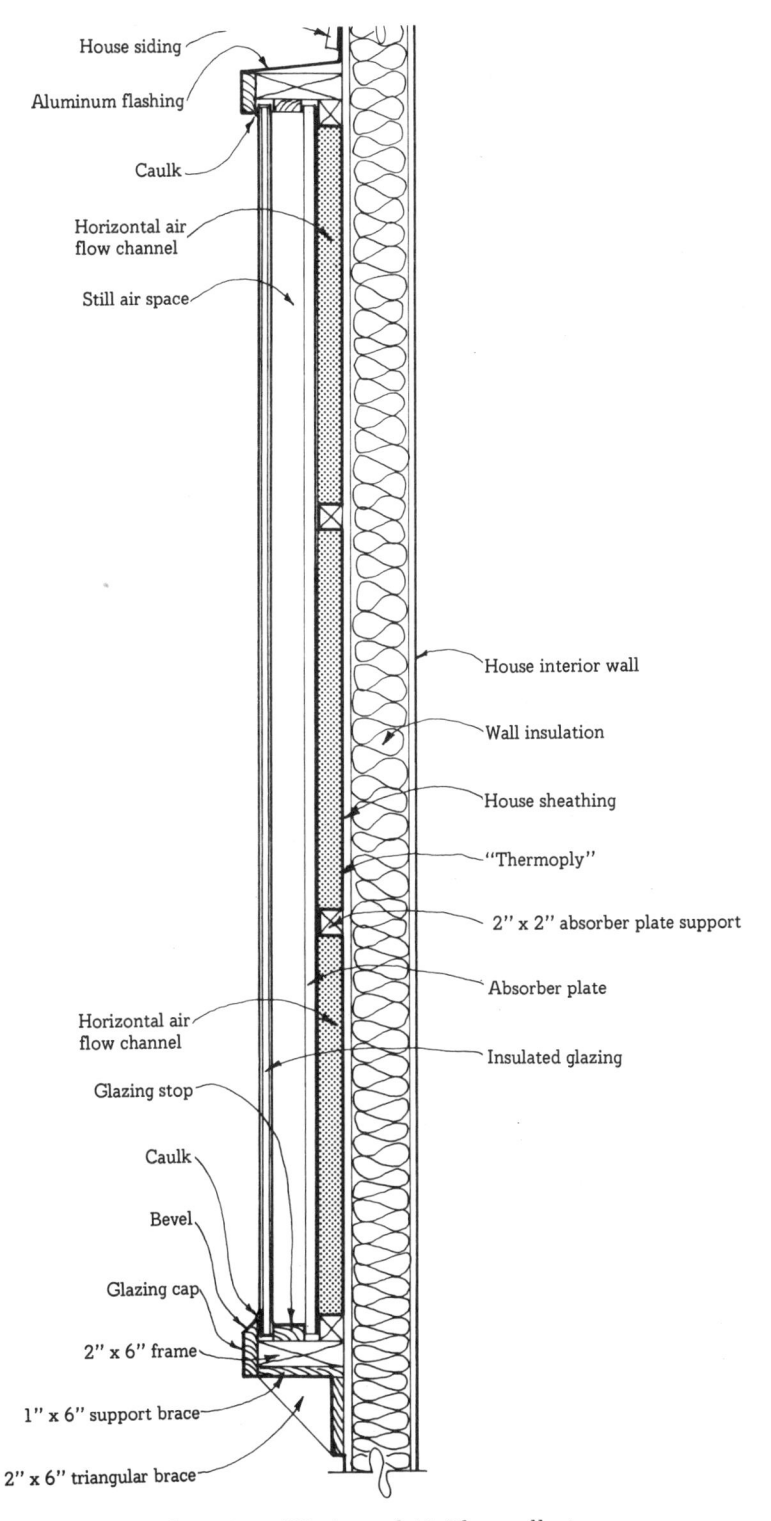

Fig. 5–10 Vertical section of Horizontal Air Flow collector

3. Connect the intake and exhaust ducting from the house to the manifolds. All connections must be airtight. Use silicone caulk to seal any air leaks inside either manifold. Once the absorber plate is secured it will be difficult to work on the manifolds.
4. Mount the collector thermostat sensor in the air channel behind the absorber plate. Do not mount the sensor to either the absorber plate or "Thermoply." The sensor must respond to quick changes in the air temperature and not be warmed by the heat stored in the absorber plate or house sheathing.
5. Mark the location of the glazing bars on the horizontal 2×2s. When using a corrugated absorber plate, position the corrugations (placed vertically) to minimize interference with the glazing bars.
6. Secure the absorber plate to the 2×2s using nails of the same material. If the absorber plate is corrugated, use silicone caulk to adhere the end closure strips to the top and bottom of each absorber plate before mounting it. The end closure strips should be able to withstand temperatures up to 200°F.

Note: Leave a 1/4 in. space between the side of the end sheets of the absorber plate and the 2 in. × 6 in. frame; and leave a 1/2 in. space between the top and bottom of all absorber plate sheets and the frame.

Glazing

1. Prefabricate the vertical glazing bars. If necessary, cut the 1 in. × 4 in. glazing stops to allow for the glazing thickness plus the 1/8 in. spacers in front of and behind the glazing. The glazing bars must be straight and true. Nail the glazing bars to the 2 in. × 6 in. frame and the 2x2s. The distance between the glazing bars must be 1/2 in. wider than the glazing. Nail the horizontal glazing stops in place.

Note: The glazing bars and stops should be constructed of spruce or fir (not pine) and be primed and painted a light color.

Fig. 5–11 Installing the absorber plates and glazing bars

The Horizontal Air Flow Active Collector

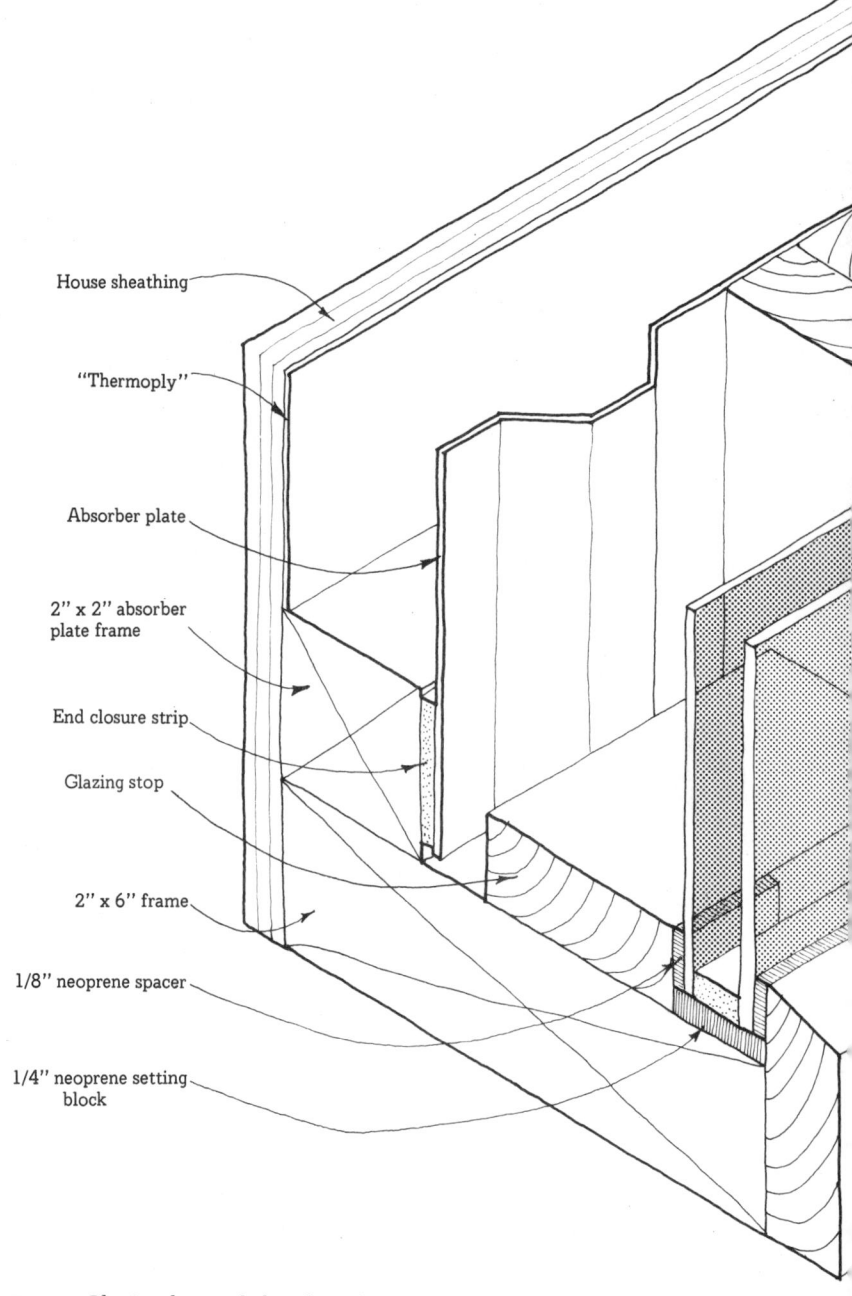

Fig. 5–12 Glazing bar and absorber plate assembly in a Horizontal Air

The Horizontal Air Flow Active Collector

Air flow behind absorber plate

1" x 5" mullion

1" x 4" glazing stop

Insulated glazing

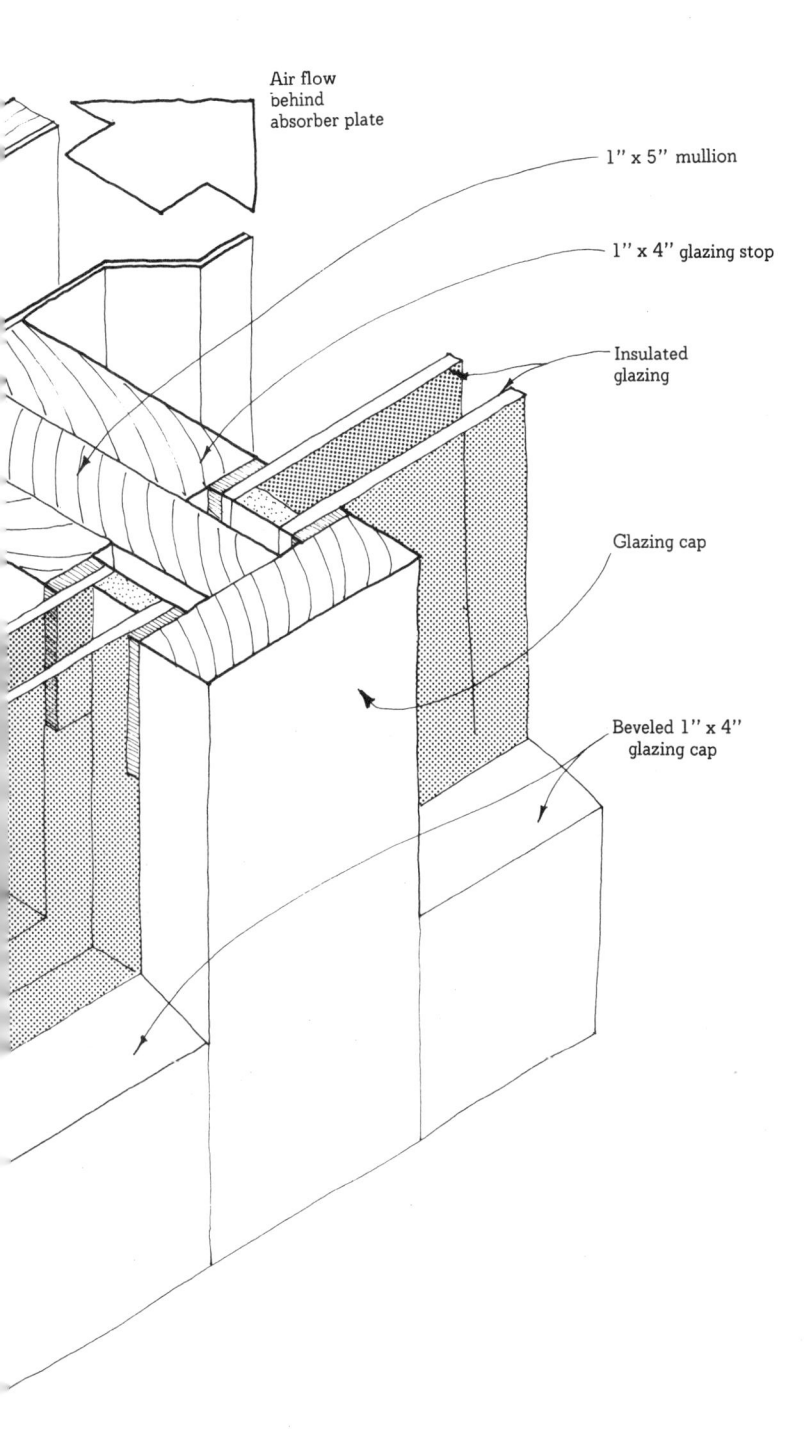

Glazing cap

Beveled 1" x 4" glazing cap

Flow Collector

Fig. 5-13 Lifting the insulated glass into place

2. Drill two 1/8 in. weep holes in the 2 in. × 6 in. frame for each sheet of glazing.

Fig. 5–14 Carefully caulk all seams. Reduce the amount of caulk needed by placing 1/4-in. diameter polyethylene rope between the end of the insulated glass unit and the wood frame.

Glass installation

1. Set the neoprene setting blocks and spacers as shown in Fig. 2–13. For a 3/4 in. thick glazing unit use 1/4 in. × 1 in. × 2 in. setting blocks at quarter points to set the glass on; and 1/8 in. neoprene spacers. Use silicone caulk to adhere the neoprene blocks in place.
2. Touch up the absorber plate paint where needed.

3. Thoroughly clean the back of the glass before putting it into the frame. Install the glass. You will need two people to lift the glass, and a third person on a ladder to guide it from above.
4. Temporarily secure the glass by toenailing several nails into the edge of the frame. Apply silicone caulk between the edge of the glass and the 2 in. × 6 in. frame.
5. Cut the glazing caps to 2¼ in. wide. Bevel cut the bottom glazing cap to shed water. Install the glazing caps being careful not to nail into the edge of the glass. Set 1/8 in. neoprene spacers between the glazing caps and the glass.
6. Paint all exterior wood.
7. Caulk between the glass and the glazing caps to form a double seal.
8. Clean the glass.

Maintenance Your Horizontal Air Flow Collector is designed to operate with high efficiency. Periodic maintenance is required to ensure full operating capacity over the years. In the fall, when the heating season begins, prune any trees and shrubs that shade the glazing during the winter months. Check and repair caulk and flashing where needed. All glazing should be thoroughly cleaned in the fall and whenever necessary throughout the heating season.

The electrical wiring, thermostat, and fan should also be checked periodically. Follow the manufacturer's instructions for fan and thermostat maintenance. The fan may require oiling every six months. Thermostat setting, calibration, and performance should also be tested to insure optimum efficiency.

Performance The amount of heat delivered from your collector can be calculated by multiplying *the amount of air delivered from the collector × the difference in temperature of air entering and leaving the collector registers × the heat capacity of air × the length of fan-on time.*

The amount of air delivered from the collector is determined by the size of your fan—measured in CFM (cubic feet of air per minute)—and the resistance to air flow within the system.

Fig. 5–15 Installing the fan and thermostat unit

The temperature of the air at each register should be measured after the fan has been operating for at least several minutes.

The heat capacity of air equals 0.0182 Btu/ft$^3\cdot$°F. That is, it takes 0.0182 Btu to raise the temperature of one cubic foot of air 1 degree Fahrenheit.

Using the first three numbers, the heat delivered can be calculated for a hour, a day or a year.

Note: Since the amount of air is measured in cubic feet per minute, you will have to multiply this number times 60 to get the cubic feet per hour.

For example, how much heat is delivered during 5 hours of fan operation if the fan delivers 400 CFM and the difference between the intake and exhaust air temperature is 30°F?

400 CFM × 30°F × 0.0182 Btu/ft$^3\cdot$°F × 300 minutes =
$$65{,}520 \text{ Btu.}$$

6
IDEAS FOR IMPROVING PERFORMANCE

Reflectors   On a sunny day, a snow field in front of your collector increases the insolation that strikes the glazing by as much as 30%. Reflection from horizontal surfaces is greatest when the sun is low in the sky, as in the winter. Vertical glazing is best for receiving this reflectance. On sunny winter days in snowy climates, ground reflectance can make vertical glazing outperform glazing that is angled perpendicular to the sun.

In climates where snow does not cover the ground during most of the winter, reflectors can be built to achieve similar

Material	% Reflectance
fresh snow	87
aluminum foil	85
white paint	80
green paint	50
red brick	45
concrete	40
galvanized steel	35
grass	31
red paint	26
water	6
flat black paint	4

Reprinted with permission from the 1972 ASHRAE Handbook of Fundamentals, New York.

Ideas for Improving Performance 149

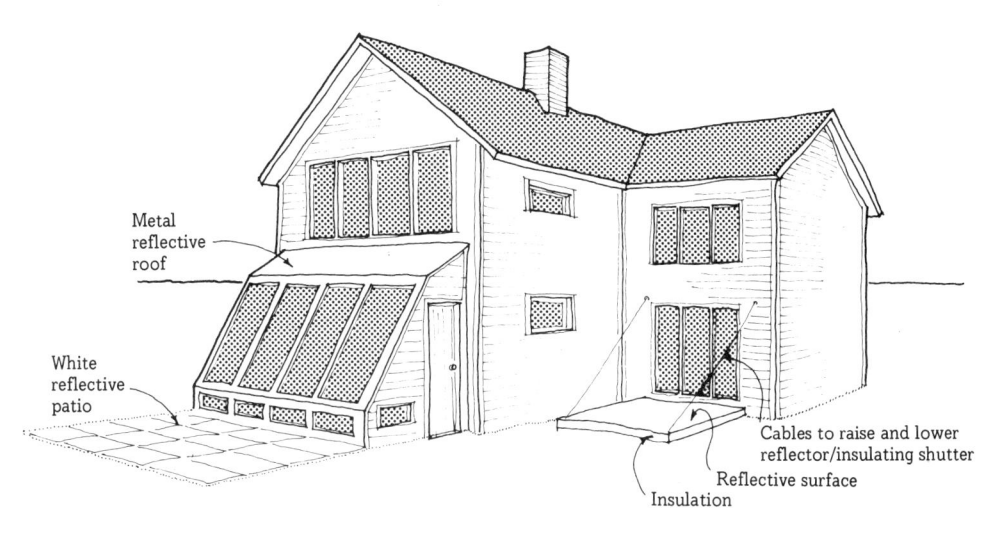

Fig. 6–1 Reflectors

results. Reflectors should be as wide as the glazing area and from one to two times the glazing height.

Direct Gain Systems and Solar Greenhouses can be further enhanced by building mechanically operated insulating shutters into the reflectors. These shutters are also excellent for shading the summer sun. In cold climates, mechanical shutters must be designed to operate despite snow and ice buildup on moving parts.

Movable reflectors are subjected to severe wind stresses and must be very well constructed.

Wind Barriers

All solar heating systems should include wind barriers.

Wind barriers are essential because an important part of the insulating value of any glazing material (glass or plastic) is the *outside air film* on the glazing surface. Wind significantly reduces the thickness of this still air film, and thereby greatly decreases the insulating value of the glazing. (This reduction of the still air film is the wind chill factor we experience on cold, windy days.)

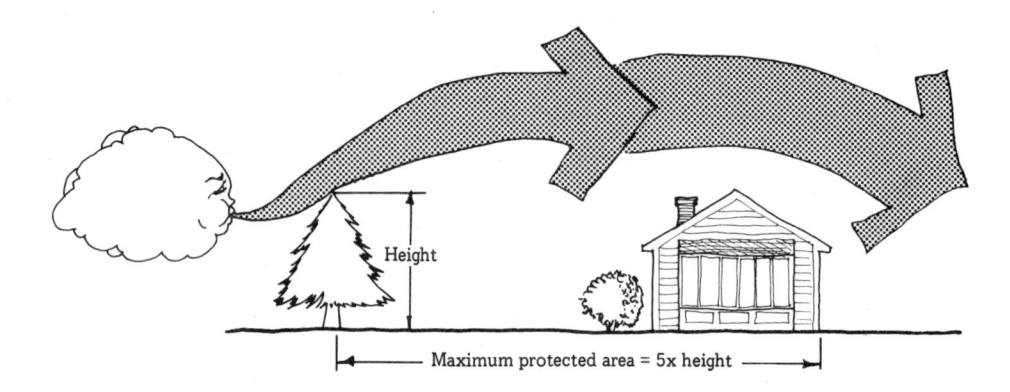

Fig. 6–2 Wind barriers (Courtesy of *The Solar Home book*, Brick House Publishing Co., Inc.)

Direct Gain and Solar Greenhouse systems are affected by wind chill both day and night. Insulating curtains dramatically reduce nighttime heat losses. Wind chill causes only daytime heat loss with TAPs and Horizontal Air Flow Collectors because at night there is no air circulating through the collectors. But, since these systems operate at high temperatures, their daytime heat loss can equal the total daily heat loss of the Direct Gain or Solar Greenhouse systems.

Good wind protection can reduce overall heat loss by as much as 30%. Wind breaks can consist of natural landscaping as well as man-made construction. If well designed, they can also provide summer shading and cooling. Hemlock, fir, and spruce, as well as smaller evergreens, are excellent wind barriers because they absorb the force of the wind. A good barrier provides protection up to a distance five times its height. Do not plant too close to the house, however, because the constant moisture around dense planting can deteriorate your home's siding.

Man-made barriers must be carefully designed to absorb the wind, not just redirect its force. Slatted construction is good for absorbing the force of the wind. Its effectiveness is demonstrated by snow fences along highways and open fields.

When building or planting wind barriers, remember that in most areas prevailing winter winds come from the *north* and *west*. You must determine the direction of the winter

Fig. 6-3 Good wind protection is an important feature of solar design.

winds around your house before designing your wind barriers. When planning a greenhouse entrance, don't locate it to face oncoming winter winds. If your entrance *must* face these winds, plan to have either a vestibule or a good wind barrier.

Summer shading

Greenhouses and Direct Gain systems often need summer shading to minimize interior overheating. TAPs and Horizontal Air Flow Collectors do not overheat in summer because of their vertical glazing, and because they can simply be turned off to prevent heat from entering the house. Although Direct Gain systems also have vertical glazing, the heat gained cannot be kept from entering the house.

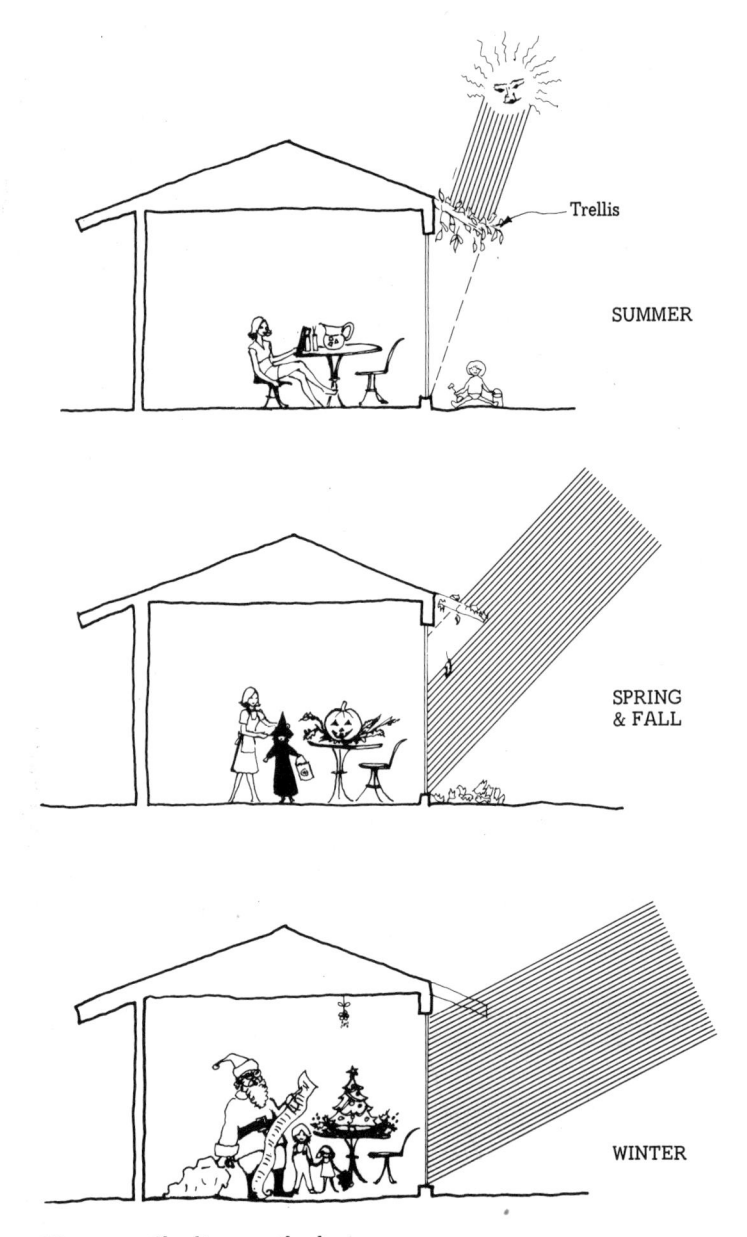

Fig. 6–4 Shading south glazing

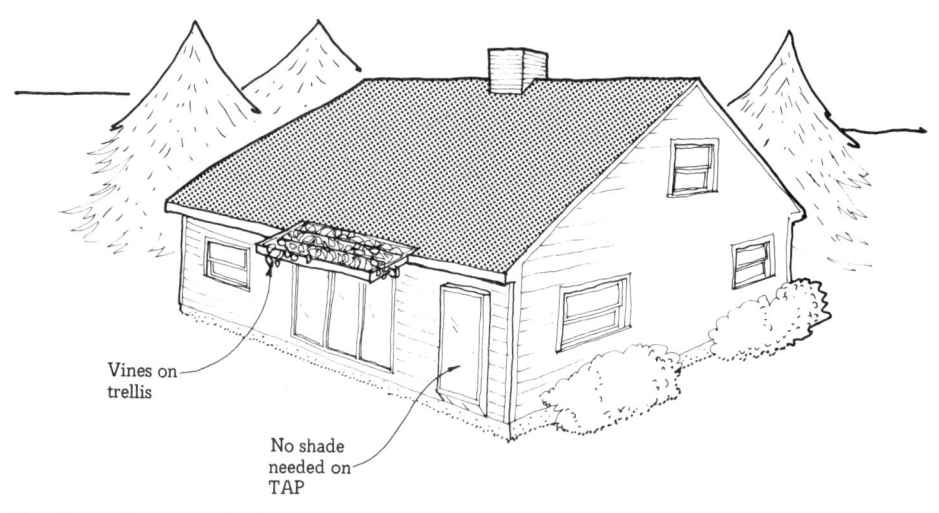

Fig. 6-5 Summer shading

Fixed overhangs and awnings can provide effective shading for your collector. Because the winter sun is low in the sky, the overhang or awning does not block much of the sun's rays. However, in the summer, when the sun is high much of the day, the overhang or awning effectively reduces the amount of direct sunlight on the collector.

One drawback of fixed overhangs and awnings, however, is that they produce the same amount of shade on September 21 and on March 21—while the need for heat is significantly greater in March. (September is warmer because of the heat storage capacity of the earth.)

Adjustable exterior shades can solve this problem, but can be expensive and difficult to maintain. Interior reflective shades can help, but they do not keep the heat out as well as exterior shades, and they reduce both your view and the amount of daylight through the glazing.

Plants are often the best way to get optimum winter sun and summer shading. Leaves on deciduous trees have a seasonal cycle closely in tune with heating demand. In summer, when you don't want so much sun, the leaves provide shade for the house; but in winter, when sun is desirable, there are no leaves to shade the house (although tree trunks and branches do slightly reduce winter insolation on the collector).

Sunflowers and other tall, quick-growing plants can make edible summer shades. Vines growing up stakes or along overhead trellises are also excellent examples of appropriate technology for the job. Be sure to prune adequately at the end of the summer to avoid any unnecessary winter shading on your collector.

Note: The four sides of your house should not be shaded equally. The east and west sides of houses north of 40°N latitude receive 2½ times more sun in summer than in winter. They should be shaded from the summer sun with bushes and small trees. Overhangs do not work on the east and west sides because of the low angles of the rising and setting sun. The north side on houses in the northern hemisphere does not need shading.

Solar Window Greenhouse

The Solar Window Greenhouse is a low-cost design combining some of the best advantages of Direct Gain and Attached Solar Greenhouse systems. It can be added to an existing south window or is an ideal way to open up a south-facing wall. With artificial lighting, the window greenhouse is ideal for secondary solar sites (although solar heat gain will be reduced). Because of its design flexibility, it can be added to upper story rooms. The Solar Window Greenhouse is a great add-on for homes with little or no outdoor space.

As an extension of your house, the window greenhouse provides a place to grow vegetables, herbs, and house plants, as well as to start outdoor plants in the early spring. During the day the continuous flow of air between the greenhouse and the house distributes oxygen, moisture, and solar heat gain to the house. At night, with thermal shades drawn, heat from the house keeps the plants warm. This heat exchange eliminates the need for thermal storage.

To construct a window greenhouse, use the sketches in this chapter and follow the construction details and material recommendations for Direct Gain and Attached Solar Greenhouse systems in Chapters 2 and 4.

Ideas for Improving Performance 155

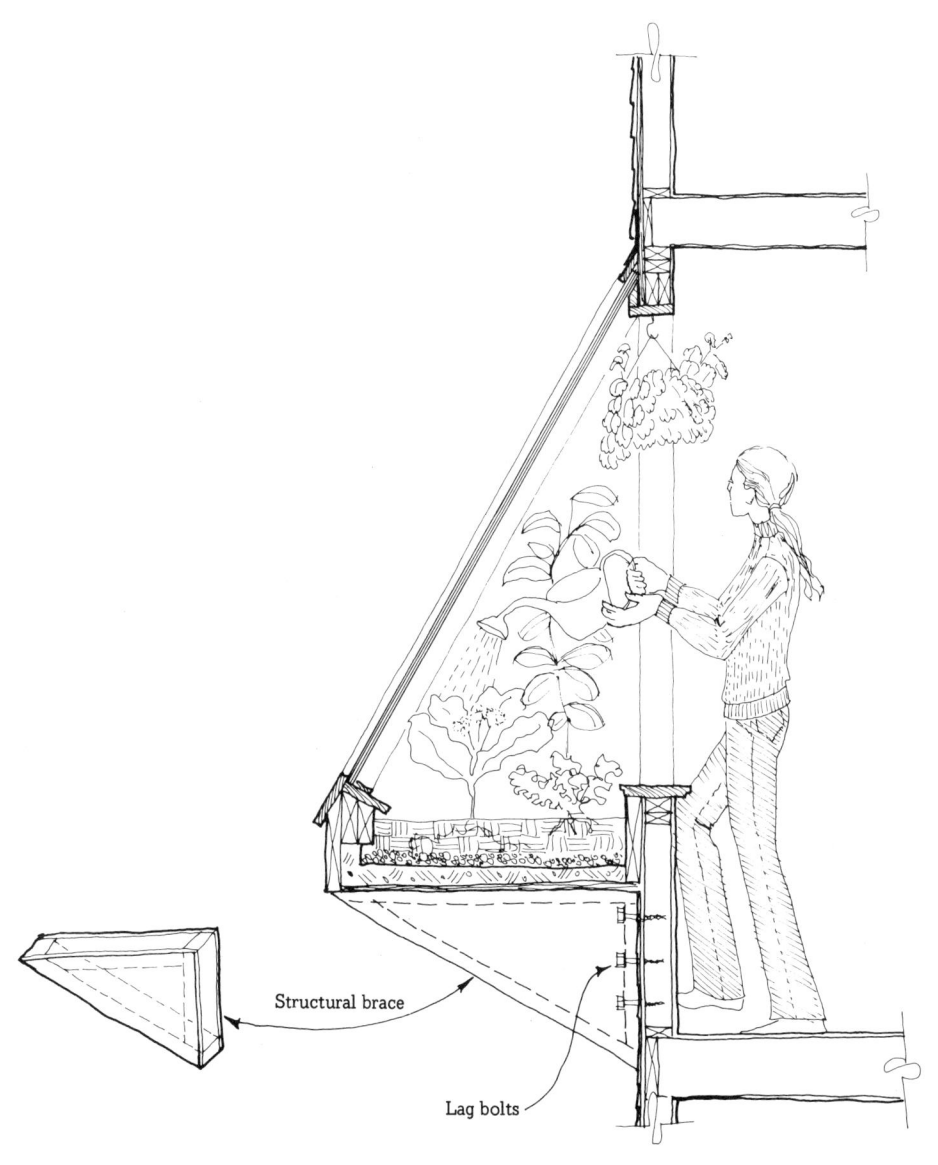

Fig. 6-6 Solar window greenhouse

Fig. 6-7 Exterior of solar window greenhouse — Foundation posts to frost line

"Acrylite" and insulated glass are recommended glazing materials. "Acrylite" sheets are 47½ inches wide and available in 8, 10, and 12 foot lengths. "Acrylite" can be cut to size, providing design freedom. When using insulating glass be sure to account for the added weight.

Improving TAP Performance

On sunny winter days, the midday insolation striking the TAP's absorber plate produces more heat than can be efficiently thermosiphoned into the house. The absorber plate becomes excessively hot and loses additional heat through the glazing. Of course, the air entering the house also becomes hotter—but overall collector efficiency is reduced.

Increasing the amount of air that flows from the house behind the absorber plate can help capture some of this otherwise lost heat. The problem is to use a fan unit whose cost is justified by the slight increase in overall collector performance. Ideally the fan speed should be in direct pro-

Fig. 6–8 Solar window greenhouse is ideal when outdoor space is limited.

portion to the amount of heat available. Automatic controls to turn the fan on and off daily and fine tune the fan motor speed add significantly to the cost of the fan installation.

A photovoltaic powered fan unit can provide the finely tuned speed control needed at a moderate cost. The photocell powers the fan speed in direct proportion to the amount of sunlight striking it. The stronger the sunlight, the faster the fan. When there is no sunlight, the fan is off. The photovoltaic cell should be placed on the absorber plate or where it will receive the same amount of sunlight as on the absorber plate. The fan should be placed in the upper vent boot where it assists the thermosiphoning air flow.

Components for this fan system are available from local solar energy dealers.

These designs are still in the development stage. Proper fan design and photocell size have not yet been determined.

The amount of air that flows through the TAP can also be increased by reducing the amount of air resistance in the panel. A large portion of the resistance to the air moving

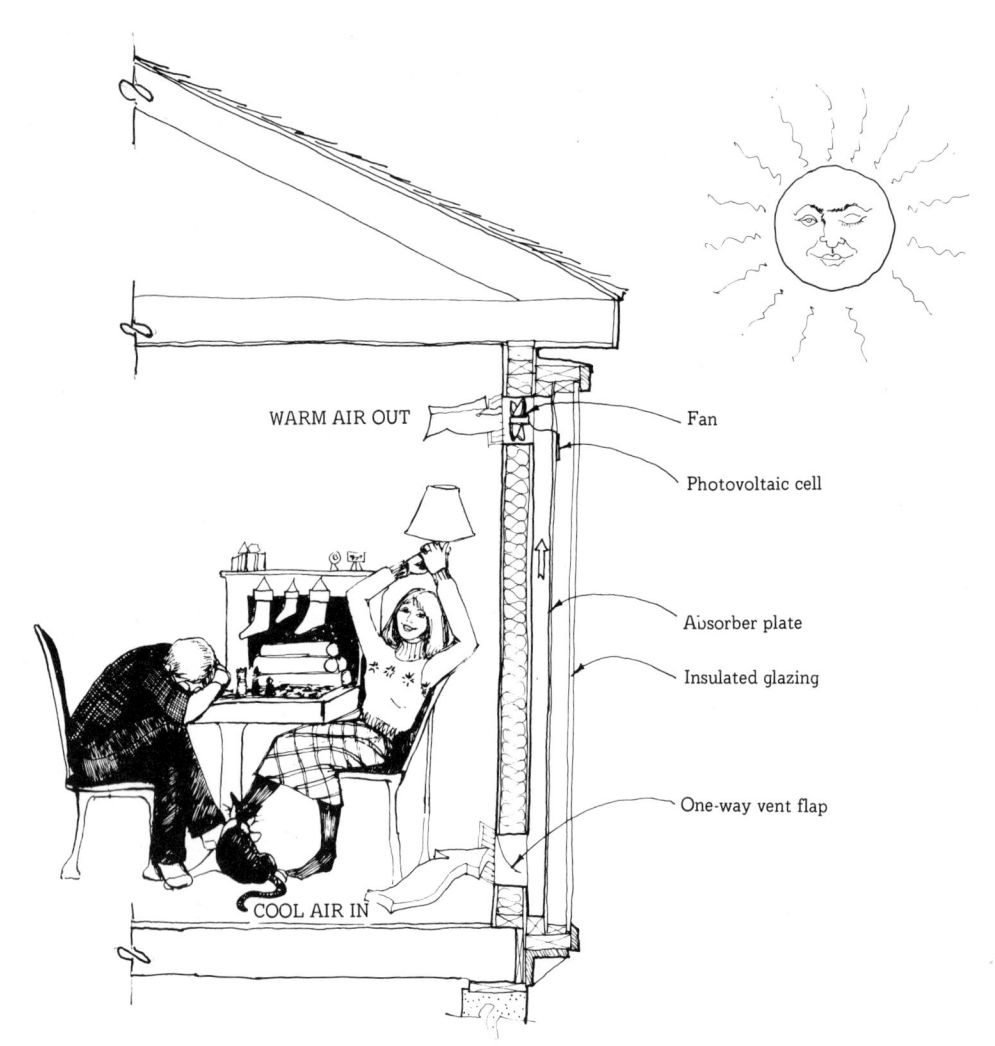

Fig. 6-9 Improving TAP performance with a photovoltaic powered fan.

through the TAP occurs where the air must make right angle turns as it travels from the lower vent to the space behind the absorber plate and from this space to the upper vent. Two techniques to reduce this air resistance are to enlarge the vents and to make the path through which the air must pass more aerodynamic.

When enlarging the vent openings, long narrow vents across the entire width of the panel are most effective. A drawback of this technique is building the continuous vents and vent boots around the wall studs.

To make the air passage between the vents and the space behind the absorber plate more aerodynamic the inside and outside corners of this passage can be rounded. Although effective, constructing these rounded corners can be an arduous task. An alternative technique is to place a thin, louvered vent diagonally across the corner of the vent boot and the air space behind the absorber plate. This angled vent acts similar to a "mirror" keeping the streams of air parallel as they turn the right angle corner into and out of the air space behind the absorber plate.

The construction details for these designs will become available as we continue to learn from our solar experiences.

7

FUNDAMENTALS OF SOLAR

Heat loss, heat gain, and heat storage calculations can be a valuable asset in designing your solar heating system. Compare heat loss and solar heat gain for your house during a typical winter day. Calculate the heat storage capacity of your house, and the rise in temperature from your solar gain. These calculations will give you insight into the performance of your system.

Heat Loss During the winter, your house loses heat in three ways: through conduction, convection, and radiation.

Conduction is the transfer of heat through a material or from one material to another in contact with it. Heat energy is exchanged from one molecule to another, and so on. For instance, the handle on a frying pan gets hot when heat is applied only to the bottom of the pan.

Convection is the transfer of heat by the movement of liquids or gases (usually air). Warm air naturally rises and is replaced by cooler air causing a thermosiphoning effect. This heat flow occurs in air spaces within your walls, between layers of glazing, and on the surface of your walls. Infiltration of air around windows and doors, and through cracks throughout your house, is also a part of convective heat loss.

Radiation is the flow of heat by electromagnetic waves such as light. Heat from the sun comes to earth by radiation.

The electromagnetic waves do not heat the space through which they travel, but release heat when they are absorbed by a cooler object. The warmth from a fireplace is radiant heat.

Calculating heat loss

To calculate the total heat loss from your house, you must combine both conductive heat loss and convective heat loss due to infiltration. Conductive heat loss calculations take into account convective heat transfer within and on the surfaces of walls, as well as radiant heat transfer.

Conductive heat loss

Conductive heat loss is usually the larger component of total heat loss from your house. When you insulate you reduce the conductive heat flow through your walls, floor, and ceiling.

$$\text{Conductive heat loss} = \frac{\text{Area} \times \text{Temperature difference}}{\text{R-value}} \times \text{Time}$$

The *area* is the square footage of the exterior wall, floor, or ceiling you are considering. To find the square footage of a wall, multiply its height, usually 8 feet, times its length. Total conductive heat loss is calculated using the total area of *all* exterior walls, windows, and doors, as well as the floor and ceiling or roof (depending on where your insulation is placed). Because the conductive heat loss from windows and doors is calculated separately, remember to subtract the area of doors and windows when calculating the square footage of walls.

Temperature difference equals the indoor temperature minus the outdoor temperature. This measure is often referred to as delta T (ΔT). If the indoor temperature is 65°F and the outdoor temperature is 25°F, $\Delta T = 40°$. When calculating daily or seasonal heat loss, use an average outdoor temperature.

R-value measures the resistance to heat flow. The higher the R-value, the greater the heat resistance. To calculate the total R-value of a wall, floor, or ceiling, add the R-value of each material including the values of the inside and outside air films. If one inch of insulation equals R3.5, then 3 inches of this insulation has an R-value of 10.5.

Note: The inverse of R-value $\left(\frac{1}{R}\right)$ equals the coefficient of heat transfer and is given the term "U-value." U-value is the rate of heat loss in Btus per hour through a square foot of wall when the temperature difference is 1°F. To convert a given U-value to an R-value, divide the U-value into 1:

$$R = \frac{1}{U}$$

The *time* is the period in hours, during which the heat loss occurs.

R-values for a common wall

Wall Construction	R-value
Outside air film (15 mph wind)	.17
1/2" Wood lapped siding	.81
1/2" Plywood sheathing	.62
3½" Fiberglass insulation (R per inch = 3.12)	10.92
1/2" Sheetrock	.45
Inside air film	.68
Total R-value	13.65

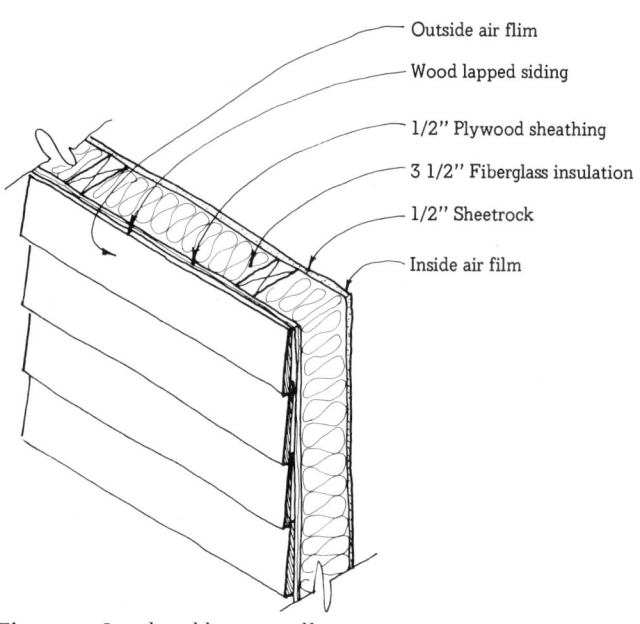

Fig. 7–1 Insulated house wall

Total Conductive Heat Loss from a Sample House

Surface	Area (ft²) ×	ΔT* ÷	R-value $\left(\dfrac{HR \cdot Ft^2 \cdot °F}{Btu}\right)$	Conductive Heat Losses (in Btu) 1 hr. when outside temperature is 25°F	24 hrs. average outside temperature is 25°F
Walls	934	40°F	13.65	2,737	65,688
Windows (10) 2' × 4'	80	40°F	1.72	1,860	44,651
Doors (2) 3' × 7'	42	40°F	2.04	824	19,765
Floor	1040	40°F	13.04	3,190	76,564
Ceiling	1040	40°F	20.02	2,078	49,870
Total				10,689	256,548

*The indoor temperature is 65°F and the outdoor temperature is 25°F, therefore ΔT = 65°F − 25°F = 40°F.

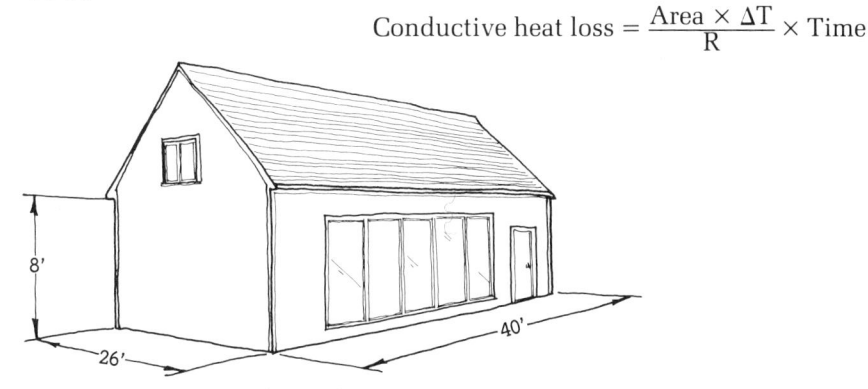

$$\text{Conductive heat loss} = \frac{\text{Area} \times \Delta T}{R} \times \text{Time}$$

Fig. 7–2 Calculate heat loss and heat gain for this house.

Convective heat loss

Air infiltration, which is convective heat loss, accounts for 10 to 50% of your total heat loss. Wherever there is a seam between two materials, there is potential for air infiltration. All the cold outdoor air that enters your house must be heated to room temperature. Most air leakage occurs around windows and doors, but some air moves right through your walls. With the skyrocketing cost of fuel, weatherstripping is one of your best investments.

Convective heat loss (Infiltration) =
   Volume of air to be heated × Temperature difference × Heat capacity of air.

Note: Calculations for convective heat loss are only approximate.

The volume of air to be heated. The volume of air in your house equals the length times the width times the height of all heated spaces. The volume of air, however, is not the same as the volume of air to be heated, because the air changes many times a day. (An "air change" means that all of the air inside your house is replaced by outside air.)

Air Changes per Hour Based on Condition of House

Condition of Your House	Number of Air Changes per Hour (ACH)
Air lock entry (vestibule); tight fitting windows and doors; storm windows and doors; all other seams well caulked.	1/2
Average fitting windows and doors; storm windows and doors.	1
Loose fitting windows and doors; some storm windows and doors; some draft	1½
Loose fitting windows and doors; drafty.	2

Once you have determined the number of air changes per hour for your house, you can calculate the volume of air to be heated. For example, the volume of air in a sample house is 40 ft. × 26 ft. × 8 ft = 8320 cubic feet (ft^3). If we assume this house has loose fitting windows and doors, and storm windows only, then the number of air changes per hour = 1½. Therefore, the volume of air to be heated each hour = 8320 ft^3 × 1½, or 12,480 ft^3.

To calculate the amount of air to be heated over a given period of time, multiply the volume per hour times the number of hours. For one day, the volume of air to be heated in the sample house =

12,480 ft^3 × 24 hours = 298,520 ft^3 per day

Temperature difference. If the outdoor temperature is 25°F and the indoor temperature is 65°F, the air must be heated 40°F. This is the temperature difference (ΔT).

Heat capacity is the amount of heat needed to raise 1 cubic foot of a material 1 degree Fahrenheit. Air is so light that it takes only 0.0182 Btu to raise 1 cubic foot of air 1°F. (One kitchen match equals one Btu and can raise the temperature of one cubic foot of air 50°F!)

When calculating heat capacity for convective heat loss, we always use the following formula:

$$\text{Heat capacity of air} = \frac{0.0182 \text{ Btu}}{1 \text{ cu. ft} \cdot {}^\circ\text{F}}$$

Therefore the convective heat loss (air infiltration) for the sample house during one 25°F day equals:

$$\frac{298{,}520 \text{ ft}^3}{\text{day}} \times 40^\circ\text{F} \times \frac{0.0182 \text{ Btu}}{\text{ft}^3 \cdot {}^\circ\text{F}} = 217{,}000 \text{ Btu per day}$$

With convective heat loss by infiltration almost as much as conductive heat loss, you should tighten up those loose-fitting windows and doors before going solar!

Solar Heat Gain

You can calculate the amount of solar energy gained from your system by knowing two factors: how much of the sun's energy strikes the collector glazing, and what is the efficiency of the solar heating system.

The amount of solar energy that strikes the collector—*insolation* (not to be confused with insulation)—depends on the collector's slope and orientation away from solar south, the amount of shading on the collector, and the amount of available sunshine. After completing your solar site analysis, you should know both the collector orientation away from solar south and the approximate amount of shading. The available insolation varies according to the weather and the slope of the collector surface.

To calculate insolation, you will have to determine the percentage of total insolation gained by your collector's orientation away from solar south *(orientation factor)*, and the *Shading Factor* and *Clear Day Insolation* for your site.

Using the figure on page 166, determine the percentage of insolation according to your collector's orientation away from solar south. Notice that collectors oriented between 0° and 20° (east or west) away from solar south receive between

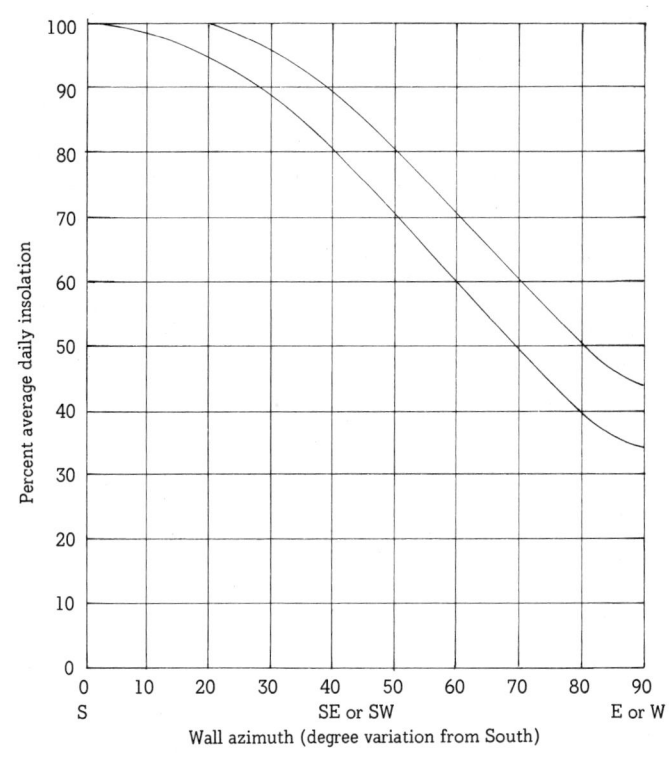

Fig. 7-3 The percentage of insolation on vertical collectors for orientation away from solar south. Redrawn from B. Anderson and M. Riordan, *The Solar Home Book*, 1976. Used with permission.

95 and 100 percent of maximum insolation; and collectors oriented 25° to 30° away from solar south receive approximately 90 percent of the maximum.

The Shading Factor can be determined by subtracting the percentage of shading on the collector from 100 percent (full sun with no shading). With 10 percent shading, the Shading Factor equals 90 percent.

Clear Day Insolation is the total direct and diffuse solar energy striking a surface on a cloudless day. It is measured in Btu per square foot of glazing surface, and is listed in the appendix for each hour of the twenty-first day of each month. Insolation varies according to latitude and the slope of glazing. The insolation for solar greenhouses with sloped glazing will differ from the insolation for Direct Gain, TAP and Solar Greenhouse systems with vertical glazing. This

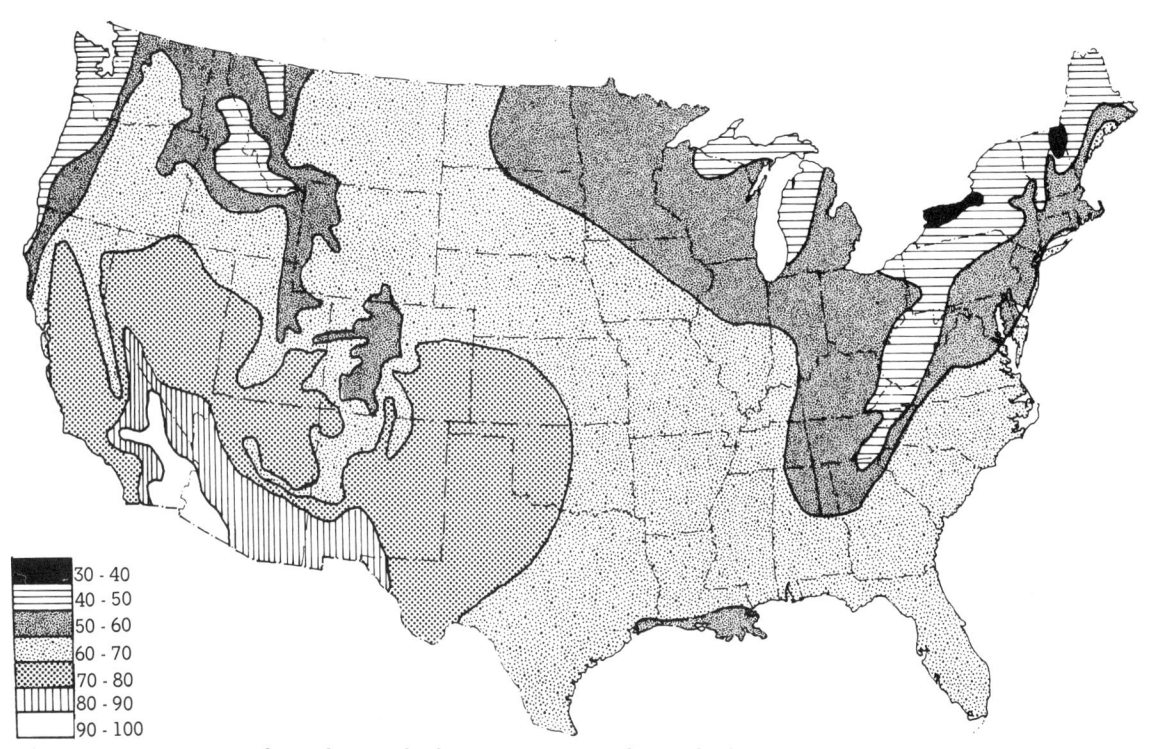

Fig. 7-4 Percent sunshine during the heating season. When calculating annual heat gain, multiply the percentage of sunshine for your area times the total clear day insolation.

Legend:
- 30 - 40
- 40 - 50
- 50 - 60
- 60 - 70
- 70 - 80
- 80 - 90
- 90 - 100

data is for clear days only; on cloudy days the amount of *available insolation* can be reduced by 30 to 90 percent.

Note: The Clear Day Insolation data does not account for increased insolation by reflectance. Since reflectance is an important part of insolation on vertical collectors, you should add an additional 10 to 30 percent to these numbers (depending on your ground reflectance) when calculating insolation on Direct Gain, TAP and vertical active collectors.

To calculate the insolation striking your collector surface, multiply Orientation Factor × Shading Factor × available insolation × area of the glazing (ft^2). Using this method you can calculate the insolation for your system during one hour, one day, one month, or a year.

For example, a house in Denver, Colorado (40°N latitude), has a collector with five 34" × 76" sliding glass door panels, which are oriented 20° east of solar south, and have 10 percent shading. How many Btus strike the glazing on a clear day in February?

$$\begin{array}{c}\text{Orientation}\\\text{factor}\end{array} \times \begin{array}{c}\text{Shading}\\\text{factor}\end{array} \times \begin{array}{c}\text{Available insolation}\\\text{(plus 20\% reflectance)}\end{array} \times \text{Glazing area (ft}^2\text{)} = \text{Insolation}$$

$$97\% \quad \times \quad 90\% \quad \times \quad 1730 + 346 \text{ Btu/ft}^2 \quad \times \quad 90 \quad = 163{,}000 \text{ Btu per day}$$

After you have calculated the insolation, you can determine the amount of solar heat (in Btus) that enters your house. TAPs and Horizontal Air Flow Active Collectors have an estimated efficiency of 40 percent. For these systems, therefore, multiply the computed insolation times 40 percent to find an estimate of the solar heat gain. For the sample house in Denver, solar heat gain is determined as follows:

$$\text{Insolation} \quad \times \quad \frac{\text{Estimated}}{\text{efficiency}} = \frac{\text{Estimated}}{\text{solar heat gain}}$$

$$163{,}000 \text{ Btu/day} \quad \times \quad 40\% \quad = 65{,}200 \text{ Btu/day}$$

Note: Burning one gallon of oil delivers 70,000–100,000 Btus depending on the efficiency of your oil burner and heating system.

You can compare this estimate with the amount of solar heat you actually gain. Formulas for calculating the actual solar heat delivered by TAP and Horizontal Air Flow Active Collector systems are provided in the chapters explaining each of those systems.

Solar heat gain from Direct Gain and Solar Greenhouse systems can also be calculated. The insolation must first pass through the insulated glazing (transmittance) and then be absorbed (absorptance). The transmittance of various glazing materials is listed in the Chapter on Attached Solar Greenhouse systems. The transmittance of a single sheet of standard 1/8 inch glass is 84 percent. For insulated glass, the transmittance equals 84 percent times 84 percent, or 71 percent.

In Direct Gain and Solar Greenhouse Systems, the sun's energy is absorbed by the walls, floor, thermal storage, and furnishings within the room. If the room is at least 12 feet deep from the glazing to the far wall, or if the room's interior color is fairly dark, between 85 and 95 percent of the sun's energy will be absorbed and converted to heat.

Let us assume the sample house in Denver has a Direct Gain system. The transmittance of two layers of glass is 71 percent, and the absorptance for the room is 90 percent. Therefore, the total heat gained on a sunny February day is:

Insolation × Transmittance × Absorptance = solar heat gain

163,000 Btu/day × 71% × 90% = 104,000 Btu/day

Note: To calculate the actual performance of Direct Gain and Solar Greenhouse systems you must subtract the heat loss through the glazing from the solar heat gain.

Heat Storage

On sunny days, particularly in spring and fall, heat gain from your solar system may exceed heat need in your home, especially if you are solar heating only a few rooms. In this case, I recommend the use of *heat storage*: materials which absorb a large amount heat and store it for later use.

All materials absorb heat as their temperature rises, and release heat as their temperature falls. The walls, floors, ceiling, and furnishings of your house all have *heat storage capacity*. Masonry houses have more heat storage capacity than lightweight houses. But the amount of heat stored this way is generally not enough to last more than a few hours. You can increase the amount of heat stored by carefully adding water, rocks, masonry, or phase change materials to your solar heating system.

Heat can be stored by both passive and active methods. Passive heat storage is usually preferred because of its simplicity and low cost. Examples of passive storage are containers of water or masonry in direct sunlight.

With active storage, fans and pumps move the heat to the storage and from the storage into the house. Blowing hot air through rocks and pumping and storing hot water from collectors are two examples of active storage systems.

For Direct Gain and Attached Solar Greenhouse systems, passive storage is recommended. However, the amount of heat storage you can add is limited by the solar room floor's ability to support the storage weight, by the amount of direct sun obtainable on the storage, and by decorative restrictions on placement of storage in the room.

Active storage can be incorporated into the Horizontal Air Flow Collector. Hot air from the collector flows through small containers of water or rock beds before returning to the collector or being distributed to the house. The size and air resistance of the storage must be carefully designed to provide good heat distribution without reducing collector efficiency.

With a TAP heat storage is limited, because TAPs directly heat the house air. Therefore, storage material in the house is heated to the same temperature as the house and will release heat only when the house temperature becomes cooler.

Phase change materials offer a way to store additional heat in *all* systems. Certain materials, such as eutectic salts, melt and solidify at near room temperatures. When these materials melt, they absorb a large amount of heat, which is released when they again become solid. Because these materials can store relatively large amounts of heat in limited spaces and with less weight than water or masonry, they provide excellent heat storage for solar retrofits. Phase change materials are becoming commercially available to meet this demand.

Calculating heat storage capacity

A material's ability to store heat is measured in two ways: by its *specific heat* and its *heat capacity*. We use these material qualities to determine the amount of heat stored.

Specific heat is the number of Btu needed to raise the temperature of *one pound* of the material 1°F. For example, raising the temperature of one pound of water 1°F requires one Btu. Therefore, water has a specific heat of 1. There are 8.4 pounds of water in one gallon. Therefore, 8.4 Btu are needed to raise the temperature of one gallon of water 1°F.

One pound of concrete, on the other hand, needs only 1/4 of one Btu to become warmer by 1°F. Concrete's specific heat is .22—much less than that of water. Therefore, 1 Btu raises the temperature of one pound of concrete 4° Fahrenheit.

Heat capacity is the number of Btu required to raise *one cubic foot* of the material 1°F. To calculate heat capacity, we

Specific Heats and Heat Capacities of Common Materials

Material	Specific Heat (Btu/lb.·°F)	Density (lb/ft³)	Heat Capacity (Btu/ft³·°F)
Water (40°F)	1.00	62.5	62.5
Steel	0.12	489	58.7
Cast Iron	0.12	450	54.0
Copper	0.092	556	51.2
Aluminum	0.214	171	36.6
Basalt	0.20	180	36.0
Marble	0.21	162	34.0
Concrete	0.22	144	31.7
Asphalt	0.22	132	29.0
Ice (32°F)	0.487	57.5	28.0
Glass	0.18	154	27.7
White Oak	0.57	47	26.8
Brick	0.20	123	24.6
Limestone	0.217	103	22.4
Gypsum	0.26	78	20.3
Sand	0.191	94.6	18.1
White Pine	0.67	27	18.1
White Fir	0.65	27	17.6
Clay	0.22	63	13.9
Asbestos Wool	0.20	36	7.2
Glass Wool	0.157	3.25	0.51
Air (75°F)	0.24	0.075	0.018

Source: ASHRAE, *Handbook of Fundamentals*, 1972. Reprinted by permission.

first need the specific heat of the material. Heat capacity equals the specific heat times the material's density (lb/ft³). For example, one cubic foot of water weights 62.5 pounds; therefore its heat capacity equals 1 × 62.5, or 62.5 Btu per cubic foot × °F (Btu/ft³·°F). It takes 62.5 Btu to raise one cubic foot of water one degree Fahrenheit. And, when this one cubic foot of water cools one degree Fahrenheit, the water gives off 62.5 Btu.

The heat capacity of concrete is 32 Btu/ft³·°F, more than half that of water. Although the specific heat of concrete is one quarter that of water, the high density of concrete compensates somewhat for its low specific heat.

To calculate heat storage capacity, multiply cubic feet of storage material × heat capacity of storage material × difference in temperature between the storage and the house.

Commercial Suppliers of Phase Change Materials

Manufacturer	Product Name	Phase Change Material	Container	Total Weight	Phase Change Temperature	Heat Storage Capacity (at phase change temperature)	Warranty
Addison Products Co. Addison, MI 49220	Solar Therm	paraffin	steel, round, 1 gallon	7.25 lbs.	115°F	80 Btu	1 year
Architectural Research Corp. 40 Water St. New York, NY 10004	Sol-Ar-Tile™	Glauber's salt	polymer resinous concrete tile, 2 feet by 2 feet	44 lbs.	73°F	1,000 Btu	2 year
Blue Lakes Engineering Pace Corp. P.O. Box 1033 Appleton, WI 54912	Thermol-81	calcium chloride hexahydrate with additives	black polyethylene tube, 6-feet long, 3½-inch diameter	35 lbs.	81°F	2,460 Btu	10 year
Boardman Energy Systems, Inc. 5720 Kennett Pike P.O. Box 4198 Wilmington, DE 19807	product available July 1980	sodium sulphate	plated steel tubes, 30-inch long and 4-inch diameter, built-in spacers, selective coating available	22 lbs.	45°, 64°, 74°, 78°, 81°, 89°,	1,444–2,000 Btu, varies with phase change temperature	will be available
Collodial Materials, Inc. P.O. Box 696 Andover, MA 01810 (617) 475-3276	Heat Pac™	sodium sulphate	3-ply aluminum foil laminate pouch, 3/4 inch by 2 feet by 2 feet	10 lbs.	73°F (may be varied between 65°F and 89°F)	350 Btu	5 year
Energy Materials, Inc. 2622 South Zuni Englewood, CO 80110 (303) 934-2444	Thermalrod-27	calcium chloride hexahydrate	black polyethylene pipe, 6-feet long, 3½-inch diameter	35 lbs.	81°F	2,542 Btu	10 year, limited
PSI Energy Systems, Inc. 1533 Fenpark Drive St. Louis, MO 63026 (314) 343-7666	Thermol-81	calcium chloride hexahydrate, with additives	black polyethylene tube, 6-feet long, 3½-inch diameter	35 lbs.	81°F	2,460 Btu	10 year
Texxor Corporation 9910 North 48th St. Omaha, NE 68152	Texxor Heat Cell	calcium chloride hexahydrate (Bisol II)	steel cylinder, 7-inch long, 4.26 inch diameter	4.56 lbs.	81°F	345 Btu	5 year
Valmont Energy Systems, Inc. Valley, NE 68064		Glauber's salt	polyethylene rectangular cube, 2 feet by 1 foot by 2 inch	16 lbs.	89°F	1,294 Btu	5 year, limited

Source: *Solar Age* Magazine, May 1980, Harrisville, New Hampshire. Reprinted with permission.

For example, how much heat is stored in 20 cubic feet of water (150 gallons), when the water is 90°F and the house is 65°F?

$$20 \text{ ft}^3 \times 62.5 \text{ Btu/ft}^3 \cdot °F \times 25°F = 31,250 \text{ Btu.}$$

How much heat is stored in an equal volume of concrete?

20 ft^3 × 32 Btu/ft^3·°F × 25°F = 16,000 Btu.

Note: To calculate the heat storage capacity of the walls, floor, ceiling, and furnishings of a conventional wood frame house multiply the square footage of the floor area times 4 Btu/°F times the temperature difference. For example, when the temperature of a typical 1500 square foot house is heated to 75°F and then allowed to cool to 60°F at night 90,000 Btu are stored then released.

1500 sq. ft. × 4 Btu/°F × 15°F = 90,000 Btu

| | | Percent Floor Area Allowed in Glass ||
Degree Days per Year	Average January Temperature °F	Average House* (UA = 600)	Well insulated House** (UA = 300)
4000	40	11	6
5000	30	13	6
6000	25	13	7
7000	20	14	7

*equals approximately R-11 walls, R-19 ceiling, double-glazed windows

**equals approximately R-25 walls, R-38 ceiling, triple-glazed windows

The above percents are for light frame houses without additional thermal storage. This chart is reprinted with permission from *The Thermal Mass Pattern Book*, Total Environmental Action, Inc.

APPENDIX 1
Caulking

The use of caulk is essential to efficient operation of solar systems. All seams where air may escape from the collector must be caulked.

Types of Caulk

Latex base caulk lasts approximately ten years. To compensate for shrinkage, it must be applied in a large bead, and only on narrow cracks. Porous and metal surfaces should be primed before applying caulk. For exterior use, latex caulk should be painted after it is applied. If properly applied, latex caulk is a good, moderately priced choice for narrow openings.

Butyl rubber caulk lasts up to ten years. It can be used on interior and exterior work and adheres well to most surfaces, but it is only suitable for narrow openings because it shrinks after application. After curing for one week, it can be painted. Because of butyl rubber caulk's shrinkage and long curing time, latex caulk is generally preferred.

Silicone caulk, recommended for all solar energy systems, is an ideal, but expensive choice. It remains weathertight for 20 years. Its long life often offsets its high cost. Also, because silicone can withstand high temperatures, it is ideal for use in solar collectors. Silicone will adhere to most surfaces, although porous surfaces should be primed. Shrinkage is minimal. Silicone caulk comes in several tones—I recommend clear for aesthetic reasons.

Polyurethane caulk, like silicone caulk, can withstand high temperatures and lasts for 20 years. Polyurethane adheres to most surfaces without the need for primer. Polyurethane differs from silicone in drying time—it remains workable for almost an hour, while silicone sets in 5 to 10 minutes. Because polyurethane sets slowly it can be messy to work with. For general purposes, therefore, silicone caulk is preferred.

Polyurethane is available as "Sears Best" caulk.

I do not recommend oil base caulk. Although it is inexpensive, it dries out in one to five years. Nor do I recommend *polysulfide* caulk because it takes several days to dry, is toxic, and needs a special primer when applied to porous surfaces.

APPENDIX 2
U-Values of Windows

Description	Winter U-values[1]
Vertical panels:	
Single pane flat glass	1.13
Insulating glass—double[2]	
3/16" air space	0.69
1/4" air space	0.65
1/2" air space	0.58
Insulating glass—triple[2]	
1/4" air spaces	0.47
1/2" air spaces	0.36
Storm windows	
1–4" air space	0.56
Single plastic sheet	1.09

[1] in units of Btu/hr·ft^2·°F
[2] double and triple refer to the number of layers of glass.

Source: ASHRAE, *Handbook of Fundamentals*, 1972. Reprinted by permission.

APPENDIX 3
Insulating Values of Materials

R-Values of Building Materials

Material and Description		Density (lb/ft^3)	R-Value* per inch thickness	R-Value* for listed thickness
Building Boards, Panels, Flooring				
Asbestos-cement board		120	0.25	—
Asbestos-cement board	1/8"	120	—	0.03
Gypsum or plaster board	3/8"	50	—	0.32
Gypsum or plaster board	1/2"	50	—	0.45
Plywood (see Siding Materials)		34	1.25	—
Sheathing, wood fiber (impregnated or coated)	25/32"	20	—	2.06
Wood fiber board (laminated or homogenous)		26	2.38	—
Wood fiber, hardboard type		65	0.72	—
Wood fiber, hardboard type	1/4"	65	—	0.18
Wood subfloor	25/32"	—	—	0.98
Wood, hardwood finish	3/4"	—	—	0.68
Building Paper				
Vapor-permeable felt		—	—	0.06
Vapor-seal, 2 layers of mopped 15 lb felt		—	—	0.12
Vapor-seal plastic film		—	—	negl.

R-Values of Building Materials

Material and Description	Density (lb/ft^3)	R-Value* per inch thickness	R-Value* for listed thickness
Finish Materials			
Carpet and fibrous pad	—	—	2.08
Carpet and rubber pad	—	—	1.23
Cork tile 1/8"	—	—	0.28
Tile (asphalt, linoleum, vinyl, rubber)	—	—	0.05
Gypsumboard 1/2"	—	—	0.45
Gypsumboard 5/8"	—	—	0.56
Hardwood flooring 25/32"	—	—	0.68
Insulating Materials			
Blankets and Batts:			
Mineral wool, fibrous form (from rock, slag or glass)	0.5	3.12	—
	1.5–4.0	3.70	—
Wood fiber	3.2–3.6	4.00	—
Board and Slabs:			
Cellular glass	9	2.70†	
Corkboard	6.5–8.0	3.45†	—
Glass fiber	4.0–9.0	4.55†	—
Expanded polyurethane (R-11 blown; 1" thickness or more)	1.5–2.5	5.88†	—
Expanded polystyrene, extruded	1.9	4.17†	—
Expanded polystyrene, molded beads	1.0	3.85*	—
Mineral fiberboard, felted core or roof insulation	16–17	2.94	—
acoustical tile	18	2.86	—
Mineral fiberboard, molded acoustical tile[1]	23	2.38	—
Wood or cane fiberboard acoustical tile 1/2"	—	—	1.19
interior finish	15	2.86	—
Insulating roof deck[2] 1"	—	—	2.78
2"	⅛	—	5.56
3"	—	—	8.33
Shredded wood (cemented, preformed slabs)	22	1.67	—
Loose Fills			
Macerated paper or pulp	2.5–3.5	3.57	—
Mineral wool	2.0–5.0	4.00*	—
Perlite (expanded)	5.0–8.0	2.94*	—
Vermiculite (expanded)	7.0–8.2	2.27	—
Sawdust or shavings	0.8–15	2.22	—

Appendix 3

R-Values of Building Materials

Material and Description		Density (lb/ft³)	R-Value* per inch thickness	R-Value* for listed thickness
Masonry Materials—Concretes				
Cement mortar		116	0.20	—
Gypsum-fiber concrete (87½% gypsum, 12½% concrete)		51	0.60	—
Lightweight aggregates		120	0.19	—
(expanded shale, clay or slate;		100	0.28	—
expanded slags, or cinders;		80	0.40	—
pumice; perlite or vermiculite;		60	0.59	—
cellular concretes)		40	0.86	—
		20	1.43	—
Sand and gravel or stone aggregate (oven dried)		140	0.11	—
Sand and gravel or stone aggregate (not dried)		140	0.08	—
Stucco		116	0.20	—
Masonry Units				
Brick, common[3]		120	0.20	—
Brick, face[3]		130	0.11	—
Clay tile, hollow				
1 cell deep	3″	—	—	0.80
1 cell deep	4″	—	—	1.11
2 cells deep	6″	—	—	1.52
2 cells deep	8″	—	—	1.85
3 cells deep	10″	—	—	2.22
3 cells deep	12″	—	—	2.50
Concrete block, 3 oval core				
Sand and gravel aggregate	4″	—	—	0.71
	8″	—	—	1.11
	12″	—	—	1.28
Cinder aggregate	3″	—	—	0.86
	4″	—	—	1.11
	8″	—	—	1.72
	12″	—	—	1.89
Lightweight aggregate	3″	—	—	1.27
(expanded shale, clay slate	4″	—	—	1.50
or slag; pumice)	8″	—	—	2.00
	12″	—	—	2.72
Concrete blocks, rectangular core				
Sand and gravel aggregate				
2 core, 36 lb[4]	8″	—	—	1.04
same, filled cores[5]		—	—	1.93
Lightweight aggregates				
3 core, 19 lb[4]	6″	—	—	1.65
same, filled cores[5]		—	—	2.99

Insulating Values of Materials

R-Values of Building Materials

Material and Description		Density (lb/ft^3)	R-Value* per inch thickness	R-Value* for listed thickness
2 core, 24 lb[4]	8"	—	—	2.18
same, filled cores[5]		—	—	5.03
3 core, 38 lb[4]	12"	—	—	2.48
same, filled cores[5]		—	—	5.82
Stone, lime or sand		—	0.08	—
Granite, marble		150–175	0.05	—
Plastering Materials				
Cement plaster, sand aggregate		116	0.20	—
Gypsum plaster				
Lightweight aggregate	1/2"	45	—	0.32
Lightweight aggregate	3/8"	45	—	0.39
Same, on metal lath	3/4"	—	—	0.47
Perlite aggregate		45	0.67	—
Sand aggregate		105	0.18	—
Same, on metal lath	3/4"	—	—	0.10
Same, on wood lath	3/4"	—	—	0.40
Vermiculite aggregate		45	0.59	—
Roofing Materials				
Asbestos-cement shingles		120	—	0.21
Asphalt roll roofing		70	—	0.15
Built-up roofing	3/8"	70	—	0.44
Slate roofing	1/2"	—	—	0.05
Wood shingles		—	—	0.94
Siding Materials				
Shingles				
Asbestos-cement		120	—	0.21
Wood, 16" with 7½" exposure		—	—	0.80
Wood, double 16" with 12" exposure		—	—	1.19
Wood, plus insulating backer board	5/16"	—	—	1.40
Siding				
Asbestos-cement lapped	1/4"	—	—	0.21
Asphalt roll siding		—	—	0.15
Asphalt insulating siding	1/2"	—	—	1.46
Wood, drop (1" × 8")		—	—	0.79
Wood, drop (1/2" × 8" lapped)		—	—	0.81
Wood, bevel (3/4" × 10", lapped)		—	—	1.05
Plywood, lapped	3/8"	—	—	0.59

R-Values of Building Materials

Material and Description		Density (lb/ft^3)	R-Value* per inch thickness	R-Value* for listed thickness
Plywood	1/4"	—	—	0.31
	3/8"	—	—	0.47
	1/2"	—	—	0.62
	5/8"	—	—	0.78
	3/4"	—	—	0.94
Stucco		116	0.20	—
Sheathing, insulating board	1/2"	—	—	1.32
(regular density)	25/32"	—	—	2.04
Woods				
Hardwoods (maple, oak)		45	0.91	—
Softwoods (fir, pine)		32	1.25	—
	25/32"	32	—	0.98
	1 5/8"	32	—	2.03
	2 5/0"	32	—	3.28
	3 5/8"	32	—	4.55
Wood Doors				
Solid core	1"	—	—	1.56
	1 1/4"	—	—	1.82
	1 1/2"	—	—	2.04
	2"	—	—	2.33

*Representative values intended for use as design values of dry building materials in normal use.
†R-value for material at 30°F.

[1] R-values of acoustical tile depend upon the board and the type, size and depth of perforations; these are average values.

[2] Roof deck insulation is made in thicknesses to meet these standards: thickness may vary somewhat with manufacturer.

[3] Face brick and common brick do not always have these densities and R-values.

[4] Weights of blocks approximately 7 5/8" high by 15 3/8" long.

[5] Vermiculite, perlite, or mineral wood insulation.

Source: ASHRAE, *Handbook of Fundamentals*, 1967. Reprinted by permission.

R-Values of Air Films

Type and Orientation of Air Film	Direction of Heat Flow	Non-reflective surface	Fairly reflective surface	Highly reflective surface
Still air:				
Horizontal	up	0.61	1.10	1.32
Horizontal	down	0.92	2.70	4.55
45° slope	up	0.62	1.14	1.37
45° slope	down	0.76	1.67	2.22
Vertical	across	0.68	1.35	1.70
Moving air:				
15 mph wind	any*	0.17	—	—
7½ mph wind	any†	0.25	—	—

*Winter conditions.
†Summer conditions.
Source: ASHRAE, *Handbook of Fundamentals*, 1972. Reprinted by permission.

APPENDIX 4
Clear Day Insolation Data *

Solar Position and Insolation, 24° N Latitude

	Solar Time		Solar Position		BtuH/Sq. Ft. Total Insolation on Surfaces					
						\multicolumn{5}{c}{South Facing Surface Angle with Horiz.}
Date	A.M.	P.M.	Alt	Azm.	Horiz.	14	24	34	54	90
Jan. 21	7	5	4.8	65.6	10	17	21	25	28	31
	8	4	16.9	58.3	83	110	126	137	145	127
	9	3	27.9	48.8	151	188	207	221	228	176
	10	2	37.2	36.1	204	246	268	282	287	207
	11	1	43.6	19.6	237	283	306	319	324	226
	12		46.0	0.0	249	296	319	332	336	232
	Surface Daily Totals				1622	1984	2174	2300	2360	1766
Feb. 21	7	5	9.3	74.6	35	44	49	53	56	46
	8	4	22.3	67.2	116	135	145	150	151	102
	9	3	34.4	57.6	187	213	225	230	228	141
	10	2	45.1	44.2	241	273	286	291	287	168
	11	1	53.0	25.0	276	310	324	328	323	185
	12		56.0	0.0	288	323	337	341	335	191
	Surface Daily Totals				1998	2276	2396	2446	2424	1476

* *Source:* Morrison, C.A. and Farber, E.A., "Development and Use of Solar Insolation Data in Northern Latitudes for South Facing Surfaces," in *Symposium on Solar Energy Applications.* New York: ASHRAE, 1974. Reprinted by permission.

Note: Ground reflection is not included in the listed values.

Solar Position and Insolation, 24° N Latitude

						\multicolumn{6}{c}{BtuH/Sq. Ft. Total Insolation on Surfaces}

Date	Solar Time A.M.	Solar Time P.M.	Solar Position Alt	Solar Position Azm.	Horiz.	14	24	34	54	90
Mar. 21	7	5	13.7	83.8	60	63	64	62	59	27
	8	4	27.2	76.8	141	150	152	149	142	64
	9	3	40.2	67.9	212	226	229	225	214	95
	10	2	52.3	54.8	266	285	288	283	270	120
	11	1	61.9	33.4	300	322	326	320	305	135
		12	66.0	0.0	312	334	339	333	317	140
	\multicolumn{4}{r}{Surface Daily Totals}		2270	2428	2456	2412	2298	1022
Apr. 21	6	6	4.7	100.6	7	5	4	4	3	2
	7	5	18.3	94.9	83	77	70	62	51	10
	8	4	32.0	89.0	160	157	149	137	122	16
	9	3	45.6	81.9	227	227	220	206	186	41
	10	2	59.0	71.8	278	282	275	259	237	61
	11	1	71.1	51.6	310	316	309	293	269	74
		12	77.6	0.0	321	328	321	305	280	79
	\multicolumn{4}{r}{Surface Daily Totals}		2454	2458	2374	2228	2016	488
May 21	6	6	8.0	108.4	22	15	10	9	9	5
	7	5	21.2	103.2	98	85	73	59	44	12
	8	4	34.6	98.5	171	159	145	127	106	15
	9	3	48.3	93.6	233	224	210	190	165	16
	10	2	62.0	87.7	281	275	261	239	211	22
	11	1	75.5	76.9	311	307	293	270	240	34
		12	86.0	0.0	322	317	304	281	250	37
	\multicolumn{4}{r}{Surface Daily Totals}		2556	2447	2286	2072	1800	246
Jun 21	6	6	9.3	111.6	29	20	12	12	11	7
	7	5	22.3	106.8	103	87	73	58	41	13
	8	4	35.5	102.6	173	158	142	122	99	16
	9	3	49.0	98.7	234	221	204	182	155	18
	10	2	62.6	95.0	280	269	253	229	199	18
	11	1	76.3	90.8	309	300	283	259	227	19
		12	89.4	0.0	319	310	294	269	236	22
	\multicolumn{4}{r}{Surface Daily Totals}		2574	2422	2230	1992	1700	204

Solar Position and Insolation, 24° N Latitude

Date	Solar Time A.M.	Solar Time P.M.	Solar Position Alt	Solar Position Azm.	Horiz.	14	24	34	54	90
Jul 21	6	6	8.2	109.0	23	16	11	10	9	6
	7	5	21.4	103.8	98	85	73	59	44	13
	8	4	34.8	99.2	169	157	143	125	104	16
	9	3	48.4	94.5	231	221	207	187	161	18
	10	2	62.1	89.0	278	270	256	235	206	21
	11	1	75.7	79.2	307	302	287	265	235	32
	12		86.6	0.0	317	312	298	275	245	36
	Surface Daily Totals				2526	2412	2250	2036	1766	246
Aug 21	6	6	5.0	101.3	7	5	4	4	4	2
	7	5	18.5	95.6	82	76	69	60	50	11
	8	4	32.2	89.7	158	154	146	134	118	16
	9	3	45.9	82.9	223	222	214	200	181	39
	10	2	59.3	73.0	273	275	268	252	230	58
	11	1	71.6	53.2	304	309	301	285	261	71
	12		78.3	0.0	315	320	313	296	272	75
	Surface Daily Totals				2408	2402	2316	2168	1958	470
Sep. 21	7	5	13.7	83.8	57	60	60	59	56	26
	8	4	27.2	76.8	136	144	146	143	136	62
	9	3	40.2	67.9	205	218	221	217	206	93
	10	2	52.3	54.8	258	275	278	273	261	116
	11	1	61.9	33.4	291	311	315	309	295	131
	12		66.0	0.0	302	323	327	321	306	136
	Surface Daily Totals				2194	2342	2366	2322	2212	992
Oct. 21	7	5	9.1	74.1	32	40	45	48	50	42
	8	4	22.0	66.7	111	129	139	144	145	99
	9	3	34.1	57.1	180	206	217	223	221	138
	10	2	44.7	43.8	234	265	277	282	279	165
	11	1	52.5	24.7	268	301	315	319	314	182
	12		55.5	0.0	279	314	328	332	327	188
	Surface Daily Totals				1928	2198	2314	2364	2346	1442
Nov. 21	7	5	4.9	65.8	10	16	20	24	27	29
	8	4	17.0	58.4	82	108	123	135	142	124
	9	3	28.0	48.9	150	186	205	217	224	172
	10	2	37.3	36.3	203	244	265	278	283	204
	11	1	43.8	19.7	236	280	302	316	320	222
	12		46.2	0.0	247	293	315	328	332	228
	Surface Daily Totals				1610	1962	2146	2268	2324	1730

BtuH/Sq. Ft. Total Insolation on Surfaces — South Facing Surface Angle with Horiz.

Solar Position and Insolation, 24° N Latitude

	Solar Time		Solar Position			BtuH/Sq. Ft. Total Insolation on Surfaces				
						South Facing Surface Angle with Horiz.				
Date	A.M.	P.M.	Alt	Azm.	Horiz.	14	24	34	54	90
Dec. 21	7	5	3.2	62.6	3	7	9	11	12	14
	8	4	14.9	55.3	71	99	116	129	139	130
	9	3	25.5	46.0	137	176	198	214	223	184
	10	2	34.3	33.7	189	234	258	275	283	217
	11	1	40.4	18.2	221	270	295	312	320	236
		12	42.6	0.0	232	282	308	325	332	243
	Surface Daily Totals				1474	1852	2058	2204	2286	1808

Solar Position and Insolation, 32° N Latitude

	Solar Time		Solar Position			BtuH/Sq. Ft. Total Insolation on Surfaces				
						South Facing Surface Angle with Horiz.				
Date	A.M.	P.M.	Alt	Azm.	Horiz.	22	32	42	52	90
Jan. 21	7	5	1.4	65.2	0	0	0	0	1	1
	8	4	12.5	56.5	56	93	106	116	123	115
	9	3	22.5	46.0	118	175	193	206	212	181
	10	2	30.6	33.1	167	235	256	269	274	221
	11	1	36.1	17.5	198	273	295	308	312	245
		12	38.0	0.0	209	285	308	321	324	253
	Surface Daily Totals				1288	1839	2008	2118	2166	1779
Feb. 21	7	5	7.1	73.5	22	34	37	40	42	38
	8	4	19.0	64.4	95	127	136	140	141	108
	9	3	29.9	53.4	161	206	217	222	220	158
	10	2	39.1	39.4	212	266	278	283	279	193
	11	1	45.6	21.4	244	304	317	321	315	214
		12	48.0	0.0	255	316	330	334	328	222
	Surface Daily Totals				1724	2188	2300	2345	2322	1644
Mar. 21	7	5	12.7	81.9	54	60	60	59	56	32
	8	4	25.1	73.0	129	146	147	144	137	78
	9	3	36.8	62.1	194	222	224	220	209	119
	10	2	47.3	47.5	245	280	283	278	265	150
	11	1	55.0	26.8	277	317	321	315	300	170
		12	58.0	0.0	287	329	333	327	312	177
	Surface Daily Totals				2084	2378	2403	2358	2246	1276

Solar Position and Insolation, 32° N Latitude

						BtuH/Sq. Ft. Total Insolation on Surfaces				
	Solar Time		Solar Position			South Facing Surface Angle with Horiz.				
Date	A.M.	P.M.	Alt	Azm	Horiz.	22	32	42	52	90
Apr. 21	6	6	6.1	99.9	14	9	6	6	5	3
	7	5	18.8	92.2	86	78	71	62	51	10
	8	4	31.5	84.0	158	156	148	136	120	35
	9	3	43.9	74.2	220	225	217	203	183	68
	10	2	55.7	60.3	267	279	272	256	234	95
	11	1	65.4	37.5	297	313	306	290	265	112
	12		69.6	0.0	307	325	318	301	276	118
	Surface Daily Totals				2390	2444	2356	2206	1994	764
May 21	6	6	10.4	107.2	36	21	13	13	12	7
	7	5	22.8	100.1	107	88	75	60	44	13
	8	4	35.4	92.9	175	159	145	127	105	15
	9	3	48.1	84.7	233	223	209	188	163	33
	10	2	60.6	73.3	277	273	259	237	208	56
	11	1	72.0	51.9	305	305	290	268	237	72
	12		78.0	0.0	315	315	301	278	247	77
	Surface Daily Totals				2582	2454	2284	2064	1788	469
Jun 21	6	6	12.2	110.2	45	26	16	15	14	9
	7	5	24.3	103.4	115	91	76	59	41	14
	8	4	36.9	96.8	180	159	143	122	99	16
	9	3	49.6	89.4	236	221	204	181	153	19
	10	2	62.2	79.7	279	268	251	227	197	41
	11	1	74.2	60.9	306	299	282	257	224	56
	12		81.5	0.0	315	309	292	267	234	60
	Surface Daily Totals				2634	2436	2234	1990	1690	370
Jul 21	6	6	10.7	107.7	37	22	14	13	12	8
	7	5	23.1	100.6	107	87	75	60	44	14
	8	4	35.7	93.6	174	158	143	125	104	16
	9	3	48.4	85.5	231	220	205	185	159	31
	10	2	60.9	74.3	274	269	254	232	204	54
	11	1	72.4	53.3	302	300	285	262	232	69
	12		78.6	0.0	311	310	296	273	242	74
	Surface Daily Totals				2558	2422	2250	2030	1754	458
Aug 21	6	6	6.5	100.5	14	9	7	6	6	4
	7	5	19.1	92.8	85	77	69	60	50	12
	8	4	31.8	84.7	156	152	144	132	116	33

Solar Position and Insolation, 32° N Latitude

	Solar Time		Solar Position		\multicolumn{6}{c}{BtuH/Sq. Ft. Total Insolation on Surfaces}
						\multicolumn{5}{c}{South Facing Surface Angle with Horiz.}
Date	A.M.	P.M.	Alt	Azm	Horiz.	22	32	42	52	90
	9	3	44.3	75.0	216	220	212	197	178	65
	10	2	56.1	61.3	262	272	264	249	226	91
	11	1	66.0	38.4	292	305	298	281	257	107
	\multicolumn{2}{c}{12}	70.3	0.0	302	317	309	292	268	113
	\multicolumn{4}{r}{Surface Daily Totals}	2352	2388	2296	2144	1934	736
Sep. 21	7	5	12.7	81.9	51	56	56	55	52	30
	8	4	25.1	73.0	124	140	141	138	131	75
	9	3	36.8	62.1	188	213	215	211	201	114
	10	2	47.3	47.5	237	270	273	268	255	145
	11	1	55.0	26.8	268	306	309	303	289	164
	\multicolumn{2}{c}{12}	58.0	0.0	278	318	321	315	300	171
	\multicolumn{4}{r}{Surface Daily Totals}	2014	2288	2308	2264	2154	1226
Oct. 21	7	5	6.8	73.1	19	29	32	34	36	32
	8	4	18.7	64.0	90	120	128	133	134	104
	9	3	29.5	53.0	155	198	208	213	212	153
	10	2	38.7	39.1	204	257	269	273	270	188
	11	1	45.1	21.1	236	294	307	311	306	209
	\multicolumn{2}{c}{12}	47.5	0.0	247	306	320	324	318	217
	\multicolumn{4}{r}{Surface Daily Totals}	1654	2100	2208	2252	2232	1588
Nov. 21	7	5	1.5	65.4	0	0	0	1	1	1
	8	4	12.7	56.6	55	91	104	113	119	111
	9	3	22.6	46.1	118	173	190	202	208	176
	10	2	30.8	33.2	166	233	252	265	270	217
	11	1	36.2	17.6	197	270	291	303	307	241
	\multicolumn{2}{c}{12}	38.2	0.0	207	282	304	316	320	249
	\multicolumn{4}{r}{Surface Daily Totals}	1280	1816	1980	2084	2130	1742
Dec. 21	8	4	10.3	53.8	41	77	90	101	108	107
	9	3	19.8	43.6	102	161	180	195	204	183
	10	2	27.6	31.2	150	221	244	259	267	226
	11	1	32.7	16.4	180	258	282	298	305	251
	\multicolumn{2}{c}{12}	34.6	0.0	190	271	295	311	318	259
	\multicolumn{4}{r}{Surface Daily Totals}	1136	1704	1888	2016	2086	1794

Solar Position and Insolation, 40° N Latitude

	Solar Time		Solar Position		BtuH/Sq. Ft. Total Insolation on Surfaces					
						South Facing Surface Angle with Horiz.				
Date	A.M.	P.M.	Alt	Azm.	Horiz.	30	40	50	60	90
Jan. 21	8	4	8.1	55.3	28	65	74	81	85	84
	9	3	16.8	44.0	83	155	171	182	187	171
	10	2	23.8	30.9	127	218	237	249	254	223
	11	1	28.4	16.0	154	257	277	290	293	253
	12		30.0	0.0	164	270	291	303	306	263
	Surface Daily Totals				948	1660	1810	1906	1944	1726
Feb. 21	7	5	4.8	72.7	10	19	21	23	24	22
	8	4	15.4	62.2	73	114	122	126	127	107
	9	3	25.0	50.2	132	195	205	209	208	167
	10	2	32.8	35.9	178	256	267	271	267	210
	11	1	38.1	18.9	206	293	306	310	304	236
	12		40.0	0.0	216	306	319	323	317	245
	Surface Daily Totals				1414	2060	2162	2202	2176	1730
Mar. 21	7	5	11.4	80.2	46	55	55	54	51	35
	8	4	22.5	69.6	114	140	141	138	131	89
	9	3	32.8	57.3	173	215	217	213	202	138
	10	2	41.6	41.9	218	273	276	271	258	176
	11	1	47.7	22.6	247	310	313	307	293	200
	12		50.0	0.0	257	322	326	320	305	208
	Surface Daily Totals				1852	2308	2330	2284	2174	1484
Apr. 21	6	6	7.4	98.9	20	11	8	7	7	4
	7	5	18.9	89.5	87	77	70	61	50	12
	8	4	30.3	79.3	152	153	145	133	117	53
	9	3	41.3	67.2	207	221	213	199	179	93
	10	2	51.2	51.4	250	275	267	252	229	126
	11	1	58.7	29.2	277	308	301	285	260	147
	12		61.6	0.0	287	320	313	296	271	154
	Surface Daily Totals				2274	2412	2320	2168	1956	1022
May 21	5	7	1.9	114.7	0	0	0	0	0	0
	6	6	12.7	105.6	49	25	15	14	13	9
	7	5	24.0	96.6	214	89	76	60	44	13
	8	4	35.4	87.2	175	158	144	125	104	25
	9	3	46.8	76.0	227	221	206	186	160	60
	10	2	57.5	60.9	267	270	255	233	205	89
	11	1	66.2	37.1	293	301	287	264	234	108
	12		70.0	0.0	301	312	297	274	243	114
	Surface Daily Totals				2552	2442	2264	2040	1760	724

Solar Position and Insolation, 40° N Latitude

| | Solar Time | | Solar Position | | \multicolumn{6}{c}{BtuH/Sq. Ft. Total Insolation on Surfaces} |
Date	A.M.	P.M.	Alt	Azm.	Horiz.	30	40	50	60	90
Jun 21	5	7	4.2	117.3	4	3	3	2	2	1
	6	6	14.8	108.4	60	30	18	17	16	10
	7	5	26.0	99.7	123	92	77	59	41	14
	8	4	37.4	90.7	182	159	142	121	97	16
	9	3	48.8	80.2	233	219	202	179	151	47
	10	2	59.8	65.8	272	266	248	224	194	74
	11	1	69.2	41.9	296	296	278	253	221	82
		12	73.5	0.0	304	306	289	263	230	98
	\multicolumn{4}{l}{Surface Daily Totals}	2648	2434	2224	1974	1670	610
Jul 21	5	7	2.3	115.2	0	0	0	0	0	0
	6	6	13.1	106.1	50	26	17	15	14	9
	7	5	24.3	97.2	114	89	75	60	44	14
	8	4	35.8	87.8	174	157	142	124	102	24
	9	3	47.2	76.7	225	218	203	182	157	58
	10	2	57.9	61.7	265	266	251	229	200	86
	11	1	66.7	37.9	290	296	281	258	228	104
		12	70.6	0.0	298	307	292	269	238	111
	\multicolumn{4}{l}{Surface Daily Totals}	2534	2409	2230	2006	1728	702
Aug 21	6	6	7.9	99.5	21	12	9	8	7	5
	7	5	19.3	90.0	87	76	69	60	49	12
	8	4	30.7	79.9	150	150	141	129	113	50
	9	3	41.8	67.9	205	216	207	193	173	89
	10	2	51.7	52.1	246	267	259	244	221	120
	11	1	59.3	29.7	273	300	292	276	252	140
		12	62.3	0.0	282	311	303	287	262	147
	\multicolumn{4}{l}{Surface Daily Totals}	2244	2354	2258	2104	1894	978
Sep. 21	7	5	11.4	80.2	43	51	51	49	47	32
	8	4	22.5	69.6	109	133	134	131	124	84
	9	3	32.8	57.3	167	206	208	203	193	132
	10	2	41.6	41.9	211	262	265	260	247	168
	11	1	47.7	22.6	239	298	301	295	281	192
		12	50.0	0.0	249	310	313	307	292	200
	\multicolumn{4}{l}{Surface Daily Totals}	1788	2210	2228	2182	2074	1416
Oct. 21	7	5	4.5	72.3	7	14	15	17	17	16
	8	4	15.0	61.9	68	106	113	117	118	100
	9	3	24.5	49.8	126	185	195	200	198	160
	10	2	32.4	35.6	170	245	257	261	257	203
	11	1	37.6	18.7	199	283	295	299	294	229
		12	39.5	0.0	208	295	308	312	306	238
	\multicolumn{4}{l}{Surface Daily Totals}	1348	1962	2060	2098	2074	1654

South Facing Surface Angle with Horiz.

Solar Position and Insolation, 40° N Latitude

	Solar Time		Solar Position		BtuH/Sq. Ft. Total Insolation on Surfaces					
						South Facing Surface Angle with Horiz.				
Date	A.M.	P.M.	Alt	Azm	Horiz.	30	40	50	60	90
Nov. 21	8	4	8.2	55.4	28	63	72	78	82	81
	9	3	17.0	44.1	82	152	167	178	183	167
	10	2	24.0	31.0	126	215	233	245	249	219
	11	1	28.6	16.1	153	254	273	285	288	248
	12		30.2	0.0	163	267	287	298	301	258
	Surface Daily Totals				942	1636	1778	1870	1908	1686
Dec. 21	8	4	5.5	53.0	14	39	45	50	54	56
	9	3	14.0	41.9	65	135	152	164	171	163
	10	2	20.7	29.4	107	200	221	235	242	221
	11	1	25.0	15.2	134	239	262	276	283	252
	12		26.6	0.0	143	253	275	290	296	263
	Surface Daily Totals				782	1480	1634	1740	1796	1646

Solar Position and Insolation, 48° N Latitude

	Solar Time		Solar Position		BtuH/Sq. Ft. Total Insolation on Surfaces					
						South Facing Surface Angle with Horiz.				
Date	A.M.	P.M.	Alt	Azm	Horiz.	38	48	58	68	90
Jan. 21	8	4	3.5	54.6	4	17	19	21	22	22
	9	3	11.0	42.6	46	120	132	140	145	139
	10	2	16.9	29.4	83	190	206	216	220	206
	11	1	20.7	15.1	107	231	249	260	263	243
	12		22.0	0.0	115	245	264	275	278	255
	Surface Daily Totals				596	1360	1478	1550	1578	1478
Feb. 21	7	5	2.4	72.2	1	3	4	4	4	4
	8	4	11.6	60.5	49	95	102	105	106	96
	9	3	19.7	47.7	100	178	187	191	190	167
	10	2	26.2	33.3	139	240	251	255	251	217
	11	1	30.5	17.2	165	278	290	294	288	247
	12		32.0	0.0	173	291	304	307	301	258
	Surface Daily Totals				1080	1880	1972	2024	1978	1720

Solar Position and Insolation, 48° N Latitude

	Solar Time		Solar Position		\multicolumn{6}{c}{BtuH/Sq. Ft. Total Insolation on Surfaces}
						\multicolumn{5}{c}{South Facing Surface Angle with Horiz.}
Date	A.M.	P.M.	Alt	Azm	Horiz.	38	48	58	68	90
Mar. 21	7	5	10.0	78.7	37	49	49	47	45	35
	8	4	19.5	66.8	96	131	132	129	122	96
	9	3	28.2	53.4	147	205	207	203	193	152
	10	2	35.4	37.8	187	263	266	261	248	195
	11	1	40.3	19.8	212	300	303	297	283	223
	\multicolumn{2}{c	}{12}	42.0	0.0	220	312	315	309	294	232
	\multicolumn{4}{r	}{Surface Daily Totals}	1578	2208	2228	2182	2074	1632
Apr. 21	6	6	8.6	97.8	27	13	9	8	7	5
	7	5	18.6	86.7	85	76	69	59	48	21
	8	4	28.5	74.9	142	149	141	129	113	69
	9	3	37.8	61.2	191	216	208	194	174	115
	10	2	45.8	44.6	228	268	260	245	223	152
	11	1	51.5	24.0	252	301	294	278	254	177
	\multicolumn{2}{c	}{12}	53.6	0.0	260	313	305	289	264	185
	\multicolumn{4}{r	}{Surface Daily Totals}	2106	2358	2266	2114	1902	1262
May 21	5	7	5.2	114.3	9	4	4	4	3	2
	6	6	14.7	103.7	61	27	16	15	13	10
	7	5	24.6	93.0	118	89	75	60	43	13
	8	4	34.7	81.6	171	156	142	123	101	45
	9	3	44.3	68.3	217	217	202	182	156	86
	10	2	53.0	51.3	252	265	251	229	200	120
	11	1	59.5	28.6	274	296	281	258	228	141
	\multicolumn{2}{c	}{12}	62.0	0.0	281	306	292	269	238	149
	\multicolumn{4}{r	}{Surface Daily Totals}	2482	2418	2234	2010	1728	982
Jun 21	5	7	7.9	116.5	21	9	9	8	7	5
	6	6	17.2	106.2	74	33	19	18	16	12
	7	5	27.0	95.8	129	93	77	59	39	15
	8	4	37.1	84.6	181	157	140	119	95	35
	9	3	46.9	71.6	225	216	198	175	147	74
	10	2	55.8	54.8	259	262	244	220	189	105
	11	1	62.7	31.2	280	291	273	248	216	126
	\multicolumn{2}{c	}{12}	65.5	0.0	287	301	283	258	225	133
	\multicolumn{4}{r	}{Surface Daily Totals}	2628	2420	2204	1950	1644	874

Solar Position and Insolation, 48° N Latitude

						BtuH/Sq. Ft. Total Insolation on Surfaces					
	Solar Time		Solar Position			South Facing Surface Angle with Horiz.					
Date	A.M.	P.M.	Alt	Azm.	Horiz.	38	48	58	68	90
Jul 21	5	7	5.7	114.7	10	5	5	4	4	3
	6	6	15.2	104.1	62	28	18	16	15	11
	7	5	25.1	93.5	118	89	75	59	42	14
	8	4	35.1	82.1	171	154	140	121	99	43
	9	3	44.8	68.8	215	214	199	178	153	83
	10	2	53.5	51.9	250	261	246	224	195	116
	11	1	60.1	29.0	272	291	276	253	223	137
		12	62.6	0.0	279	301	286	263	232	144
	Surface Daily Totals				2474	2386	2200	1974	1694	956
Aug 21	6	6	9.1	98.3	28	14	10	9	8	6
	7	5	19.1	87.2	85	75	67	58	47	20
	8	4	29.0	75.4	141	145	137	125	109	65
	9	3	38.4	61.8	189	210	201	187	168	110
	10	2	46.4	45.1	225	260	252	237	214	146
	11	1	52.2	24.3	248	293	285	268	244	169
		12	54.3	0.0	256	304	296	279	255	177
	Surface Daily Totals				2086	2300	2200	2046	1836	1208
Sep. 21	7	5	10.0	78.7	35	44	44	43	40	31
	8	4	19.5	66.8	92	124	124	121	115	90
	9	3	28.2	53.4	142	196	197	193	183	143
	10	2	35.4	37.8	181	251	254	248	236	185
	11	1	40.3	19.8	205	287	289	284	269	212
		12	42.0	0.0	213	299	302	296	281	221
	Surface Daily Totals				1522	2102	2118	2070	1966	1546
Oct. 21	7	5	2.0	71.9	0	1	1	1	1	1
	8	4	11.2	60.2	44	86	91	95	95	87
	9	3	19.3	47.4	94	167	176	180	178	157
	10	2	25.7	33.1	133	228	239	242	239	207
	11	1	30.0	17.1	157	266	277	281	276	237
		12	31.5	0.0	166	279	291	294	288	247
	Surface Daily Totals				1022	1774	1860	1890	1866	1626
Nov. 21	8	4	3.6	54.7	5	17	19	21	22	22
	9	3	11.2	42.7	46	117	129	137	141	135
	10	2	17.1	29.5	83	186	202	212	215	201
	11	1	20.9	15.1	107	227	245	255	258	238
		12	22.2	0.0	115	241	259	270	272	250
	Surface Daily Totals				596	1336	1448	1518	1544	1442

Clear Day Insolation Data

Solar Position and Insolation, 48° N Latitude

	Solar Time		Solar Position		BtuH/Sq. Ft. Total Insolation on Surfaces					
					Horiz.	South Facing Surface Angle with Horiz.				
Date	A.M.	P.M.	Alt	Azm.		38	48	58	68	90
Dec. 21	9	3	8.0	40.9	27	87	98	105	110	109
	10	2	13.6	28.2	63	164	180	192	197	190
	11	1	17.3	14.4	86	207	226	239	244	231
	12		18.6	0.0	94	222	241	254	260	244
	Surface Daily Totals				446	1136	1250	1326	1364	1304

Solar Position and Insolation, 56° N Latitude

	Solar Time		Solar Position		BtuH/Sq. Ft. Total Insolation on Surfaces					
					Horiz.	South Facing Surface Angle with Horiz.				
Date	A.M.	P.M.	Alt	Azm.		46	56	66	76	90
Jan. 21	9	3	5.0	41.8	11	50	55	59	60	60
	10	2	9.9	28.5	39	135	146	154	156	153
	11	1	12.9	14.5	58	183	197	206	208	201
	12		14.0	0.0	65	198	214	222	225	217
	Surface Daily Totals				282	934	1010	1058	1074	1044
Feb. 21	8	4	7.6	59.4	25	65	69	72	72	69
	9	3	14.2	45.9	65	151	159	162	161	151
	10	2	19.4	31.5	98	215	225	228	224	208
	11	1	22.8	16.1	119	254	265	268	263	243
	12		24.0	0.0	126	268	279	282	276	255
	Surface Daily Totals				740	1640	1716	1742	1716	1598
Mar. 21	7	5	8.3	77.5	28	40	40	39	37	32
	8	4	16.2	64.4	75	119	120	117	111	97
	9	3	23.3	50.3	118	192	193	189	180	154
	10	2	29.0	34.9	151	249	251	246	234	205
	11	1	32.7	17.9	172	285	288	282	268	236
	12		34.0	0.0	179	297	300	294	280	246
	Surface Daily Totals				1268	2066	2084	2040	1938	1700

Solar Position and Insolation, 56° N Latitude

| | Solar Time | | Solar Position | | \multicolumn{6}{c}{BtuH/Sq. Ft. Total Insolation on Surfaces} |
| | | | | | | \multicolumn{5}{c}{South Facing Surface Angle with Horiz.} |
Date	A.M.	P.M.	Alt	Azm	Horiz.	46	56	66	76	90
Apr. 21	5	7	1.4	108.8	0	0	0	0	0	0
	6	6	9.6	96.5	32	14	9	8	7	6
	7	5	18.0	84.1	81	74	66	57	46	29
	8	4	26.1	70.9	129	143	135	123	108	82
	9	3	33.6	56.3	169	208	200	186	167	133
	10	2	39.9	39.7	201	259	251	236	214	174
	11	1	44.1	20.7	220	292	284	268	245	200
	12		45.6	0.0	227	303	295	279	255	209
	\multicolumn{4}{r}{Surface Daily Totals}		1892	2282	2186	2038	1830	1458
May 21	4	8	1.2	125.5	0	0	0	0	0	0
	5	7	8.5	113.4	25	10	9	8	7	6
	6	6	16.5	101.5	71	28	17	15	13	11
	7	5	24.8	89.3	119	88	74	58	41	16
	8	4	33.1	76.3	163	153	138	119	98	63
	9	3	40.9	61.6	201	212	197	176	151	109
	10	2	47.6	44.2	231	259	244	222	194	146
	11	1	52.3	23.4	249	288	274	251	222	170
	12		54.0	0.0	255	299	284	261	231	178
	\multicolumn{4}{r}{Surface Daily Totals}		2374	2374	2188	1962	1682	1218
Jun 21	4	8	4.2	127.2	4	2	2	2	2	1
	5	7	11.4	115.3	40	14	13	11	10	8
	6	6	19.3	103.6	86	34	19	17	15	12
	7	5	27.6	91.7	132	92	76	57	38	15
	8	4	35.9	78.8	175	154	137	116	92	55
	9	3	43.8	64.1	212	211	193	170	143	98
	10	2	50.7	46.4	240	255	238	214	184	133
	11	1	55.6	24.9	258	284	267	242	210	156
	12		57.5	0.0	264	294	276	251	219	164
	\multicolumn{4}{r}{Surface Daily Totals}		2562	2388	2166	1910	1606	1120
Jul 21	4	8	1.7	125.8	0	0	0	0	0	0
	5	7	9.0	113.7	27	11	10	9	8	6
	6	6	17.0	101.9	72	30	18	16	14	12
	7	5	25.3	89.7	119	88	74	58	41	15
	8	4	33.6	76.7	163	151	136	117	96	61
	9	3	41.4	62.0	201	208	193	173	147	106
	10	2	48.2	44.6	230	254	239	217	189	142
	11	1	52.9	23.7	248	283	268	245	216	165
	12		54.6	0.0	254	293	278	255	225	173

Solar Position and Insolation, 56° N Latitude

| | Solar Time | | Solar Position | | \multicolumn{6}{c}{BtuH/Sq. Ft. Total Insolation on Surfaces} |
| | | | | | | \multicolumn{5}{c}{South Facing Surface Angle with Horiz.} |
Date	A.M.	P.M.	Alt	Azm	Horiz.	46	56	66	76	90
Aug 21	5	7	2.0	109.2	0	0	0	0	0	0
	6	6	10.2	97.0	34	16	11	10	9	7
	7	5	18.5	84.5	82	73	65	68	45	28
	8	4	26.7	71.3	128	140	131	119	104	78
	9	3	34.3	56.7	168	202	193	179	160	126
	10	2	40.5	40.0	199	251	242	227	206	166
	11	1	44.8	20.9	218	282	274	258	235	191
		12	46.3	0.0	225	293	285	269	245	200
	\multicolumn{4}{r}{Surface Daily Totals}	1884	2218	2118	1966	1760	1392
Sep. 21	7	5	8.3	77.5	25	36	36	34	32	28
	8	4	16.2	64.4	72	111	111	108	102	89
	9	3	23.3	50.3	114	181	182	178	168	147
	10	2	29.0	34.9	146	236	237	232	221	193
	11	1	32.7	17.9	166	271	273	267	254	223
		12	34.0	0.0	173	283	285	279	265	233
	\multicolumn{4}{r}{Surface Daily Totals}	1220	1950	1962	1918	1820	1594
Oct. 21	8	4	7.1	59.1	20	53	57	59	59	57
	9	3	13.8	45.7	60	138	145	148	147	138
	10	2	19.0	31.3	92	201	210	213	210	195
	11	1	22.3	16.0	112	240	250	253	248	230
		12	23.5	0.0	119	253	263	266	261	241
	\multicolumn{4}{r}{Surface Daily Totals}	688	1516	1586	1612	1588	1480
Nov. 21	9	3	5.2	41.9	12	49	54	57	59	58
	10	2	10.0	28.5	39	132	143	149	152	148
	11	1	13.1	14.5	58	179	193	201	203	196
		12	14.2	0.0	65	194	209	217	219	211
	\multicolumn{4}{r}{Surface Daily Totals}	284	914	986	1032	1046	1016
Dec. 21	9	3	1.9	40.5	0	3	4	4	4	4
	10	2	6.6	27.5	19	86	95	101	104	103
	11	1	9.5	13.9	37	141	154	163	167	164
		12	10.6	0.0	43	159	173	182	186	182
	\multicolumn{4}{r}{Surface Daily Totals}	156	620	678	716	734	722

Bibliography

Anderson, B., and Riordan, M. *The Solar Home Book.* Andover, Mass.: Brick House Publishing Co., 1976.

Baer, S. *Sunspots.* Albuquerque, N. Mex.: Zomeworks, 1976.

Mazria, E. *The Passive Solar Energy Book.* Emmaus, Pa.: Rodale Press, 1979.

MuCullagh, J. *The Solar Greenhouse Book.* Emmaus, Pa.: Rodale Press, 1978.

Shurcliff, W. *New Inventions in Low Cost Solar Heating.* Andover, Mass.: Brick House Publishing Co., 1979.

———. *Thermal Shutters and Shades.* Andover, Mass.: Brick House Publishing Co., 1980.

Solar Age Magazine, Harrisville, New Hampshire.

Wagner, W. *Modern Carpentry.* South Holland, Ill.: Goodheart-Willcox Co., 1976.

Yanda, B., and Fisher, R. *The Food and Heat Producing Solar Greenhouse.* Santa Fe, N. Mex.: John Muir Publications, 1976.

697
qR361
c.1

697 qR361 c.1
Reif, Daniel K.
Solar retrofit :

DATE DUE	
APR 0 5	MAY 1 4 1997
MAR 0 5 1992	
AUG 3 1 1992	NOV 1 7 1997
APR 2 8 1993	OCT 2 2 1998
JUN 1 4 1993	MAR 2 2 1999
OCT 0 4 1993	
MAY 1 8 1994	APR 0 8 2002
AUG 1 6 1994	NOV 2 6 2004
Sept 6	MAR 1 0 2007
APR 2 9 1996	
JUL 2 2 1996	SEP 0 6 2008